THIS
BOOK
BELONGS TO

Ann Brunton

LADIES OF INFLUENCE

A. Susan Williams

LADIES OF INFLUENCE

Women of the Elite in Interwar Britain

ALLEN LANE
THE PENGUIN PRESS

ALLEN LANE
THE PENGUIN PRESS

Published by the Penguin Group
Penguin Books Ltd, 27 Wrights Lane, London W8 5TZ, England
Penguin Putnam Inc., 375 Hudson Street, New York, New York 10014, USA
Penguin Books Australia Ltd, Ringwood, Victoria, Australia
Penguin Books Canada Ltd, 10 Alcorn Avenue, Toronto, Ontario, Canada M4V 3B2
Penguin Books (NZ) Ltd, Private Bag 102902, NSMC, Auckland, New Zealand

Penguin Books Ltd, Registered Offices: Harmondsworth, Middlesex, England

First published 2000
1 3 5 7 9 10 8 6 4 2

Set in 10.5/14 pt PostScript Linotype Sabon
Typeset by Rowland Phototypesetting Ltd, Bury St Edmunds, Suffolk
Printed and bound in Great Britain by The Bath Press, Bath

A CIP catalogue record for this book is available from the British Library

ISBN 0-713-99261-1

To Elizabeth Patience,
with gratitude

Contents

Illustrations

(Photographic Acknowledgements in Brackets)

1. Edith Londonderry at the *Fête de Dom Perignon* (Hulton Getty)
2. Edith Londonderry, undated photograph by Lucien Aigner (Corbis)
3. Prime Minister Ramsay MacDonald with Edith Londonderry (Public Record Office Image Library)
4. Lucy Baldwin, Stanley Baldwin and Neville Chamberlain (Topham Picturepoint)
5. Lucy Baldwin with a newborn baby (Hulton Getty)
6. Cover of pamphlet issued by the British Oxygen Company concerning the Lucy Baldwin Apparatus (Public Record Office Image Library)
7. Violet Milner (By kind courtesy Mrs Margaret Edmonds)
8. Violet Milner, then Lady Edward Cecil, with a party on the verandah of Cecil Rhodes's mansion (The Bodleian Library, Oxford)
9. Joan Grigg on safari in Kenya (By kind courtesy John Grigg)
10. Joan Grigg visiting Boran desert villagers, Kenya (By kind courtesy John Grigg)
11. Joan Grigg giving a speech at the Indian Maternity Home, Nairobi (By kind courtesy John Grigg)
12. The Duchess of Atholl giving a speech in Perth (Topham Picturepoint)
13. Front cover of *The Tatler* featuring the Duchess of Atholl (*The Illustrated London News* Picture Library)
14a. Child refugees from Bilbao, Spain, arriving in Southampton (Hulton Getty)
14b. Front cover of *Searchlight on Spain* by the Duchess of Atholl (Penguin Archives)
15. Nancy Cunard, by Beaton (© Cecil Beaton Photograph, courtesy Sotheby's, London)
16. Nancy Cunard and Henry Crowder working at The Hours Press, Paris (The Photography Collection, Harry Ransom Humanities Research Center, The University of Texas at Austin)

Acknowledgements

My first acknowledgement must be to those who helped me select the 'ladies of influence' who feature in the following chapters. With characteristic generosity, Dennis Dean suggested the Duchess of Atholl and Charles Webster proposed the idea of Stella Reading. Gervase Hood suggested that I devote a chapter to the question of Empire, which made me think of Joan Grigg. This led to the pleasure of meetings with John and Patricia Grigg, who suggested in turn that I write a chapter on Violet Milner. Discovering the neglected story of Lucy Baldwin was a result of earlier research that was funded by the National Birthday Trust Fund/WellBeing. Carol Savage assisted at a critical stage of the decision-making process.

Relying heavily on private records, I was most fortunate to be given access to family papers and permission to quote from these. The chapter on Lucy Baldwin was dependent on the kindness of the Baldwin family, notably the Fourth Earl Baldwin and Countess Baldwin, Mr Miles Huntington-Whiteley, Mrs Molly Anderson and Sir Julian and Lady Ridsdale. With warm hospitality, John and Patricia Grigg let me consult documents and photographs relating to Joan Grigg, and also assisted my research on Violet Milner. Joan, Lady Zuckerman generously shared some of her memories of Stella, Marchioness of Reading, her step-grandmother, and Simon, Marquess of Reading, gave his support for my study. Lady Warner went to considerable and much appreciated efforts to assist my research on her aunt, the Duchess of Atholl. Lady Mairi Stewart responded helpfully to my inquiries about the papers of her mother, Edith, Lady Londonderry. The Hon. Mrs Dawnay offered every help and lent some documents relating to

Iris Capell. Many of the descendants mentioned above were kind enough to read and comment on chapter drafts.

My study of Lady Milner was facilitated by Kinn McIntosh and Margaret and Robin Edmonds, who lent me papers and commented usefully on the Milner chapter. On a delightful visit to Sturry in Kent, they arranged for me to visit Milner Court. Mrs Edmonds's information on Lady Milner resulted from her friendship in later years with Mrs Emily Cork, Lady Milner's personal maid; in order to preserve Mrs Cork's memories for future generations, Mrs Edmonds interviewed her on several occasions, recording these interviews on audiotape. Mr Richard Barton, headmaster of Junior King's School, Canterbury, and Mr P. Pollak, School Archivist of The King's School, put me in touch with Miss McIntosh and Mrs Edmonds and also helped in other ways.

Over the last decade, I have interviewed a number of people who were alive in Britain between the wars, who shared with me their recollections of the time. I remember with gratitude their welcome and the hours I spent listening in their homes. Where these interviews have been used in this book, they are acknowledged in the endnotes to the chapters.

Research for the book was heavily dependent on record collections, which are listed at the end of the book in the section on Archive Sources. I am indebted to the Contemporary Medical Archives Centre (CMAC) at the Wellcome Library in London for permission to quote from papers held in their archive collections; Lesley Hall and Julia Sheppard, archivists at CMAC, gave me considerable and much appreciated help. Siobhan Abbott, archivist at the Women's Royal Voluntary Service (WRVS), was unstinting in her efforts to assist my research and the WRVS let me borrow a number of key publications. Mrs Jane Anderson, the archivist at Blair Castle, was most helpful, as were the staff of the Modern Papers Reading Room at the Bodleian Library in Oxford. The London Library deserves not only gratitude but also high praise for its very efficient service.

Some individuals deserve a special mention. First and foremost, I owe a debt of gratitude to Mrs Margaret Wynn, who has taught me not to judge the people of the past by the certainties of today and tomorrow, but to appreciate *their* spirit and *their* aims as separate from our own. In the case of interwar Britain, this meant understanding the possibilities of real female power and influence in a world where the idea of full enfranchisement for women was still a novelty. It was a messy and complicated picture, but one which Peggy understood well, as someone who had taken an active role in the politics of the Thirties.

I am grateful to Elizabeth Murray, who unearthed some elusive pieces of information. With his usual kindness, James Thomas worked out for me the present-day values of interwar currency. Professor Geoffrey Chamberlain sought information on my behalf from a hospital in Nairobi, Kenya, and the British Red Cross Museum and Archives produced a record of Lady Grigg's service as a VAD in the First World War. Some useful references were supplied by Kevin Jefferys and David Smith. Andrew and Malini Maxwell-Hyslop produced a systematic bibliography out of my endnotes. Denis Judd and Elizabeth Murray helped with the illustrations.

Criticism of one's work by others offers the best way of improving it and pushing it forward. I am therefore immensely grateful to those who were kind enough to read and to comment on my chapters. Dennis Dean, Gervase Hood and Peggy Wynn read the whole book in draft form and gave me invaluable comments and guidance. I am especially indebted to Philip Williamson for his detailed comments on the Londonderry, Baldwin and Milner chapters. He made many crucial suggestions and I am extremely grateful to him for his generosity. Dame Mary Smieton commented helpfully on an early draft of the Stella Reading chapter.

At every stage of the book, Margaret Bluman, my editor at Penguin, has been an important source of ideas on content and direction. I always walked away from our meetings refreshed and excited by her clear-thinking and rigorous approach.

I should like to thank Richard Aldrich, my head of department in the History and Philosophy Group at the Institute of Education, University of London, for his understanding while I was engrossed in the book. Judy Morrison and Anne-Marie Peacock, the department's administrative staff, were always helpful.

My partner Gervase Hood walked by my side as I wrote the book. My best critic, his comments invariably advanced my thinking and the quality of my analysis. I have also enjoyed many conversations concerning the book with Benedict Wiseman. The support and friendship of Jackie Lee have meant a great deal to me, as always. Stuart Jacobs and Julian Webber rescued me from dental torment at a critical period. The book is dedicated to Elizabeth Patience as a mark of my deep gratitude to her.

Finally, I thank my daughter Tendayi Bloom, whose enthusiasm for life casts a glow of delight over everything I see and do. On one hot day, when I was starting to despair of ever finishing the book, she energetically reorganized my workroom to give me better access to my computer and my books. From this day forward, it was easier to write. She has also offered fresh and unexpected perspectives on many of the book's concerns. Tendi makes everything in my life wonderful and I thank her from my heart.

Introduction

'THE NOBLEST WOMEN IN ENGLAND'

Women in Britain were living in a 'moment of transition on the bridge', wrote Virginia Woolf in the late 1930s in *Three Guineas*, an essay which looked at male society through women's eyes. It was a bridge, she explained, 'which connects the private house with the world of public life'.[1] Throughout history, public life had been the territory of men and the domain of women was the home. Now, for the first time, women had won the right to vote and to hold public office. In 1918, the franchise had been extended to women aged thirty and over; ten years later, the age limit was lowered to twenty-one, which put women on an equal electoral basis with men. The Sex Disqualification Removal Act of 1919 had also made women eligible for any profession and for the holding of any civil or judicial post. 'Doors that were shut, opened,' enthused the feminist writer Winifred Holtby in 1934.[2] 'The door of the private house was thrown open,' echoed Virginia Woolf in 1938.[3] 'A whole world,' said the Duchess of Atholl, who was a Member of Parliament between 1924 and 1938, 'is waiting to see what we make of it.'[4]

But there were still massive obstacles to direct political power for women. 'Can you see a woman becoming a Prime Minister?' asked Margot Asquith in 1943, who thought she ought to know as the widow of the former Liberal Prime Minister, H. H. Asquith. 'I cannot imagine a greater calamity for these islands,' she added in horror, 'were they to be put under the guidance of a woman in 10 Downing Street.'[5] At the start of the twenty-first century, following the prime ministership of Margaret Thatcher, an opinion like this seems eccentric. But it was widely held between the wars and reflected the very low number of women Members of Parliament. Nancy Astor was not only the first but the sole woman to take her seat as an MP in the House of Commons in 1919. In the election of 1922, only two women MPs were elected. Eight women were elected in 1923, but only half that number in 1924. Double figures were reached in 1929 (fourteen) and 1931 (fifteen), but fell back to nine in 1935.

But a lack of visible power in the public sphere is not the same thing as a lack of power altogether. Other channels of influence on national life had always been available to *some* women – namely, to women of the social and political elite. To them, Virginia Woolf's model of the 'moment of transition on the bridge' does not properly apply. It is a useful way of charting the overall evolution of women's status in Britain and has a special relevance for the 'daughters of educated men',[6] for whom Woolf was writing in *Three Guineas* and who came from her own social background. But the model fails to take account of the extent to which this bridge simply did not exist for women of the highest social rank, whose private houses were *already* connected to the world of public life. Because of their class, background, wealth and connections, these women were free of many of the restrictions placed on their sex and they had more real power, in many ways, than most men in Britain. The long history of power held by the women of the British aristocracy was well understood by Edith, Marchioness of Londonderry. Though an active campaigner for women's suffrage, she did not think that women like *herself* needed the vote. 'It is not for the noblest women in England as such, that the vote is really desired, except for the recognition of the principle,' she wrote in a letter to *The Times* in 1912.[7]

In the world of politics, women of the elite have always been able to wield an influence, albeit sometimes through channels that are indirect and invisible. 'All through history,' observed Harold Macmillan in 1975, 'the political power of women has been displayed sometimes openly, sometimes behind the scenes. Queens and courtiers, wives and mistresses, have at different stages all played dominant roles.'[8] Macmillan had married into the aristocracy and was a Conservative MP between the wars (becoming Prime Minister in the 1950s), so was well placed to make this observation. Other means of national influence, too, were available to women of wealth and social prestige. One of these was philanthropy and good works: by giving their names and their time to a cause in which they believed, the Great and the Good were able to draw attention to their own concerns and to leave a mark on public life. Patronage was another way for rich women to exert an influence, in the worlds of art, music and literature. In some cases, women were able to achieve this kind of influence through the production of their own writing or art. Few women of the elite had been to school, but they were well educated by governesses and in many cases had been encouraged to develop their artistic and literary talents.

This book looks at seven women living between the wars for whom the notion of Woolf's bridge had little personal relevance. All of these women occupied the highest stratum of the social and political elite, through either birth or marriage or both, and all of them sought to have an influence on national life in some way. Although each woman had various interests and concerns, the book picks out for each one the particular role that best illustrates the nature of their influence. Some relied entirely on traditional methods, while others engaged more directly with the new political reality for women.

This was a period of great social and political change. In 1924, the first Labour government in Britain was elected into power; in 1926, the first General Strike brought Britain to a standstill for nine days; then, in 1929, the crash of the New York Stock Exchange produced a severe economic depression. The overwhelming backdrop to these events was the terrible legacy of the 1914–18 war. Edith Londonderry described the war as 'the holocaust that buried two generations of hapless young men, whose ideas and manners perished with them'.[9] The Labour MP Ellen Wilkinson drew attention to the massive loss of men in her *Peeps at Politicians*, which was published in 1930. 'It is only at times you notice it,' she wrote, 'but when you do it comes as a shock to realize that a whole generation has dropped out of the House of Commons. In the seats of the mighty in all parties are the men over sixty. The criticisms come from the under or early forties. And of the intermediaries, the men who should be bridging the generations, there are just a scattered few, the survivors of the Great War.'[10] Viscountess Milner, whose only son George was killed on active service, marked the twentieth anniversary of Britain's declaration of war by commenting in the *National Review* that

There can be few men and women over 35 who, during the time that has elapsed since the end of the War, have seen the advent each year of this month without emotion. This August, 1934, coming, as it does, twenty years after the great cataclysm, finds them more aware of the date of the immense tragedy than ever before. Each year during August we have lived in the memories of 1914, recalling the emotions of that fateful month.[11]

The first lady of influence in this book is Edith, Lady Londonderry. An aristocrat of enormous wealth, she continued the tradition of previous Marchionesses of Londonderry by acting as a great Tory hostess and she held lavish receptions at Londonderry House in London to mark the opening of Parliament. By these means, and also through an intimate relationship with the socialist Prime Minister Ramsay MacDonald, she had a considerable impact on national affairs. Being a political hostess was a serious alternative to high political office for women, at least for very rich and patrician women. In 1958 Lady Londonderry wrote a biography of her forebear Frances Anne Londonderry, an important Tory hostess in the nineteenth century, in which she observed that had Frances Anne 'been a man, she would have been a statesman. Indeed had she lived in modern times she might even have been a Prime Minister.'[12] Maybe Edith was thinking of her own life when she made this observation of Frances Anne.

The subject of the next chapter is Lucy Baldwin, with a particular focus on her campaign to provide all women in Britain with pain relief in childbirth. Mrs Baldwin cared passionately about maternal welfare and was a leading member of the National Birthday Trust Fund for the extension of maternity services, an organization of titled ladies that was set up by Lady Londonderry and Lady George Cholmondeley in 1928. Women of all classes were united in their concern about the high rate of maternal death: in England and Wales in the mid-1920s, the death rate was 400 to 500 for every 100,000 live births, which meant that as many as one in every 200 women lost their lives in childbirth every year.[13] Every pregnant woman at this time was aware that she might not survive to care for her baby and just about everyone had suffered the loss of a friend or a loved one in childbirth. The overall rate of maternal death had been rising steadily since 1911 and did not start to fall until 1935. The Birthday Trust aimed specifically to help poor women, although not one single working-class woman sat on its committee and there were only a few middle-class members as necessary hospital representatives. The Birthday Trust ladies had little contact with anyone outside their class apart from the mistress/master–servant relationship. Typical of this relationship was Lady Bessborough's offer to lend her servants for a day to sell flags and stamps for the Trust:

My Maid, my Cook, and 1 of the Kitchen maids, and 1 Hse [sic] maid would love to sell flags for you . . . I'm sorry I can't help myself, but I shall have a hectic day with my boy, who doesn't go back to Eton till the evening.[14]

As a special branch of the Trust, Lady Baldwin created an Anaesthetics Fund. To raise its profile, she drew attention to her role as the wife of the Conservative leader Stanley Baldwin, who was Prime Minister for eight years. She did not simply set up committees and raise funds, but exploited the new political climate in which women had the power of the vote: for the first time, male politicians had photographs taken of themselves with their wives and children and declared a special interest in matters relating to women. She accompanied Stanley everywhere and was visibly the Prime Minister's wife, even broadcasting messages about maternal welfare from Chequers. This was good for his political career – and it was also good for her anaesthetics campaign, which appeared to carry the full weight of the elected government behind it.

Lucy Baldwin liked the way that women did things and regarded the House of Commons as 'essentially a man's institution evolved through centuries by men to deal with men's affairs in a man's way';[15] if she advocated any kind of direct political participation for women, it was a 'Women's Council', devoted to the affairs of women and children.[16] Ideally, she would have liked maternity service provision to be organized exclusively by women. 'Now, we women are temperamental,' she told her audience at a fundraising event, 'as I think a good many men friends here would agree – (laughter) – some of us more so, some less, but never more so than when a baby is on its way. You are up against that mystic psychology of motherhood. And therefore I venture to think that you cannot run the maternity services the same way as you can the health services.'[17] In discussions over the administration of the 1936 Midwives Act, many women – including Lady Baldwin – objected to the idea of the state being in charge, on the grounds that the government was run by men. The Independent MP Eleanor Rathbone said she wanted to see the role of the voluntary organizations maintained because they were 'naturally very largely' composed of women, as compared with the local authorities.[18]

The next lady of influence is Violet, Viscountess Milner, an exponent of strong imperial views who sought to impress upon the nation the importance of the Empire. Between the wars, Britain was still a great imperial power. In 1929 the under-secretary of state for the colonies, Dr Drummond Shiels, reported to the House of Commons that

this House is directly responsible for the welfare of from 50,000,000 to 70,000,000 of human beings, scattered all over the earth, whose conditions of life may be adversely or happily affected by decisions which are taken here.

He added that there were 'some 36 British colonies and protectorates, including the mandated territories' and that about '60,000 colonial public service officials were engaged'.[19] Despite growing nationalist movements in India, Egypt and elsewhere and the emergence of self-governing dominions, vast areas of the world map were coloured pink to signify British rule.

Lady Milner derived the means to influence national thinking from the three most important men in her life: her two husbands and her brother. Marriage to her first husband, Lord Edward Cecil, son of the Third Marquess of Salisbury, brought her into one of England's great Conservative families and its family seat of Hatfield House in Hertfordshire; in the year following their marriage, Salisbury began his third period of office as Prime Minister. This gave Lady Edward Cecil (as she was then) high social status, wealth, and a sophisticated understanding of political life. After Lord Edward's death she married Viscount Milner, a distinguished statesman, who shared her view of the imperial mission as a sacred duty. Finally, the death of her brother Leo Maxse caused her to take over the editorship of the *National Review*, which she edited for fourteen years.

When German nationalism developed in the thirties, Lady Milner used the *National Review* to warn her readers of this danger to Britain and to Europe. Edith, Lady Londonderry, took a different approach, developing close friendships with high-ranking Germans; in 1936 she and her husband Lord Londonderry visited Germany for discussions with Hitler and Goering and to see the Munich Olympics. Italy under Mussolini attacked Abyssinia in 1936 and, in the same year, Franco led a coup against Spain's legally elected Republican government. Adolf Hitler was appointed Chancellor of Germany in 1933 and proceeded to lead his National Socialist Party towards a monopoly of power; extremely nationalist and anti-Semitic, Hitler and his Nazis sought to establish a Third Reich, in which Germany would be the dominant force in world politics. When Hitler annexed Austria and marched into Czechoslovakia in 1938, the British Prime Minister Neville Chamberlain met Hitler in Munich and agreed to let him keep these territories. His attempt at appeasement failed: Hitler invaded Poland on 1 September 1939 and, two days later, Britain and France declared war on Germany.

Fascism was still a distant menace when Joan, Lady Grigg, went to Kenya as the wife of Sir Edward Grigg, who was Governor of Kenya between 1925 and 1930. Like Lady Milner, she contributed to the imperial mission, but from within the territory of a British colony and in a practical way. She was appalled by the lack of medical care for Kenyan women and, to help meet this need, she created the Lady Grigg Welfare League as a way of training midwives and providing some basic medical services. She relied heavily on her role as Governor's wife to give official authority to her League and to compel people to listen to her. This role and her elevated social status enabled her to establish connections with the key women of the colony and to raise funds for the League, both in Kenya and in Britain. She was a Lady Bountiful in the most traditional way, but within a colonial context.

The Duchess of Atholl entered the public sphere more directly than any of the women mentioned so far. She was initially opposed to female suffrage but in 1923 sought election as a Conservative Member of Parliament and joined the small band of pioneer women MPs: Lady Astor, Miss Horsbrugh and Dame Irene Ward among the Conservatives; Eleanor Rathbone as an Independent; and Jennie Lee, Ellen Wilkinson, Margaret Bondfield, and Susan Lawrence in the Labour

Party. The Duchess herself became the first Conservative woman Minister, as Parliamentary Secretary at the Board of Education between 1924 and 1929. This book looks in particular at her efforts to support the Republican government during the Spanish Civil War, on account of which she was widely dubbed 'The Red Duchess'. In this cause she encountered hostility from her own party, many of whom tried to block her efforts for Spain. This brought her parliamentary career to a sudden end, just as she was trying to put pressure on the government to abandon its policy of appeasement. Putting her beliefs into practice in the political world required tremendous courage, especially when she drew the attention of the House of Commons to the issue of female circumcision in Africa, which was also of concern to Joan Grigg.

Nancy Cunard was an intellectual like Lady Milner, but her interests were cultural as well as political and she was left-wing rather than right-wing. Her mother, Lady Emerald Cunard, was a social hostess of the old-fashioned type like Lady Londonderry, although she was more interested in the patronage of writers and musicians than of politicians. Nancy, too, devoted much of her life to patronage, but in a new way. She went to France in 1920 to join the movement of the avant-garde and then bought a printing press to publish literature that she believed was important artistically and politically. Her Hours Press did not make a profit but this was of no real consequence as she had the family money of the Cunard shipping empire behind her. She then used her wealth and her connections with key intellectual figures to produce a massive anthology called *Negro*, containing a wide range of materials on the history and culture of black people. It also made a moving plea for civil rights. She lived openly with a black man, which was highly unusual for a white woman at this time and scandalized many members of her mother's circle.

The final lady of influence in this book is Stella, Marchioness of Reading, who employed old-fashioned methods of charitable influence in order to build something completely new. In 1938, she created the Women's Voluntary Service for Civil Defence (WVS) as a way of preparing the civilian population of Britain to meet the threat of another war. In order to set it up, she exploited to the full the extensive network of titled connections she had developed as the wife and then widow of the Marquess of Reading. But having done this, she then developed the WVS into an organization that gave the ordinary women of Britain an opportunity for active service in public life. Stella Reading was uniquely placed for this achievement, because she understood the world of ordinary people: she was not a privileged woman by birth and had first met Lord Reading when she was employed as his first wife's secretary.

Lady Reading was forty-four when she started the WVS. With the exception of Joan Grigg, who was a youthful twenty-eight when she went to Kenya, and Nancy Cunard, who was thirty-two when she started her Hours Press, all the women in this book were most influential when they were mature in years. Lucy Baldwin was sixty when she set up her Anaesthetics Fund; Lady Londonderry was forty-five years of age when she first met Ramsay MacDonald; Lady Milner was sixty when she embarked upon her sixteen-year editorship of the *National Review*; and the Duchess of Atholl was sixty-two when the Spanish Civil War broke out in 1936. Their longevity was one of the many privileges that came with wealth. Good food, fresh air and leisure, as well as expert medical care, all helped to keep these women vigorous in their years of maturity.

Servants were another privilege of wealth. Lady Milner relied heavily on her personal maid, Miss Hillman (known as 'Hillman' and 'Hilly'), who stayed with her for twenty-four years. At Astley Hall in Worcestershire, Mrs Baldwin employed eight indoor servants, a butler, ten gardeners, a chauffeur and a housekeeper. Nancy Cunard self-consciously opted for a simple life but, all the same, she employed a Breton maid called Anna to look after her when she moved to Paris. For Joan Grigg in Kenya, the army of staff at Government House must have been a headache at times. Even so, it released her from many routine activities and gave her the freedom to develop her Lady Grigg Welfare League. 'I am teaching a small Swahili boy of 13 to wait on John,' she wrote to her mother, while she was waiting for her young son to arrive from Britain. 'All our native servants are simply longing for John's arrival,' she added. 'I have got two quite tiny boys of 9 and 11 who run messages and bring round coffee cups.'[20]

How different were the lives of the seven women in this book from the majority of women in Britain between the wars. 'The emancipation for which many thousand women have worked in the last hundred years, has had little or no effect on the domestic slavery of mind and body of the millions with whom rests the immediate care of a home and family', wrote Margery Spring Rice in *Working-Class Wives* at the end of the 1930s. 'The poorest women,' she added, '*have no time to spare* (sic).'[21] Many of them longed for an opportunity to read and study. One woman wrote sadly in 1915 to the Women's Co-operative Guild (a campaigning organization of working-class women who were married and belonged to the Co-operative Movement) that she 'could give no time to mental culture or reading'. With five children to care for on her husband's meagre weekly wage of 32 to 40 shillings, the best she could do was to prop a book above the sink:

I bought Stead's penny editions of literary masters, and used to put them on a shelf in front of me on washing-day, fastened back their pages with a clothes-peg, and learned pages of Whittier, Lowell, and Longfellow, as I mechanically rubbed the dirty clothes, and thus wrought my education.[22]

Once she had paid off her debts, she hoped to have more time to read. 'I'd like to develop mentally', she said, 'but I must stifle that part of my nature until I have made good the ills of the past.'[23]

These contrasts in quality of life became even more extreme as a result of the Depression, which made the living conditions of the poor almost intolerable. In many areas, almost the whole population was unemployed and dependent on insurance benefit and help from the Unemployment Assistance Board. Families were hungry and cold and often there was no running water, so that mothers had to carry pails of water from an outside tap up many flights of steps. Strikes, national hunger marches, and campaigns against the Means Test and the Unemployment Assistance Board were commonplace in the 1930s. The average weekly wage in 1939 was 77 shillings per week, which is equal to just over £130 at the end of the twentieth century.[24] But throughout this period of hardship, the women in this book were largely unaffected. Lady Londonderry continued to hold her glittering receptions on the eve of Parliament and Nancy Cunard still stayed up till the early hours drinking cocktails in the cafés of Paris.

Yet another stark contrast between the ladies of the elite and most people of Britain was the extent of their mobility: while working-class women were generally confined to their own neighbourhoods and many middle-class women were pleased if they could manage one annual visit to London, women of the upper class moved routinely between their London houses and country estates. They travelled frequently to Europe and many of them were brought up to be as comfortable in French, as in British, society. Lady Milner, for example, would have her hair dressed in Paris and nowhere else; according to her servant 'Hilly', she 'went to Paris for everything'. Shortly before her marriage to Alfred Milner, she journeyed to Paris especially to have underclothes made with the initials 'V.M.', to replace those marked 'V.C.' from her previous marriage.[25] But the travel of the upper classes was not limited to Europe. Rather, they inhabited a vast territory that stretched across the world, from America to Africa to Asia. The Empire offered particularly exotic opportunities for adventure and travel: 'We have just got back from Safari, 100 miles off through the Kikuyu reserve – it was so lovely – we camped in a green valley beside the Gouya River', wrote Joan Grigg in Kenya.[26] The Londonderrys went to India shortly after their marriage as guests of Lord Curzon, the Viceroy, where Edith went on a tiger shoot and pig-sticking in the early mornings:

This was the greatest fun. The Maharajah gave me a beautiful little Arab horse, and one day in hot pursuit of a boar – it knew far more about the sport than I did – it ran away with me through a prickly-pear hedge in pursuit of the pig . . . We visited Jaipur, also Jodhpur, where a lot of polo was played, and we did some more pig-sticking. One morning also we went out with a tame cheetah after black buck.[27]

The lives of these seven women were certainly privileged, but they were not frivolous. They amounted to much more, for example, than the daily routine of E. M. Delafield's heroine (who was upper class, but not top drawer) in the *Diary of a Provincial Lady*:

November 12th: Home yesterday and am struck, as so often before, by immense accumulation of domestic disasters that always await one after any absence. Trouble with kitchen range has resulted in no hot water, also Cook says the mutton has gone, and will I speak to the butcher, there being no excuse in weather like this. Vicky's cold, unlike the mutton, hasn't gone. Mademoiselle says, '*Ah, cette petite! Elle ne sera peut-etre pas longtemps pour ce bas monde, madame.*' Hope this is only her way of dramatizing the situation.

Robert reads *The Times* after dinner, and goes to sleep.[28]

This is pretty much the beginning and end of life for Delafield's heroine: marriage, motherhood, and managing the servants. Of course, the seven ladies of this book also had domestic concerns, like most women: Mrs Baldwin's diary regularly includes entries like 'Doctor, dress-making & dentist'[29] and 'Bank & paid wages'.[30] But they did so much more, as well. They engaged with real problems as they saw them: unnecessary pain in childbirth; maternal welfare for women of all races; imperial duty; female circumcision; the legal and moral rights of the democratically elected Spanish Republican government; racism against black people; the threat of war against the civilian population. Many people have disapproved of Lady Londonderry's intimacy with Ramsay MacDonald, but no one can deny the seriousness with which she approached that relationship.

Many rich and patrician women between the wars made no mark at all on national life. But in any social class at any historical moment, there are always at least some people who are able to take advantage of the opportunities that are available to them. In the case of the seven women in this book, those opportunities were furnished by nobility and wealth.

I

'A GREAT POLITICAL HOSTESS'
Edith, Marchioness of Londonderry

Edith, Marchioness of Londonderry, 1878–1959, was born Edith Helen Chaplin, the second of three children of Henry, Viscount Chaplin, a prominent Conservative politician, and Lady Florence Leveson-Gower, daughter of the third Duke of Sutherland. She spent much of her childhood at Dunrobin Castle in Sutherland, the home of her mother, who died when she was almost three; when in London, she and her brother lived with their grandparents at Stafford House (now Lancaster House). Although she enjoyed 'coming out', she also relished behaviour that was unconventional: on a visit to Japan, when she was twenty-five, she had her left leg tattooed with the figure of a snake (which proved to be a problem when fashion raised the length of skirts). In 1899, at the age of twenty, Edith married Charles Stewart, Viscount Castlereagh, heir to the massive Londonderry estates. He succeeded his father as Seventh Marquess of Londonderry. A Conservative politician, Londonderry's ministerial career (from 1920) culminated in his period of office as Secretary of State for Air between 1931 and 1935. He and Edith had five children: Maureen, Edward (known as Robin), Margaret, Helen and Mairi. The family had three great bases: Londonderry House in London, Wynyard in County Durham and Mount Stewart in County Down in Northern Ireland; they also owned Plas Machynlleth in North Wales.

Lady Londonderry was an active suffragist, despite opposition from her father and her mother-in-law. In 1938, she referred with satisfaction to the 'absolute emancipation of the female sex': she believed that in the relations of the sexes, there had been 'an almost complete rupture with pre-war ideas, which expressed itself . . . in an entirely new code for conduct and thought'.[1] She took a leading role in putting women into uniform in the First World War. Within a few weeks of the outbreak of war in 1914 she became Colonel-in-Chief of the Women's Volunteer Reserve; then, in the following year, she founded the Women's Legion, specifically to recruit women cooks to the army. She became Director-General of the Legion, which expanded to include an Agriculture Section and a Motor Transport Section. In 1917 she became the first woman to be appointed Dame of the British Empire (Military Division).

After the war, Lady Londonderry began her glittering role as a political hostess, for which she is best known and which lasted over twenty-five years. She knew the great political figures of her time and gave regular receptions at Londonderry House to mark the opening of Parliament. She was an intimate friend of Ramsay MacDonald, who was Prime Minister of the first and second Labour governments (1924 and 1929–31) and the first and second National governments (between 1931 and 1935). In the lead-up to the Second World War, Lord and Lady Londonderry became friendly with high-ranking Nazis and in 1936 they visited Germany, where they held private discussions with Hitler and Goering and also attended the Munich Olympics. In 1938, Lord Londonderry published a book advocating détente *with Germany and Lady Londonderry published a memoir,* Retrospect, *in which she criticized the British people for a lack of faith and complained that, 'The more positive "isms" are taboo, like Nazi-ism or Fascism, because they imply doing something.'*[2] *However, when Hitler occupied Prague on 16 March 1939, the Londonderrys' support for Nazism came to an end. Lady Londonderry died at the age of eighty.*

On the evening of 6 February 1928, Edith, Marchioness of Londonderry, gave a grand reception at Londonderry House to mark the new session of Parliament. She stood at the top of the grand staircase in the centre of the house to receive her guests, with Stanley Baldwin, the Conservative Prime Minister, at her side. *The Times* reported that

Lady Londonderry, with whom were the Prime Minister and the Marquess of Londonderry, wore a Velasquez gown of black chiffon velvet, with full panniered skirt and a fitting corsage, and a diamond necklace, a diamond rivière, and long diamond-drop earrings. Pale yellow mimosa, massed on the mantelpieces and in the fireplaces, decorated the long picture gallery and reception rooms.

About a thousand people were present and the guest list took up nearly two full columns of *The Times*.[3] This was just one of the regular receptions given by Lady Londonderry to mark the start of a new session of Parliament, which were always lavish and always on a grand scale. After the eve-of-session reception in February 1924, Lucy Baldwin wrote in a letter to her mother-in-law that 'Stan hurried off to assist Lady Londonderry to receive for the party. – There were about 1100 people who had to get up the staircase & I was told that some gave the attempt up and got up the back stairs instead!'[4] This was a world in which Lady Londonderry was pre-eminent: etiquette, issues of precedence and fine manners required deference to the lady of the house from all guests, however elevated their social or political position. In the world of government, men were in charge; but at Londonderry House, it was Edith. It was she who stood at the top of the staircase, next to the Prime Minister, while her husband stood behind them.

Lady Londonderry belonged to the highest level of the British elite. She was a granddaughter of the Duke of Sutherland and had married Charles, the Seventh Marquess of Londonderry, whose mother was the eldest daughter of the Earl of Shrewsbury, the premier Earl of England. The wealth of the Londonderry family was vast, involving 50,000 acres of land in England, Ireland and Wales and coalfields in Durham that employed 10,000 miners. This level of wealth and prestige enabled Lady Londonderry to set a standard in entertaining and fashion. A few days after her reception in February 1928, *The Times* commented that 'To such a reception as that held on Monday night at Londonderry House an interest other than political attaches. The mirror of fashion reflects the best that can be found in the dress of today.' It noted a 'friendly rivalry' between the 'slim willowy draped gown . . . and the crisp picture frock with bouffant skirt' and observed that at Londonderry House 'the real flowers won their way. Not in single blossom, but as a spray of three or more flowers, they were to be seen in every hue, mauve and green orchids first, carnations second, and violets frequently.'[5]

Londonderry House on Park Lane, in the exclusive London district of Mayfair, was ideal for entertaining. According to William Buchan, who accompanied his father John Buchan to some of the receptions, it had many high rooms communicating with one another from either side of a grand staircase. He marvelled at the 'feeling of Ruritanian splendour, the gilding and the crystal, the wigged footmen moving so dexterously'.[6] Patrick Donner, a Conservative MP between 1931 and 1955, has described Londonderry House as a home that was a political centre, efficiently run by Lady Londonderry; he attended one of the receptions and 'was astonished to know how much could be accomplished by a purposeful individual in the course of a single evening'.[7] As the title of Edith Londonderry's obituary in *The Times* put it many years later, she was 'A great political hostess'.[8]

Edith had been prepared for the role of hostess long before her marriage into the Londonderry family. Her own family had always been at the centre of social and political influence and her aunt Millicent, Duchess of Sutherland, 'had the gift of bringing all sorts of people together' at Stafford House. She entertained the royal family and their foreign relations, as well as visiting potentates and the society of the day: Edith recalled that 'You met or saw at Stafford House every one you ever heard of or hoped to meet.'[9] Both her own and her husband's family were closely associated with the Conservative Party and her entertaining at Londonderry House was carried out on behalf of the party. This specific role as Tory hostess had a long history in the Londonderry family: Edith's predecessor Frances Anne Vane-Tempest, the Third Marquess's second wife, had presided as hostess for the Tory Party for more than forty years, from the time of the building of Londonderry House (then called Holdernesse House) in 1825. More recently, Theresa Chetwynd Talbot, wife of the Sixth Marquess and Edith's mother-in-law, had established herself as the foremost Tory political hostess of her day and had welcomed to her home friends who ranged 'from crowned heads and prime ministers to poets and sculptors and men of letters', wrote Edith in her memoir.[10] Austen Chamberlain once said that he could gauge the state of his own political fortunes by the number of fingers that Theresa Londonderry extended to him when they met.[11]

Edith's own role as a political hostess began in 1919, following the death of her mother-in-law, when Lord Londonderry was asked if they would give a political reception for the Coalition Government. The apparatus of the role was ready for her: the palatial setting of Londonderry House, the experienced servants and the suppliers of food and fresh flowers. But Edith lived at a very different time, when lavish and glittering receptions seemed too obviously at odds with the eked-out existence of working-class families. This was especially the case after the start of the economic depression in 1929. 'Such entertainments,' observed Buchan's son, 'were becoming rare; possibly, in the middle of a serious economic recession, they were inappropriate.'[12] Stanley Baldwin remarked in 1936 that the Marchioness's political entertaining was 'very magnificent and beautifully done, but to me it was out of date and at times in dubious taste'.[13]

The 'Great Hostess', wrote Lady Milner sadly in 1930 in an editorial for the National Review, 'has passed with the Great House.' The loss to the community, she added, 'is immense. London is disfigured. Consider the present Devonshire House! The retreat of the great aristocrat from London ... has caused a real revolution in social existence.'[14] With few exceptions, the 'great' houses of London were gone, commented a gossip column in the Bystander in 1931: 'They are either demolished, with gargantuan hotels in their place – such as Grosvenor House, Devonshire House, and the Dorchester – or, like Montagu House and Stafford House (now Lancaster House), they are put to other uses.' About the only important London house that still continues to remain open in the grand manner, added the Bystander, 'is Londonderry House, and ... Lord and Lady Londonderry still continue to give big political receptions in the old style, and to let their house be the social headquarters of the Conservative Party.'[15] Lady Londonderry regarded the role of hostess as a duty that came with her class position. 'There is still ... an Upper Class, its ranks diminished and impoverished by the war,' she wrote in 1938, who 'still wield a certain influence behind the scenes, and, in times of crisis, their presence will still be felt, something solid and very British and, above all, they are people who were born and bred to the old tradition – that possessions carry duties with them, before pleasure.'[16]

As well, Lady Londonderry hosted literary and artistic occasions at the various family seats, especially during the parliamentary recess; indeed, she was an interested patron of several writers. She was not the only 'society hostess' of this type. Others included Sybil, Lady Colefax, who collected people and information and was nicknamed 'old Coalbox' by those who sneered. 'Colefaxismus' was coined as a term to describe a remark that was intended to impress with privileged knowledge of people and events; and Virginia Woolf referred to gossip about Sybil Colefax as 'Colefaxiana'.[17] Emerald, Lady Cunard, was a much less frivolous hostess than Lady Colefax. She was a patron of the opera (who was in love with the conductor Sir Thomas Beecham) and used her skills as a hostess to regenerate British interest in opera; Harold Acton commented respectfully that 'She was the only consistent patron of musical talent in London'.[18] Ethel, Lady Desborough, a particular friend of Lord Londonderry, has been described as the last Whig hostess in the tradition made famous in the eighteenth century by Georgiana, Duchess of Devonshire. But none of Edith Londonderry's contemporaries managed to carry off the role of hostess with quite the same style and élan as she did.

The Ark Club was one of Lady Londonderry's entertaining triumphs. Every week, she brought together the key figures of the day – and their wives – at the Club's weekly sessions. The Ark had been set up to amuse officers during the 1914–18 war, when Londonderry House was used as an officers' hospital, but after the war sought less to amuse than to bring prominent figures together in an informal setting – 'Ambassadors and Ministers, and a big sprinkling of Cabinet Ministers.' Londonderry House was called the Ark and its members were given the name of a bird, insect, beast or reptile, or else a mythological or magical creature. Charley Londonderry was 'Charley the Cheetah' (because of his 'many amatory successes', according to one source[19]), while Lady Londonderry was 'Circe the Sorceress'. Churchill was 'Winston the Warlock', Lord Balfour was 'Arthur the Albatross', Sir Samuel Hoare was 'Sam the Skate' (because he liked skating), Sir John Simon was 'Simon the Silkworm', Sir John Lavery ('with his lovely Hazel Hen') was 'John Dory', Lady Astor was 'Nancy the Gnat' and John Buchan was 'Buck'.[20] 'Mention of the London-derrys caused my mother a delicate wrinkling of the nose,' recalled John Buchan's son. 'She thought the Ark business silly and vulgar, and was not pleased to see JB mixed up in it.'[21]

One member of the Ark – 'Hamish the Hart' – was an unlikely guest. In real life he was Ramsay MacDonald, the first Labour Prime Minister of Britain, a socialist who was the leader of the Labour governments of 1924 and 1929–31 and then of the National Governments between 1931 and 1935. It was during his first premiership that he first met Lady Londonderry, when they sat next to each other at a dinner at Buckingham Palace; he was fifty-eight and she was forty-five, by now a grandmother. 'We got on exceedingly well,' wrote Edith much later in her memoir.[22] This mutual liking surprised them both, since he was a socialist and she was a high Conservative. Socially, too, they came from opposite worlds. While Lady Londonderry was very rich and very upper class, MacDonald came from a background that was at least as humble as that of Londonderry's miners. He had grown up in a little cottage in Lossiemouth, a fishing port, the illegitimate child of a woman who had been a domestic servant and then earned her living in the fields and as a dressmaker. MacDonald was always hard-up and, even when he was Prime Minister, he had to struggle to provide for his family.

Shortly after their first meeting, MacDonald invited the London-derrys to Chequers, the official country house of the Prime Minister. Edith and Ramsay then started to correspond and found ways of visiting each other.[23] Many Labour supporters were appalled. 'Alas!' exclaimed Beatrice Webb, a left-wing social reformer, when she read in her newspaper in 1930 that the Prime Minister would be the guest of the Londonderrys in Scotland on his way to Balmoral to visit the King.

Balmoral is inevitable, but why the castles of the wealthiest, most aristocratic, most reactionary and by no means the most intellectual of the Conservative Party? 'Because', JRM [she meant MacDonald] would answer if he laid bare his heart, 'I am more at home with them than I should be with you or with any other member of the Labour Party'. . . .

This silly little episode 'will do the PM untold damage with the non-commissioned officers of the Labour Movement,' observed Mrs Webb. In her view, 'he *ought* not to be more at home in the castles of the great than in the homes of his followers. It argues a perverted taste and a vanishing faith.'[24] This view is understandable: the Marquess was not simply a Tory, but extremely right-wing. He took little interest in the welfare of his miners, who were among the poorest in Britain, and was ruthless in negotiations over pay and hours. 'We have a desperate struggle before us in the next few years,' he wrote angrily to Baldwin in 1924, 'and I am proposing to devote a great deal of my time to defeating the Socialist menace in one of the reddest portions of the kingdom [by which he meant County Durham].'[25] In 1926 Londonderry and the other coal-owners threatened to cut wages, which were already barely adequate for a family's survival, and to lengthen the hours of work, which were already long; this brought the miners out on strike and sparked off the General Strike. The miners were eventually forced back to work by cold and starvation, having to accept both longer hours and lower wages. But throughout this episode, Londonderry refused to make any compromises with his workers. Even his family thought he was harsh and unsympathetic. 'Before the last war,' wrote his son Robin in the *Spectator* in 1946, 'over half of all industrial disputes were to do with coalmining. The average owner is rarely seen by his men; in fact, the only times they see him are when there are differences of opinion which call for strikes. The miner can hardly be blamed for regarding his employer as a man who is more interested in profits than welfare.'[26]

But despite these sharp differences between Edith and Ramsay, a profound mutual attraction drew them together. Edith's letters to him reveal a kind of desperate need for his affection, which may have been linked to the loneliness she felt at her husband's unfaithfulness. Charley's frequent absences and affairs shaped much of their marriage, right from the start. Edith discovered only a few months after their wedding that Charley had not only had a premarital affair with another woman, a married American actress (known as the 'Eternal Flapper' because she never seemed to age), but also had a child by her, Dorothé, who was born six weeks after his marriage to Edith. One of many adulterous love affairs involved Consuelo Vanderbilt, the American heiress who had married Londonderry's second cousin, the Ninth Duke of Marlborough – 'Consuelo, adrift, beautiful and alluring,' writes Lady Londonderry's biographer, Anne de Courcy, 'was too much for Charley. Caught in the throes of a sudden passion, they ran off to Paris.'[27] Charley's affair with Eloise Ancaster, yet another American woman and the wife of the Earl of Ancaster, was the most lasting and serious and both Edith and Charley referred to her as his 'wife'. Over time, Edith grew to manage the situation through tolerance. She became a firm friend to Charley's daughter Dorothé and arranged for his various female friends to visit their home. She even bought presents for him to give Olive Murray-Smith, his mistress in the 1930s: 'I have bought you a small bottle of scent to give to Olive called Ce Soir ou Jamais,' she told him.[28] But however well she coped with his infidelities, she could never feel that he was her loyal friend and companion; and it was this gaping hole in her life that Ramsay filled so successfully. MacDonald was lonely, too. He had been devastated by the death of his beloved wife Margaret in 1911. He wrote sadly to Lady Londonderry from Chequers on 6 October 1933, 'No one is with me here today, and by the fire in the Long Gallery I sit alone. The Cromwell portraits look down through the shadowy light and are the only company I have.'[29]

Edith thought MacDonald had a 'magnificent head and fine presence' and was 'really a very brave man', she wrote in *Retrospect* after his death.[30] He, for his part, was moved by her gracious beauty and intelligence. No doubt, too, their attraction to each other was enhanced by the power he held as Prime Minister, and by the gloss of her high social status and the splendour of her life. But he was also impressed by her independence of spirit, which had made her an ardent suffragist and the founder and Director General of the Women's Legion. She had also shown a concern for those suffering from the Depression by founding the Personal Service League (for the Distressed Areas), a non-political and non-denominational charity run by very rich ladies to distribute clothing to the unemployed. She was chairman and other League members included Lady Reading, Lady Peel and other society stars. MacDonald thought the League was 'over-classy'[31] but was probably impressed by Edith's charitable intentions, which were markedly absent from her husband's approach to the poor. Lady

Londonderry easily tired of these good works, however. The Personal Service League had only been going for a couple of years before she retired from the position of chairman, in 1932, in favour of Lady Reading (though Edith was not the only member of the League to find it tedious: Lucy Baldwin wrote that she 'Went to the Annual Meeting of the Personal Service League – I was there 1 hr & 20 minutes, much too long'[32]).

Edith tried to make some sense of her intimacy with MacDonald by looking for ways to square their differences. In a letter entreating MacDonald to fly over to Northern Ireland to visit her at Mount Stewart, she observed that,

If friends must always think the same on evy [sic] minute detail how dull the friendship would be and nothing to discuss or talk about . . . and you and I think – practically the same in the end – only that you are far more autocratic – I can see you smile – but fundamentally you are – and you are either – because you have that in you to lead and to compel – If I wasn't myself – I might do both – but in the days in which we live – to be born an aristocrat – means that it must be something vy [sic] exceptional to be allowed to lead at all – and to compel – hardly ever – in the great aristocracy of brain – a leader is accepted when found – with enthusiasm – but leaders are rare – rarer still like yourself.[33]

MacDonald 'loved beautiful things – books, pictures, beautiful women, and lovely jewels and colours', wrote Edith in her memoir, asking defensively, 'And why shouldn't he? He was, for these days, an old-fashioned Socialist. His aim was to improve, not to destroy. He fought against privilege and inequality of opportunity.' He was unlike most of the leaders of his party, she said, because 'being a Celt and Highlander [he] was of different blood and outlook to most of them'. She frequently referred to this Scottish connection as a reason for their friendship – 'The mutual bond between us being Scotland, and especially the Highlands, which we both loved.'[34] This Highlands bond sounds romantic, but it must have been something of an affectation, even fantasy, given the enormous difference between their Scottish backgrounds. Edith had spent much of her early childhood in the imposing grandeur of Dunrobin Castle with her maternal grandparents, the Duke and Duchess of Sutherland. The Sutherland family was actually English, with extensive land holdings in England, but had been given large tracts of the Highlands after the failure of the Jacobite rebellions in the eighteenth century. The Sutherlands were largely responsible for the Highland clearances, which converted Highland agriculture into pastoralism; this creation of large-scale sheep farms had been a major factor in the death of traditional peasant society in Scotland. MacDonald, on the other hand, was a genuine Scot who came from a small fishing port on the edge of the Highlands. The Highlands connection, therefore, was exaggerated and seems to have functioned more as an *expression* of a bond, than as a bond in itself. When it appears in their correspondence, it is charged with a suggestive sexuality. 'The Highlands are to me, rather in the nature of someone we are much in love with – unlawfully almost –', wrote Edith to Ramsay. 'Ty [sic] are ever present in my thoughts – deep down in my nature, is incessant longing to be there – a thirst to drink the air there – This longing never leaves one – and haunts one's thoughts. Altogether,' she added,

– it can be quite a nuisance – I believe this is always so – to anyone who has the call of the blood in their veins, and explains why all Highlanders always return, whenever thy [sic] can, to their native place – Even when, like myself of mixed blood – it will not be gainsaid – This anyhow – you and I know and understand, and share together.[35]

MacDonald was more realistic than she was about the contrasts between the worlds to which they belonged. He wrote in the autumn of 1932 that, 'The day is sure to come when I shall again be of the sea and the mist, & you will continue to reign at your fireside & *amongst your own people.* "I once knew him," you will say & maybe sigh. And that will be all.'[36]

The Highlands motif was commonly associated with MacDonald, in a way that imbued his working-class background with a kind of ethnic charm. He was 'not really a Socialist in the academic sense', wrote George Bernard Shaw to Lady Londonderry in 1938, after MacDonald's death, but 'a seventeenth-century Highlander who was quite at home in feudal society and quite out of it among English trade unionists. As a leader of English labour he was, as Beatrice Webb put it, a façade: amid chieftains and ladies bright he was himself.'[37] If Londonderry House cast a spell over him, said William Buchan, 'it was very likely because he had grown out of all sympathy with the self-conscious cloth-cappery of his own followers. They were naturally disgusted when, for instance, he insisted upon court at certain functions; but then the majority of them were not romantic Highland Scots.'[38] Baldwin, too, used the Highlands motif as a euphemism for her intimacy with MacDonald. In a conversation in 1935 with her son, Robin Castlereagh, Baldwin referred to the public's doubts about their relationship by commenting 'I have Highland blood in me and I understand the bond which unites all Highlanders, but ninety per cent of people do not.'[39]

The friendship gradually drew MacDonald away from the world of the Labour Party and the trade unions and into the drawing rooms of the aristocracy. 'It was characteristic,' wrote Beatrice Webb acidly in 1928, that he told her husband Sidney Webb that he had 'a *personal* invitation from Lady Londonderry to her official party the night before the meeting of Parliament . . . The official Labour gathering . . . was a deadly affair and no wonder MacDonald with his artistic sense hankered after the gorgeous company of "the Haves" in their splendid showrooms.'[40] MacDonald became a regular guest at Londonderry House and attended the intimate small dinners at which, said John Buchan's son William, many believed that 'important political strings were pulled. The importance of that string-pulling,' he added, 'was probably exaggerated but, as can be imagined, it gave no pleasure to the Prime Minister's party to see him apparently at the beck and call of what some would certainly have seen as arch-enemies of the Labour movement.'[41]

In 1931, following the Wall Street crash of 1929, the financial recession and rising unemployment reached a crisis, creating social and economic distress on a national scale. 'To-day millions of working-class people in this country,' observed B. Seebohm Rowntree in 1937, 'are inadequately provided with the necessaries of life, simply and solely because the fathers of families are not in receipt of incomes large enough.'[42] A woman who grew up in Birmingham at that time recalls that the impossibility of surviving on parish relief forced her to relinquish her children to Dr Barnardo's homes; it was eight years before she could offer them a home again.[43] A woman living in the Midlands remembers starting work in 1924 at the age of fourteen in a hosiery factory, earning seven shillings and eleven pence for tying knots on a long winding machine all day long. Her family ended up on the Means Test and her sister, proud of her home and her little girls, 'had to suffer the visits of the Means Test man and his probing questions, even looking into the pan on the stove because something smelt particularly appetizing.'[44]

This was a terrible time for MacDonald. 'My dearest H – I feel so worried about you,' wrote Edith. 'What is it? Shall I come and see you tomorrow morning – or what would you like me to do. You wrote me such a vy [sic] charming and dear letter – I can not bear to think of you worried and wretched. This letter carries all my love to you and the flowers – Ring me up sometime this evening about 9 o['] c[lock]. Bless you – and more love from C.'[45] In a desperate bid to keep the country going, proposals were put forward to cut all public expenditure and to raise taxes. The Labour Cabinet was divided over this strategy, especially over a plan for a 10 per cent cut in unemployment benefit. Unable to resolve its differences, it resigned on 23 August 1931. On the next day, a National Government was formed, with Cabinet Ministers from all three parties, in order to rescue the situation and to save the Gold Standard (although this turned out to be futile). MacDonald was very much in two minds as to whether he should lead the new government, but finally agreed to remain as Prime Minister.[46] The King was instrumental in this decision: he had the highest opinion of MacDonald and believed that he was the only man who could tackle the current crisis, so urged him to remain in post.

MacDonald's fellow members in the Labour movement were disgusted. The election of the first Labour government in 1924 had offered tremendous hope to millions of working people, whose lives were made so difficult by poverty and hunger. A woman working in the Midlands at this time has recalled that when the first Labour Government came to power, 'I carried the photos of the Cabinet around with me as others might of their favourite film stars.'[47] MacDonald's willingness to lead the National Government was seen as a betrayal of the Labour movement and the working class; and with the exception of Snowden, Thomas and Sankey, the whole of the former Labour Cabinet deserted him. The 'general opinion amongst my friends here', wrote MacDonald to Edith, 'is that I have committed suicide. I shall soon awaken in the shades.'[48] Many of his former friends never forgave him, Clement Attlee referring bitterly in 1937 to 'the desertion of prominent leaders at a critical moment'.[49] This proved to be a watershed step in MacDonald's career as a politician and, in late September 1931, he was officially expelled from the Labour Party. He claimed to have put his country before his party, but many of his former colleagues accused him of putting personal ambition before everything. The idea of him consorting with a woman who was so ostentatiously rich and Conservative made his decision even more unpalatable.

Directly following the election in 1931, the Prime Minister retired to Chequers to make choices about his new government. He invited Lady Londonderry to join him and they had a long walk together – and after this, he decided to include her husband Charley in the Cabinet. H. Montgomery Hyde comments in his study of the Londonderry family that,

Edith Londonderry's day at Chequers had not been in vain. During the evening of 5 November 1931, it was announced from No. 10 Downing Street that Lord Londonderry had been appointed Secretary of State for Air in the new National government with a seat in the Cabinet.

'The choice of this ministry,' adds Hyde, 'was certainly not Baldwin's.'[50] The Marquess himself was well aware of the reason for his selection. 'I got the Air Ministry through Ramsay and I am eternally gratefully [sic],' he wrote to Edith much later. He added, 'That was part of the assistance you gave Ramsay at a very critical time when your help and support and mine too in a much smaller way was vital to him.'[51] It is possible that Edith was feeling some measure of guilt at this time about the growing warmth of her relationship with MacDonald; if so, the securing of a Cabinet post for her husband provided him with a form of compensation that he evidently appreciated. MacDonald's benefits from the triangle were Edith's love and affection. In the autumn of 1931 he wrote:

The best Christmas gift that anyone in these islands got came to me when you told me that when you prayed in church in the morning and thought only of what belonged to the goodness & beauty of the heart & soul you would ask blessings for me. I press your hand to my heart . . . I stood by you in church wrapped in the bliss which is the heart of the eternal. Bless you, my dear.[52]

The National Government had been set up as an emergency measure until a General Election could be held. MacDonald was inclined to get out before the election and told Edith, 'I am in some doubt as to whether an election is inevitable. Your folks are not behaving too well. The chances they now have as a party are too tempting for them.'[53] But again, MacDonald stayed on. When an election was set for October, he stood as a 'National Labour' candidate in the Seaham Harbour division of Durham, the home of the Londonderry mines. He was already MP for Seaham, having been elected there – a Labour safe seat, formerly held by Sidney Webb – as Labour MP in 1929. MacDonald turned to Lady Londonderry for assistance: 'Do see that all your following vote', he wrote, while electioneering at Seaham. 'This is looking an ominous thing at the moment. They must do it quietly, however'.[54] The Londonderry following *did* turn out to vote for him and he was returned with a majority of nearly 6,000 over his official Labour opponent. In the rest of the country, the Conservatives won 470 out of an overall total of 615 seats. This meant that the next administration was largely Conservative, with the official Labour Party firmly in opposition. National Labour was represented in the Cabinet by MacDonald as leader and by Philip Snowden and J. H. Thomas.

In effect, MacDonald had become dependent on his 'lover's' husband for a constituency, just as Londonderry had been dependent on him for a Cabinet seat. This sort of conduct was described by Virginia Woolf as a kind of prostitution. The influence created by rank, wealth and great houses, she wrote, was 'either beyond our reach, for many of us are plain, poor and old; or beneath our contempt, for many of us would prefer to call ourselves prostitutes simply and take our stand openly under the lamps of Piccadilly Circus rather than use it'.[55] Woolf was probably thinking of Lady Londonderry when she made this comment. She was herself an occasional guest at Londonderry House and well understood the Londonderry way of doing things. In February

1930 she wrote to Sybil Colefax, 'How does one refuse the M. of Londonderry? Aren't I rising in the scale!'[56] She was certainly scathing about Londonderry life, but also intrigued. Invited yet again in June 1931, she told Ethel Smyth that she was preparing 'for a party at Lady Londnderrys [sic] – for which I shall buy a new dress, all spangles . . . I count upon splendour in Park Lane.'[57] But she did not always find it: 'Lady Londonderry gave a party and did ask me', she wrote to Clive Bell, 'at which my heart leapt up, as you can imagine, until I discovered it was to meet 500 Colonial dentists and to hear Mr [Alfred] Noyes read his own poetry aloud.'[58]

On the eve of session in 1931, Lady Londonderry gave her traditional after-dinner reception in Londonderry House, but this time for the National Government. She stood at the top of the grand staircase, while Ramsay MacDonald stood beside her as Prime Minister and Lord Londonderry took up a position just behind them. This was perceived by some as a political triumph for Lady Londonderry: that she had captured and tamed the enemy and was now producing him for display. 'A few months ago', commented an Opposition Labour member with some bitterness, in the House of Commons lobby, MacDonald 'sang the Red Flag. Now he whistles the Londonderry Air!'[59] MacDonald does not appear to have enjoyed the occasion very much and remarked in dismay to Edith, 'If I stick to this job and be your supporter at the top of the stairs, I shall be a more solitary figure than ever – a mule, in short, with a hybrid ancestry and no possible posterity.'[60] He was regarded as a traitor by large sections of the working class and Labour supporters all over Britain, many of whom believed that he was, quite literally, sleeping with the enemy. Margot Asquith even described him as 'what one might call a "Diehard Tory"'.[61] Since the government was in effect a Conservative administration, it was as if he was participating in a reception that was little different from the long tradition of Tory receptions hosted by the Londonderry family. On the eve of the session in February 1932, *The Times* reported that

Lady Londonderry, wearing a dress of deep cherry-red georgette, with a coatee to match, and pearls and diamonds, stood at the top of the staircase with the Prime Minister and Mr Stanley Baldwin [who was Conservative party leader]

to receive the guests. The staircase was decorated with large bowls of mimosa, the receptions rooms with yellow daffodils and mimosa, and on the tea-tables there were red tulips.[62]

By now, MacDonald and Edith were writing to each other or seeing each other every day and, on Sunday evenings, it was his custom to call in for supper at Londonderry House on his way back from Chequers. He was also a frequent guest at Mount Stewart. While visiting France in 1932, she missed him dreadfully.

Dearest H . . . I tremble when I consider how many precious ½ hours of yours I have wasted – yet – not wasted – because I derived untold good from them, and I yet hope – you may have not have wasted your time – and feel better for a mutual talk – for however eminent you may – be – and you are – yet you are the most human – lovable human being – I have chanced to meet – on this glorious earth . . . Much love – and 1,000 blessings, Love from Circe.[63]

Another letter ends, 'My vy fond love to you. You dear and great soul – I love you vy much and admire you more. From C.'[64] The flattery and deference in these letters are marked: possibly Edith, as MacDonald's social superior, was seeking to reassure him of his value to her. Equally, she may have been genuinely impressed by MacDonald's achievements. After he telephoned her with news of the Lausanne agreement in July, she wrote:

Your telephone message gave me *such* joy – not only for the greatest event, but on account of the success of you vy [sic] dear self . . . My whole heart goes out to you in joy and admiration at the manner in which you have pulled it off – Bless you – all my love is yours . . . To hear it, in our own dear words – was wonderful, I still feel breathless – I always knew you were a great man – so I am not surprised – but I am doubly proud and pleased – All my love dearest H.[65]

By 1932, Lady Londonderry was fifty-three and MacDonald was sixty-six. None the less, their letters to each other bristle with the 'breathlessness' of an infatuation that is almost adolescent. In March, MacDonald wrote that his letter had 'to be a queer mixture of gratitude

& regret. I have to tell my hostess how she mothered, & try & tell her how I loved it. One evening she rubbed a startled nerve & soothed it by the magic of her hand & I could hardly bear her going away, I felt so miserable & deserted.' He had a sense, he added, 'that my hostess & I had known each other from the beginning when there was only the Word & nothing but the Word, & would know each other until the Word resumed its empire, that with her I wandered in rich autumn pastures where gentle winds blew & and the air was benign.'[66] Less than two months later, he sent her a letter with the following scrap of writing, enclosed in a separate envelope.

My Dear

You were very beautiful, and I loved you. The dress, dazzling in brilliance & glorious in colour and line, was you & my dear, you were the dress. I just touch its hem, & pray for your eternal happiness wondering at the same time what generous hearted archangel ever patted me on the back & arranged that amongst the many great rewards that this poor unwelcome stranger to this word was to receive was that he would be permitted before he returned to his dust to feel devotion to *you*.[67]

Lady Londonderry's good looks were remarked upon by others, too. Thomas Jones remarked in 1934, 'She is 54 and still handsome and a few years ago must have been extremely so. She is perfectly dressed. . . .'[68]

It is impossible to know whether or not Lady Londonderry and MacDonald consummated their love for each other sexually. Although there is a strong physical and sexual charge in their letters to each other, there is no conclusive evidence, one way or the other. But of course, there would not have been any evidence, whatever happened: sophisticated people like Lady Londonderry knew how to be discreet. When she went to Geneva in 1934 for the Prime Minister's speech at the Disarmament Conference, joining her husband at his hotel, Robert Bruce Lockhart wrote in his diary that 'Ramsay used to go into Lady Londonderry's bedroom every night and talk to her from 11.30 until two.' He added that 'the visits . . . were quite innocent. Ramsay calls her his fairy godmother'.[69] But how did he know this? Anne de Courcy comments that London gossip often made Edith and Ramsay into lovers, but adds that this was almost certainly not the case. One of Edith's letters ends, 'Do, dearest, let us try and meet soon. I do want to see your dear self, and to hold your hand', and de Courcy believes that 'this is probably all they did'.[70] She may be right: but in a way, it does not matter. Their correspondence reveals that they were certainly lovers, whatever form was taken by this love.

Although Edith Londonderry appears to have been MacDonald's favourite woman friend during this period, he also enjoyed close friendships with other women: Lady Margaret Sackville, Mrs Molly Hamilton, Cecily Gordon-Cumming, and Marthe Bibesco, a Rumanian princess. There are various precedents in British history of Prime Ministers having intimate relationships with women to whom they were not married. One recent example was that of H. H. Asquith's love for Venetia Stanley, the youngest child of Lord Stanley of Alderley (later Lord Sheffield). This friendship began in 1907, the year before Asquith became Prime Minister; by 1914, he was obsessed by her, although it appears almost certain that he never became Venetia's lover in the physical sense.[71] They maintained a regular correspondence and he filled his letters to her with personal, political and military secrets of every kind. Asquith anxiously sought Venetia's counsel and needed her badly when faced with political crises. 'We had a heavenly drive, and you were never more wonderful,' wrote Asquith at the time of threatened civil war in Ireland, pleading, 'Do keep close to me beloved in this most critical time of my life. I know you will not fail. *Write*. – dearest love.'[72] In 1915, Asquith's happiness was shattered when Venetia told him of her engagement to Edwin Montagu, one of his Cabinet.

This kind of romantic friendship appears to have been widely accepted between the wars among the upper classes. Certainly Margot, Asquith's wife, appears to have been relaxed about it – or, at least, gave the impression that she was. Referring not only to Venetia but to her husband's later women friends, including Venetia's sister Sylvia, she commented that, 'No woman should expect to be the only woman in her husband's life. The idea of such a thing appears to me ridiculous . . . I not only encouraged his female friends, but posted his letters to them if I found them in our front hall . . .'[73] Charley Londonderry himself enjoyed a friendship with Ethel ('Ettie') Grenfell, Lady

Desborough, that was intimate but apparently not sexual; he wrote to her on a regular basis, sharing his innermost feelings and concerns. She had several relationships like these, one of them with Arthur Balfour when he was Prime Minister. These romantic friendships may have been regarded by the participants as a twentieth-century form of the courtly love of the Middle Ages, in a way that is almost inconceivable following the development of Western postwar psychology and the sexual revolution of the 1960s. But the notion of courtly love does help in a way to make sense of the way that the attraction between Lady Londonderry and MacDonald, two highly romantic individuals, was articulated. His own romantic sensibility relished old customs and tradition. 'One evening when I was dining alone at Londonderry House,' recalled Edith in *Retrospect*,

the telephone rang just about dinner time. Ramsay himself spoke, and asked if he could look in for coffee on his way to the Palace. When he arrived he was arrayed as an Elder Brother of Trinity House in full dress. This was the first occasion on which he had worn it, and he had come especially to show it off. He was so simple and so naive about it. After he and it had been duly admired he went off with the serene countenance of a happy child.

While Edith and Ramsay's love for each other grew in strength, the Labour Party slipped back to its pre-war status as a minor party in Parliament, weak and divided. Given the achievement in 1924 of its first government in history and then a second government between 1929 and 1931 (albeit both minority governments), this was a clear reversal of fortune, depriving the nation of an opposition. But it was reassuring to the ruling classes. Behind the nascent Labour Party and the strikes and marches of the period, the classes of wealth glimpsed the threat of revolution, which had transformed Russia and given impetus to communist teachings all over Europe. One strategy for neutralizing this threat, believed Beatrice Webb, was the creation of the National Government, which was 'acclaimed by the whole of the Conservative Party and newspapers as the one and only bulwark against the spread of Socialism, and against the coming into power of the Trade Union and Co-Operative Movements'.[74] This is a convincing argument, given that out of the twenty members of the second National

Cabinet, only four were National Labour and there were no representatives of the official Labour Party whatsoever. 'Within the new Ministry,' added Mrs Webb, 'are the most prominent enemies of the Labour Movement, such as Mr Baldwin and Mr Neville Chamberlain.'[75]

Would MacDonald have acted differently if he had not been so enamoured of Lady Londonderry? Probably. It is hard to imagine, for instance, that he would have adopted the same approach to the political crisis of 1931 if his wife Margaret had still been alive, who had shared his socialist ideals and been President of the Women's Labour League. Ramsay himself understood full well the obstacles created by his feelings for Edith and to some degree he resented them: 'the silly fact is that I love you. Isn't it a nuisance?' he wrote to her in September 1932.[76] If his class loyalty had been corrupted, it is far less likely to have been corrupted by frank social ambition than by love – love for Lady Londonderry, who was the most important woman in his life at the time he was making these decisions. But little importance has been attached to her influence, and his intimacy with Londonderry House is generally explained away as a symptom of social corruption or simply as a weakness for pomp and splendour. 'Timid, indecisive, vain of applause', wrote the leftwing intellectual Harold Laski, 'he shrank from the price of unpopularity among a society he had growingly come to esteem'.[77] Philip Snowden wrote in his autobiography in 1934:

I do not think that Mr MacDonald felt any regret that the break with his Labour colleagues had come to pass . . . The day after the National Government was formed he came into my room at Downing Street in very high spirits. I remarked to him that he would now find himself very popular in strange quarters. He replied, gleefully rubbing his hands: 'Yes, to-morrow every Duchess in London will be wanting to kiss me!'[78]

However, since Snowden was eager to attach blame to MacDonald for all the problems he himself had caused as Labour Chancellor, his report is unreliable.

It was generally understood that Edith and her entertaining had oiled Londonderry's path and Birkenhead went so far as to say he was 'catering his way to the Cabinet' (which rather missed the point, since it was Edith who organized both the catering and the way to the

Cabinet).[79] From the earliest days of their marriage, Charley had been indebted to Edith for his advancement: when war was declared in 1914, she arranged an appointment for him as aide-de-camp, with the rank of Captain. Lord Londonderry did not only make use of his own wife, though. He used other men's wives, too, to get what he wanted. When in 1942 Winston Churchill opposed the publication of Londonderry's autobiography *Wings of Desire*, he did not negotiate directly with Winston – even though he was his second cousin – but appealed to 'My dear Clemmie' to intervene on his behalf (which she did, successfully).[80]

Another sign of Edith's influence on MacDonald was his support for her charitable work. He was instrumental in arranging for the Queen to be patron of the Personal Service League, which was finding it difficult to raise funds. When it was suggested that royal patronage would improve matters, Lady Londonderry wrote to MacDonald in August 1932:

The object of this letter is to ask you first of all privately, and secondly openly, whether you think the Queen would be our patroness? It would make all the difference to us financially ... Please let me know if you think it would be better for me to write direct to the Queen, but I thought it best to write to you to see if you could say a word to her yourself.[81]

She preferred him to speak on the League's behalf rather than herself, because this would carry the weight of government approval; in addition, the King and Queen were very fond of MacDonald. He duly made the request and it was granted. In fact, though, MacDonald had some reservations about the League and thought it ought to co-operate with the state, in the form of the National Council for Social Service. Thomas Jones, formerly Assistant Secretary of the Cabinet and now secretary of the Pilgrim Trust, was deputed to try to co-ordinate the two organizations and had the following meeting with Lady Londonderry:

I saw her Ladyship in Park Lane. The butler took me up in a narrow lift to a study or boudoir in the roof of the house and I had half an hour or 40 minutes with her Ladyship who talked at me about starving and dying children, ordered cocktails, 'phoned to a servant to take the dogs out for their exercise ... all with a ceaseless volubility and an attempt to charm and hypnotise which entirely failed in its object.[82]

His proposal also failed in its object, since Lady Londonderry blocked the plan.

A cynical view of Lady Londonderry's interest in MacDonald might be that it was deliberately cultivated – to be close to power, to weaken the Labour Party, and to advance Charley's political career. There is no doubt that MacDonald's desertion of the Labour Party and willingness to lead a Conservative-dominated National Government helped to maintain the *status quo*, in which she and her family had huge investments, both ideological and material. This would have had an even greater impact on Britain if war had not been declared in 1939: for in such a scenario, which is likely to have involved a General Election in 1939 or 1940, the National Government would almost certainly have stayed in power.[83] Certainly Baldwin was cynical about Lady Londonderry's motives. In 1935, after he had stepped into Mac-Donald's shoes as Prime Minister, he told her son, Robin Castlereagh, that to most people,

your Mother's friendship with Ramsay is an act of political expediency to help your Father's political career. All his life Ramsay has fought against everything your Father stands for . . . Poor old Ramsay was a doughty fighter in his early days. It was tragic to see him in his closing days as PM, losing the thread of his speech and turning to ask a colleague why people were laughing – detested by his old friends, despised even by the Conservatives.[84]

It does seem that Charley's appointment in the Cabinet was due to favouritism from MacDonald. But this happened as a consequence – not as a cause – of Edith's and Ramsay's feelings for each other, and Edith enjoyed exercising power and being seen to do so.

MacDonald was finally defeated by ill health and hostility from his Conservative colleagues. He retired as Prime Minister in June 1935 and Baldwin took over, installing Sir Philip Cunliffe-Lister in Londonderry's place as Secretary of State for Air; Londonderry was demoted to the position of Lord Privy Seal and leader of the House of Lords.

Londonderry was seen as weak both administratively and politically, and this was not helped by his wife's close relations with MacDonald. He was pushed out of government altogether after Baldwin's electoral victory in November 1935. Even his wife could do nothing for him, now that MacDonald (still in the National Government, but as an isolated Lord President) was out of power. This was a bitter blow to Londonderry, from which he never recovered. He told MacDonald in 1936 that he had been 'slighted and left out which has been my lot ever since Baldwin unceremoniously kicked me out of his Government'.[85] Right up to his death, he was writing resentful letters to Baldwin. 'With one stroke,' he accused him in 1938, 'you wiped me off the political map.'[86] His political decline was accelerated by his and Edith's visits to Germany and cultivation of high-ranking Nazis, including Hitler and Goering. 'Now I admire Londonderry in a way,' commented Harold Nicolson drily, 'since it is fine to remain 1760 in 1936; besides, he is a real gent. But I do deeply disapprove of ex-Cabinet Ministers trotting across to Germany at this moment. It gives the impression of secret negotiations and upsets the French.'[87]

Londonderry and MacDonald were in similar straits by the second half of the 1930s. On the one hand, Londonderry had been firmly placed at the centre of the establishment by virtue of his birth, status and wealth; but on the other hand, he was like MacDonald – an outsider, unwanted by the party with which he identified and by the political world that he regarded as his natural home. 'I do not think your Mother has been a very happy influence on your Father in politics', Baldwin told Robin Castlereagh in 1935. 'She has great charm, vitality and courage – priceless assets,' he said, but added that these assets become even greater liabilities 'if allied to faulty judgment'.[88] Whether or not this was a fair criticism depends on one's point of view and in Baldwin's case, it may have been influenced by a defensive unease at having thrown Lord Londonderry, Castlereagh's father, out of the Cabinet.

After MacDonald's retirement as Prime Minister, his eyesight and general health deteriorated rapidly. His handwriting was unclear and his diary entries were often marred by spelling mistakes and omitted words. In November 1936 he collapsed during a speech by Baldwin at the Lord Mayor's Banquet and had to be carried out.[89] In May 1937, he resigned as Lord President of the Council, bringing his political career to a final end. He was offered a peerage and although he admitted he was a little bit tempted, he turned it down and would not agree even to a knighthood. He and Edith saw less and less of each other. They continued to correspond and Edith sent him occasional gifts, but the infatuation was over. Had there been any real and deep affection on her side, Lady Londonderry might have cared for him in some way in his sad old age. Instead, she continued to busy herself in her role as Tory hostess. It had not been possible to hold an eve-of-session reception while Baldwin was Prime Minister, because of the odium in which he was held by her husband. But when Baldwin resigned in 1937, she held a reception with 2,000 guests for Neville Chamberlain, the incoming Prime Minister. MacDonald, though, was not well enough to attend.

Not long afterwards, MacDonald left Britain on a sea voyage to South America, hoping to restore his health and spirits. In his final letter to Edith, he said he 'was sorry to leave without a real goodbye' and added sadly:

I shall have to take your memory away with me. The result of the journey will remain uncertain, though I shall face it whatever it may be and make the best of it. So let us 'greet the unseen with a cheer', whatever it may be. I shall think much of you as I go along from pagan to saint and pray do not altogether forget me.[90]

After just two days at sea, he died – an old man of seventy-one. This was only thirteen years after his first meeting with Lady Londonderry at Buckingham Palace, when she had been so charmed by his vigour and his romantic Highlands spirit. The day after that dinner, wrote Lady Londonderry in her memoir many years later, a 'Socialist lady friend had warned him against her as a "dangerous woman"'.[91] If that warning is seen to have been justified by later events, then Lady Londonderry well deserved her Ark name of 'Circe the Sorceress'.

Just two years after MacDonald's death, the start of the Second World War ended the grand receptions and dinners at Londonderry House. In 1959, Lady Londonderry held a splendid eightieth birthday party, which was attended by Harold Macmillan (the seventh Prime

Minister to be a close friend), but this was a rare reminder of her lavish entertaining before the war. The Londonderry family had fallen on hard times: when a music concert was held at Londonderry House in 1955 to raise funds for a charity, a fee was charged for the use of the house. Coffee and light refreshments, an announcer and a 'woman for the ladies cloakroom' cost extra.[92] In 1962, Londonderry House was demolished and replaced by the Londonderry House Hotel.

2

'DAILY, HOURLY . . . "OVER THE TOP"'
Lucy, Countess Baldwin of Bewdley

Lucy Baldwin, 1869–1945, was born Lucy Ridsdale, daughter of Edward Ridsdale, a former Master of the Mint and a scientist. She was the elder of two girls and also had three brothers. The Ridsdale family lived in the Sussex village of Rottingdean and were 'the centre-piece in a tiny fragment of idyllic society that had survived like some Ruskinite experiment on a village green by the sea'.[1] All the Ridsdale children loved cricket and hockey and Cissie, as Lucy was known to family and friends, was a very good and enthusiastic cricketer; she became a member of the White Heather Club, a cricketing club for ladies.

In 1891 Lucy met Stanley Baldwin, who was visiting the Burne-Jones family in Rottingdean and was a partner in his family's iron and steel business. They married in 1892 and had six children: Diana, Leonora (known as Lorna), Margaret (Margot), Oliver, Esther (Betty), and Windham (Little). Stanley Baldwin became a Conservative MP in 1906 and in 1923 he succeeded Bonar Law as Prime Minister. He was leader of the Conservative Party for fourteen years and Prime Minister for eight. He relied heavily on his wife throughout his political career and her support for him was unstinting.

Mrs Baldwin was an early advocate of votes for women and took a keen interest in ways to improve the lives of girls and women. She was on the board of management of the YWCA Central Club. Her particular concern, though, was the lot of mothers. She was the first vice-chairman of the maternity charity, the National Birthday Trust Fund, and was instrumental in the passing of the Midwives Bill in 1936, which created a national service of salaried midwives. During debate on the Bill in the House of Commons, the Independent MP

Eleanor Rathbone remarked that it owed a good deal to a number of people, but 'to none more than the lady who is the wife of the head of the Government', by whom she meant Mrs Baldwin.[2] However, Mrs Baldwin's greatest achievement was her national campaign for the provision of anaesthesia for childbirth, which is the subject of this chapter.

Stanley Baldwin was elevated to the peerage in 1937 and Mrs Baldwin became the Countess Baldwin of Bewdley. She was made a Dame Grand Cross of the Order of the British Empire, as a tribute to her own contribution to public life. Her tiny annual diaries, which she kept almost daily between 1894 to 1945, typically start and end with thanks for the blessings in her life. 'Please God Bless this year for England', she wrote at the start of the diary for 1928, '& guide & guard & keep us through it. Amen.'[3]

Lucy Baldwin drew even closer than Edith Londonderry to the position of Prime Minister. For she was not only the intimate friend of the nation's leader, as was Lady Londonderry of Ramsay MacDonald, but also his wife – the wife of Stanley Baldwin, who was the Conservative Prime Minister of Britain in 1923, from 1924 to 1929, and then from 1935 to 1937. But Mrs Baldwin was a very different sort of woman from the patrician Marchioness of Londonderry. Her background was that of the professional and upper-middle class; there were no inherited titles in her family and she only became Lady Baldwin when her husband was created Earl in 1937. He was not from noble stock either: his family was small gentry by origin, who became rich through trade from an iron-foundry business. Their style of life was different from that of the Londonderrys, too. Instead of grand receptions and balls, the Baldwins held only parties: Astley Hall, their home in Worcestershire, has been described as a 'household without worldly show'.[4] All the same, Mrs Baldwin was guaranteed a high level of public visibility and was well placed to exert an influence over national life. She made full use of her position as the Prime Minister's wife to campaign for a cause that she cared passionately about – the need to improve maternal welfare. The high rate of maternal death, she said, was an unacceptable evil and she regarded the level of maternity care that was available to most women as dangerously inadequate.

In particular, she thought it was barbaric that so few women in childbirth were offered any kind of pain relief. At a speech to raise money for this cause in 1929, she told her audience that pregnant women were as likely to die as soldiers in the trenches in the 1914–18 war. 'Do you realize,' she asked, 'that our women daily, hourly, are "going over the top"?' When a mother gave birth, she added, it was just like 'going into battle – she never knows, and the doctor never knows, whether she will come out of it alive or not'.[5] With this bold reference to the horror of the war, which was still fresh in everybody's mind, she created a vivid picture of the fear, pain and death suffered by mothers.

Mrs Baldwin had suffered herself from the tragedy of a failed pregnancy. Two years after her marriage, she gave birth to a stillborn son, which she movingly recorded in her diary with a plain black cross;[6] the second anniversary of his death was recorded with the sad words, '2 years to-day'.[7] But when Stanley Baldwin first became Prime Minister in 1923, Mrs Baldwin had long since given birth to her last of six children and so the maternity issue was no longer of relevance to her personally. Even so, she was determined to use her position to help other women. In 1928, at the age of fifty-nine, she joined Lady Londonderry and Lady George Cholmondeley in the leadership of the newly established National Birthday Trust Fund. She was an active member of its policy arm, the Joint Council of Midwifery, and was instrumental in the passing of the 1936 Midwives Act, which created a national service of salaried midwives. 'Of course, if there was a married woman who had had a difficult labour at the head of affairs or at the Ministry of Health,' argued a leader of the Maternal Mortality Committee in 1934, 'our work would practically be done.'[8] Mrs Baldwin was the next best thing – the *wife* of a key political figure.

But her top priority in the maternity campaign was the need to deliver pain relief to women in childbirth. In 1929 she set up an Anaesthetics Fund, as an offshoot organization of the Birthday Trust. Some other efforts to provide mothers with analgesia were started at about the same time: in 1927, Lady Rhys Williams, the daughter of the novelist Elinor Glyn, set up a fund to pay for a resident anaesthetist at Queen Charlotte's Hospital in London; and in 1930, Lord Buck-master, a Liberal, initiated a short-lived scheme to raise funds for the provision of pain relief in London's voluntary maternity hospitals. But these smaller anaesthetics schemes never really took off, while Mrs Baldwin's Anaesthetics Fund grew into a massive and national cam-paign. She believed that pain relief was a democratic right, just like the vote. 'In Finland, that little progressive nation which was the first in Europe to give the franchise to women,' she liked to point out, 'they always give anaesthetics to women in childbirth.'[9] This link between the pain of birth and the franchise seemed highly relevant in the period leading up to 1928, when the vote was extended to women on the same basis as men. It was underlined by Lord Buckmaster in a letter to *The Times* on 27 January 1929 (to which Mrs Baldwin added her name, as did the Duchess of Atholl). Appealing for donations to his anaesthetics fund, he insisted that 'women surely cannot refuse to help their poorer sisters at the moment when all womanhood is one'. Mrs Baldwin, too, wanted to 'secure for the poorer mother the same relief from suffering as is invariably offered to her well-to-do sister'.[10] The issue of pain relief, argued a number of feminists, was fundamental to the struggle for women's rights. If rich women were as common as rich men, suggested Virginia Woolf, 'You could provide every mother with chloroform when her child is born.'[11]

Today, women giving birth in the West generally expect to be offered pain relief for childbirth. But before the 1930s, chloroform and Twilight Sleep were the only methods available, and only to those women who could afford the care of a doctor. Efforts to diminish the pain of women in labour have been controversial. Over the centuries in Western culture, the agony of childbirth has been regarded as woman's punishment for her natural sinfulness and has been sanc-tioned by the Bible: 'In sorrow,' states the Book of Genesis, 'thou shalt bring forth children.'[12] The common view, especially of men, observed the Public Health Committee of the London County Council in 1933, was that a woman would be doing 'something morally wrong' in evading the pain of labour.[13] Mrs Baldwin had only contempt for this kind of attitude. 'When a man shewing prejudice talks to me on this subject,' she said briskly at a fundraising event, 'I have very great difficulty in preventing myself from telling him what I think.' She added with feeling that it was 'rather a tremendous thing if a man once hears what a woman thinks of him, because he so rarely does'.[14]

The beginning of anaesthesia in midwifery followed the discovery of the anaesthetic properties of ether in 1846. In 1847, the English obstetrician Simpson abandoned ether for chloroform, which is less safe but easier to administer. Queen Victoria gave birth to Prince Leopold under light chloroform anaesthesia in 1853. Following her example, it was not uncommon for Victorian middle- and upper-class women to ask for chloroform for the delivery of their babies. In 1902, Twilight Sleep was developed, which required the administration of scopolamine and morphine. It produced a state of semi-consciousness, in which the woman appeared to feel pain but retained no memory of it. Mainly used by middle- and upper-class women, it was more popular in the USA than Britain and became less frequently used in the 1920s because it was difficult to administer safely. At this time, pain relief for childbirth was generally described as anaesthesia, not analgesia. But as the movement to widen its use developed over the 1930s, efforts were made to distinguish between these two terms. 'In the state of *anaesthesia*,' explained a letter to *The Times*, 'the patient is quite unconscious of what is going on, and does not respond to any stimulus. In the state of *analgesia*, the patient can hear and understand instructions, and can move in response, but does not feel the sensation of pain.'[15] This distinction was useful to Mrs Baldwin's campaign, since analgesia was generally regarded as safer than anaesthesia (though this argument was misleading, since analgesia can also produce side-effects).

The Ministry of Health did little in the 1930s actually to increase the provision of analgesia, though it made a commitment to do so in the Reports of the Departmental Committee on Maternal Mortality and Morbidity between 1928 and 1930. Provision by local government was patchy and most doctors 'won't trouble about it', complained a mother to the Birthday Trust.[16] One reason for this was the lack of financial incentive. 'In the majority of cases,' observed an article in the *British Medical Journal*, 'the practice cannot be made economically sound.'[17]

Mrs Baldwin herself knew well the pain of childbirth, even though she was given chloroform. The birth of her stillborn son in 1894 was preceded by an abnormally long labour. In 1896, before her daughter Leonora was born, she was in pain for several days: 'Ill & in pain all night. Didn't sleep . . . Lay on the sofa still in pain more or less. Stan came in reply to telegram.'[18] Oliver's birth in 1899 was especially painful: 'At 10 minutes to 2 o'clock, the boy was born. – I had a very bad time. – 45 min under chloroform. Thankful he was born alive!'[19] She was still feeling the effects of this birth a week later and had to be 'rolled on to a sofa for tea'.[20] The birth of her son Little in 1904 was also 'Very uncomfortable & in pain'.[21] She was taken ill about 10 o'clock[22] and 'went on in pain more or less' until he was born on the following day: 'At 6.30 Stan went for the Dr . . . Pains started again about tea and went on . . . At 5 to midnight my 3rd boy was born'.[23] This pain and the other kinds of suffering produced by pregnancy and childbirth linked her, she believed, to all women, regardless of their social class. In a BBC broadcast in 1935, given to raise funds for the Birthday Trust, she asked her listeners, 'For a moment or two, please forget that I happen to be Mrs Stanley Baldwin, for I want to speak to you *just as a woman and a mother*.'[24]

Mrs Baldwin did not regard herself as a feminist, though. 'She would be horrified to be dubbed a Feminist', said Thomas Jones, who was Deputy Secretary of the Cabinet, 'but she does battle manfully for women's rights.'[25] It was her belief that women were spiritually and morally superior to men. 'I always feel that woman is the light-bearer in life', she told a meeting of the Girls' Council of the YWCA Central Club in 1929, adding that, 'A man is made and constituted differently, and we women have got to help along the spiritual side of life. So often we come in contact with it – especially where children are concerned, and it is always a disappointment to me when a woman has let down my ideal of what a woman should be.'[26] But in any case, not all feminists were willing to identify themselves with the issue of anaesthesia – not even Lady Londonderry, who had been willing to court family disfavour in her struggle for women's suffrage. She and Lady George Cholmondeley, as leaders of the Birthday Trust, were afraid that a link with anaesthetics might be controversial and might also offend people by drawing attention to the physical side of childbirth. They were therefore anxious to prevent her from mentioning the topic in her Broadcast Appeal for the Fund's Empire Crusade on 28 April 1929.

Lady George's secretary wrote anxiously to Judith Jackson, Mrs Baldwin's private secretary, to explain that 'Lady George Cholmondeley most urgently asked me to ask you to persuade Mrs Baldwin *not to mention anaesthetics*.'[27] Lady George complained to Lady Londonderry that Mrs Baldwin was being 'persistent' about mentioning this 'controversial point' in her imminent broadcast – which 'would be too shattering!!!' She wondered if it might be possible for Mrs Baldwin just to say 'that personally' she hopes anaesthetics will be used in future, without involving the NBTF?[28] The tension was defused when Lady Londonderry was reassured that, 'There is nothing in the constitution against the use of anaesthetics so we are all right there.'[29] In the end, Mrs Baldwin replaced a specific reference to the pain of labour ('We know the *agony* we have had to face in giving birth') with a vague reference to the experience of mothers ('Mothers know *what we have had to face*'); her only mention of pain relief was a plea for funds 'to provide more beds, but also *eventually* anaesthetics.'[30]

Mrs Baldwin may have given in over the first wireless appeal, but she was not going to let Lady Londonderry and Lady George interfere with her ambitious plans for the anaesthetics campaign. In her next wireless appeal, which took place in 1935, she was more direct. 'I am especially interested,' she said, 'in making anaesthetics available in normal cases of childbirth.'[31] The haughty attitudes of Lady George and Lady Londonderry towards Mrs Baldwin may have been the product of their differences in social status: they were aristocrats, while Mrs Baldwin was only upper middle class ('I always had the impression that your Mother looked down on my wife and myself,' commented Stanley Baldwin to Robin Castlereagh, Lady Londonderry's son, in 1936[32]). But their different ways of approaching the issue of analgesia may also have reflected a different attitude towards medicine and science. Mrs Baldwin, as the daughter of a scientist, is likely to have had a greater faith in the potential of scientific development to improve women's lives.

But Mrs Baldwin was also a no-nonsense sort of woman who had the courage of her convictions and was not bothered about social status or personal popularity. This made her rather formidable at times. Lord Norwich (Duff Cooper) later recalled that during a luncheon in 1931 at Aix-les-Bains in France, to which Mr and Mrs

Baldwin had been invited, she made him feel very small. Mr Baldwin had just returned from an interview with the Prime Minister in England and Diana, Duff's wife, was eager to hear what had happened. 'We had hardly sat down', explains Lord Norwich in his autobiography, before Diana said gaily, 'Come on now, tell us every word that Ramsay MacDonald said.' At this, 'Mrs Baldwin looked horrified and exclaimed, "I would never dare ask him such a question."' Lord Norwich explained that this, 'combined with the fact that Diana, despite my protest, was wearing trousers, which were less conventional than now, made me feel that my political future was at the bottom of the lake'.[33]

Mrs Baldwin certainly never wore trousers and her own dress was severe. While other women bobbed their hair or Eton-cropped it and wore toques or bandeaux, Mrs Baldwin's dressed her hair in a bun and her hats were large and majestic. At the Inaugural Meeting of the National Birthday Fund on 12 November 1928, which was held at Wimborne House in London, she was noticeably unfashionable. The *Daily Express* reported that Lady Londonderry looked 'extremely well in black velvet, with a helmet hat. Another was Lady Islington [the mother of Joan Grigg), who also wore black. So did Lady Carlisle. Black is being rapidly restored to the favour of the *chic* – if, indeed, it ever lost it'. It was perhaps inevitable, given the fashionable status of black, that 'Mrs Baldwin wore brown'.[34] She was not prepared to conform to current trends for the sake of it – but she *was* ready to strike out on her own and to take risks, for a worthwhile purpose. This was a tremendous asset to the anaesthesia campaign, for it meant that she was unconcerned about opposition and simply looked around for allies. One of these was Lady Rhys Williams, another member of the Birthday Trust who had already done work for analgesia in labour.

Few women could afford access to pain relief. It was Mrs Baldwin's plan, therefore, that a way should be found to make it available to all women, regardless of their income or social position. Poor women were even more likely to suffer severe pain than their wealthier sisters, since inadequate nutrition in childhood led to a small pelvis and narrow birth canal.[35] Many desperate women sent letters to Mrs Baldwin in the 1930s. 'I have had to have all my children in the horrible pangs of childbirth,' complained a 'Mother in York', 'because I never have had money, not even to pay for a doctor.' Pregnant again, she felt that 'after what I have gone through year after year I cannot go through with it. My nerves are terrible.' A woman expecting her third baby lay awake at night dreading the delivery: 'I can of course only afford a Midwife. She is very good, and very kind and very efficient, but oh for the knowledge that the last hellish pains could be lost in an anaesthetic.' Yet another woman begged for two pounds to pay a doctor's bill so that she could have some relief from pain: 'I am a coward and cannot sleep at night,' she explained, 'for thinking of the time to come.'[36] A mother of seven children wrote to Mrs Baldwin: 'I am looking forward with dread to another confinement next month . . . I'm sure God will bless your efforts to bring this merciful thing [of chloroform] nearer to poor creatures. Then childbirth will not be dreaded nearly so much.'[36]

Mrs Baldwin's own role in her Anaesthetics Fund was threefold: raising funds to support the clinical work; helping to develop criteria for an appropriate method of pain relief; and educating public opinion. The first of these tasks was fairly straightforward, because Mrs Baldwin was careful to link fundraising to her social and political prestige – a notice about a Bridge Ball advertised the sale of tickets from 'Mrs Stanley Baldwin, OBE, 10 Downing Street, SW.' 'At Homes' were bound to be popular at such an address, even in the years of the Depression. On 19 July 1930 she organized an Aerial Meet and Rally at Hanworth Airfield to raise money for her Fund, which was attended by a number of foreign ambassadors. It was 'not only a most successful gathering from the flying point of view', observed the *Sketch* on 30 July, 'but was attended by many notable people, both of airy and earthly distinction'. Funds from the public at large were raised by the sale of stamps and flags bearing the message, 'Help our Mothers with Anaesthetics.'[38] Mrs Baldwin's wireless appeals in 1929 and 1935 brought in many gifts of money and warm wishes of support. A contribution of ten guineas was accompanied by a letter of admiration for 'your work to see that poor women were also given anaesthetics'.[39] 'A Small Giver' wrote to Mrs Baldwin: 'You speak, dear Lady, very kindly of the suffering . . . We heartily hope and pray that God will support you all in this effort, that the people through the mighty Press will be touched to the heart, and the result will be a great and glorious victory over pain and suffering.'[40] One mother sent all she could spare but hoped to have more to give later: 'I enclose a small cheque and will you kindly let me know where to send later on as this is all I can afford just now.'[41]

Larger sums of money came from rich individuals, such as Sir Julien Cahn, the eccentric millionaire businessman who became Chairman of the Birthday Trust in 1930. He liked the fact that Mrs Baldwin was a keen lady cricketer, since he himself was passionate about the game and had his own private cricket team, which he took to Jamaica in 1929 and to the Argentine in 1930. In honour of their friendship, Cahn paid for an up-to-date maternity hospital to be built at Stourport, near her home, which was called the Lucy Baldwin Maternity Hospital. However, there may have been an additional motive behind the generosity of Sir Julien. Although he was very wealthy – having inherited a fortune from his father's hire-purchase furnishing empire and been very lucky in the Stock Exchange Derby Sweep of 1929 – he had no natural access to the higher echelons of society. Mrs Baldwin's friendship gave him an entry point. It also gave him an indirect relationship with the leader of the Conservative Party, which must have been attractive to a man who was President of the City of Nottingham Conservative Association. Another generous contributor was the flour magnate Robert McDougall. 'My special interest', he wrote to Mrs Baldwin on the day after her Wireless Appeal in 1935, 'is in the Anaesthetic Appeal Fund section of the work of your Fund', and he asked her to create an 'Elizabeth McDougall Trust', in memory of his mother.[42]

By October 1935, the Anaesthetics Fund amounted to over £7,786, a sum that is comparable in value to well over a quarter of a million pounds at the end of the twentieth century.[43] With this kind of money coming in, it was possible to start work on the development of appropriate methods of pain relief. Since most British women could not afford to give birth in hospital, promoting the use of analgesia in hospitals would have little impact. The only way forward, realized Mrs Baldwin, was to develop a method of relief that was suitable for use at home, by midwives. She urged the scientists and health professionals working with the Birthday Trust to find a way of helping women that did not require the attendance of a doctor. She was delighted with their first result in 1932 – crushable chloroform capsules, which were manufactured under the name of 'Brisettes' and 'Chloroform Zombs'[44] and tried out in many parts of Britain and in some parts of the Empire. Lady Grigg, who now sat on the Executive Committee of the Birthday Trust, made arrangements for some capsules to be sent to one of the maternity clinics she had founded in Kenya – the Lady Grigg African Maternity Welfare and Training Centre in Pumwani, Nairobi. In October 1933, the matron of the hospital in Pumwani reported on her patients' disappointing reaction to these capsules: 'I have tried them on many cases, in the first stage, in the second stage, and Episiotomy and stitching,' she said, 'but the native women flatly refuse to inhale.'[45] Not everyone in Britain was keen on them, either. While some mothers were grateful and pleased to report that they 'did not know the baby was born', the Medical Officer of Health for Greenwich complained that the capsules made women wave their arms about and turn over; a hospital in Wolverhampton said that the capsules made women 'very hysterical and difficult to manage'.[46] There were technical problems, too. 'The capsules were anything but crushable', observed one doctor,[47] while the Matron at Alexandra Maternity Home reported that some of her capsules had exploded.[48] In 1936, the British College of Obstetricians and Gynaecologists ruled that the capsules were too dangerous for use by midwives acting alone.

Mrs Baldwin promptly abandoned the capsules and shifted her allegiance to the Minnitt Gas and Air apparatus, a new method of pain relief that had been developed in 1933 and was preferred by the British College for use by midwives in the home. The concentrations of the Minnitt machine were originally 45 per cent nitrous oxide and 55 per cent air, but this was later altered to 50 per cent of each. The apparatus consisted of a reduced pressure regulator attached to a small rubber bag in a metal drum, with an automatic valve shutting off the flow of gas when the patient did not inhale.[49] The Trust embarked on an energetic campaign to distribute these gas-and-air machines and responded particularly swiftly to requests on the grounds of economic need, such as one from a nurse working near Nottingham: 'We are a very poor colliery district and wide rural areas and it is difficult to get necessary expenses and certainly no margin for such things as this.

Is there any means of producing one free of cost?'[50] A midwife in independent practice in North London pleaded, 'Please help me to get one of the bags, as I do not like to see these poor women suffer, knowing as I do, there is something I could give them, if only allowed to.'[51] Wallsend Infirmary appealed for a machine on the grounds that it was serving mothers in 'a very badly depressed area'.[52] The machines were gratefully received, judging by the many letters that were sent to the Trust headquarters. 'We are very proud of the Gas and Air apparatus you gave us,' wrote two midwives in the Rhondda, 'and hope to do good work with it.'[53] Like the short-lived chloroform capsules, gas-and-air machines were sent all over the world, to places as far afield as Hong Kong, Calcutta, Mexico and Singapore. Whenever Sir Julien went abroad with his cricket team, he took an apparatus with him as a gift for a hospital. By the time the National Health Act came into force after the Second World War, 1,775 Minnitt machines had been distributed all over Britain and to various parts of the Empire, either free or through a grant from the Birthday Trust.

But many of these machines were not being used, as there were few courses of instruction available for midwives. 'I have seen gas apparatus provided free of charge by the National Birthday Trust standing in the corner of the labour ward, covered with rust and dust,' reported one doctor to the *Manchester Evening News*.[54] There were two main reasons for this slow progress, one of which was simple resistance to the idea of midwives providing pain relief. The other was the stipulation by the Central Midwives Board that gas and air should not be administered unless two trained midwives were in attendance – and most nursing associations found it hard enough to send one midwife to a delivery, let alone two. Consequently, only twenty-nine out of 188 local authorities had provided their domiciliary midwives with training by 1939.[55]

These clinical obstacles were difficult to overcome. Even harder, though, was the challenge of educating the public at large. In most cases, as one mother wrote in a letter to Mrs Baldwin in 1938, 'the mothers don't know such a thing exists'.[56] This was particularly true of mothers who were poor: the Public Health Committee of the London County Council reported that, 'Anaesthesia in labour is still outside the experience of the class of women coming into municipal hospitals.'[57] This level of ignorance was holding up the anaesthetics campaign, believed Vera Brittain. After enduring a difficult childbirth herself in the 1930s, she wrote in *Testament of Experience* that she 'wanted to batter down the solid walls of the Ministry of Health; to take the Minister himself and give him a woman's inside, and compel him to have six babies, all without anaesthetics'. But then she realized that the Minister could not be held responsible: '*I remembered that he, after all, could only go as fast as the public insisted.*' She realized that the force for change had to come from the mass of the people themselves, which was not likely to develop with any speed when 'all women were cursed with such an infinite capacity for resigned endurance'.[58] Mrs Baldwin tried in every way possible – over the wireless and in speeches – to encourage women to expect something better from life. A key goal of her campaign was to eradicate the common assumption that women who accepted the benefit of anaesthesia did not care about their children. The stamps and flags that were sold for the Anaesthetics Appeal sought to counter this message: the words 'Help Our Mothers With Anaesthetics' surround a veiled mother holding her baby in her lap, looking down in a devoted manner. This image of a loving mother is heightened by the placement of mother and child at the centre of a sun and its rays of light, as if she were surrounded by a halo – thus drawing on centuries-old iconography of the Madonna.

Mr Baldwin's support as Prime Minister was invaluable. Simply by associating himself publicly with the desirability of pain relief in childbirth, he gave it a kind of official authority. Lucy Baldwin understood this well and, right from the start, drew attention to the connection. When she made a broadcast appeal for the Birthday Fund in 1929, she did so from Chequers, the Prime Minister's official country home. He was more than willing to contribute to the campaign in this way and when Lord Beaverbrook and Lord Rothermere (who were using their newspapers to conduct a campaign of hostility against him in the run-up to the Government of India Act of 1935) refused to publish an appeal by his wife for donations to her Anaesthetics Fund, he was outraged. 'Some time ago my wife wished to make an appeal in connection with a subject in which she is keenly interested – that of maternity services and the provision of anaesthetics for mothers in confinement', he explained in an address to electors in 1931. He added that 'the whole of the Press rallied to her support', with the exception of the *Daily Mail*, the *Daily Express* and also the *Daily Herald*, which was the paper of the trade unions and the Labour Party. 'I can only attribute it,' he concluded, 'to the fact that Lord Rothermere must be a man who dislikes women.'[59] Lord Beaverbrook promptly sent Mr Baldwin a letter stating that Mrs Baldwin's campaign for the welfare of motherhood – although not the appeal itself – had been mentioned eight times in the *Daily Express*.[60] This heavily defensive reaction gives a sense of the growing popularity of the anaesthetics campaign.

It is not clear to what extent Stanley shared his wife's distress about the anguish of women in labour. As Prime Minister, though, he is likely to have welcomed her campaign as a means of arresting the fall in the birth rate, since the dread of labour was thought to be an important cause. A letter to the Minister of Health from one member of the public insisted that 'the chief cause of the low birthrate is the *fear* of bearing children, which is a ghastly experience given good conditions'.[61] One doctor wondered in a letter to the *British Medical Journal* if the medical profession had contributed to the decrease in the birth rate, by the unnecessary withholding of anaesthetics during labour.[62] A connection between the pain of childbirth and the birth rate was drawn right up until the time when the population trend was reversed, shortly after the Second World War. In 1945, Lady Rhys Williams received a letter claiming that, 'Practically the first sentence the average woman says when the ordeal is over is, "Thank God – Never Again", which is one of the chief reasons for the one-child problem.'[63]

But in any case, Baldwin had a debt of obligation to his wife, who supported him in everything throughout their long marriage. 'Without Lucy Baldwin', argue his biographers Middlemas and Barnes, he 'would probably never have had a political career, perhaps had nothing more than a repetition in a minor key of his father's excellent but obscure fame . . . Ambition . . . was hers, and in the slack dead periods which tended to follow nervous effort, it was her energy, sympathy and even temper which sustained him.'[64] Kenneth Young, another biographer, makes the same point: that it was Lucy who, 'when Baldwin faltered, urged him, "Go on, Tiger", and she was the real trigger to his latent political ambition.'[65] Lucy knew how important she was. In a letter to her mother-in-law in 1923, she reflected, '*I feel that I am Stan's "Trainer" for the Arena* and I have to see that he husbands his strength for the fighting times'; later that year she wrote that it was 'very exhausting hearing Stan make these big speeches. I am so anxious for him to do well'.[66] She identified completely with Stanley's success and failure and referred to his political persona as 'we' – a unit comprising herself as well as him.[67] After the election defeat in May 1929 she wrote in her diary, 'So *we* are beaten. But God willing *we'll* flourish again.'[68] On 20 October 1922, Lucy wrote to her mother-in-law to tell her about Stan's resignation from the Cabinet and his break with Lloyd George as leader: 'I knew Stan wasn't happy at the way things were going under the PM's leadership . . . But just this last peril of war and the way it had been brought about, was too much for him. So *we* decided we must make *our* protest, knowing that *we* should probably go under and of course Stan wouldn't get office again as long as the PM was Prime Minister . . . Stan told them that he always consulted me and they talked to me as though I was a Cabinet Minister too!'[69]

Lucy's role as Stan's 'Trainer' took various forms, one of which was a kind of mothering. As Baldwin's biographers have observed, periods of intense effort left him exhausted and weak, in need of revival by her. She watched out for him constantly and at one dinner party she rescued him from a young woman 'whose effect was to make him wither under my eyes': at last, she wrote to her mother-in-law, 'I could endure Stan's SOS no longer . . . and took Stan from the hands of the pretty figure-head.'[70] During elections she took some of the pressure off her husband by going out herself on the campaign trail. 'I was speaking at Willesden on Tuesday', she wrote, '. . . and was speaking at Salisbury yesterday. So your mother is on the stump, and again I go to S. Battersea on Wednesday. Just heard that we have won Shipley!!'[71] Lucy was not only Stan's 'Trainer', but also his hostess. Her first in a series of 'At Homes' was an 'awful day',

but about 180 people turned up. – Stan came in for about an hour which pleased the guests very much and had about half a dozen trusty lieutenants who went about introducing people to each other . . . I am rather amused for I hear that Mrs Lloyd George has followed my example and is giving At Homes to the Liberal Ladies – and Lady Salisbury told me last night that she is going to give a series of lunches to the wives of members of the party and wants me to come & lend a hand so we are trying to tighten the bonds that connect us all and make a strong united party.[72]

'I am giving a dinner party to wives of the Government the same night that the Prime Minister is giving to the Government,' she told her mother-in-law, '& so husband & wives will dine next door to each other & then proceed to Lady Londonderry's At Home. It is rather a good thing as we shan't have a long time after dinner to pow-pow to each other.'[73]

Lucy supported Stanley in his public life because he was the centre of her world. This is manifest in all her diaries, whether in connection with the most routine activities ('Lovely day. – Pottered with Stan') or an event of national importance ('Unpleasant foggy day. Stan and I walked . . . Great anxiety about the King's Health. His heart seems failing. We kept awake until 8.30 a.m. to hear the latest').[74] Whenever possible they were together: 'Bank & paid wages. Stan and I lunched with Lady Milner, Helen Hardinge there';[75] 'Stan and I dined at the Londonderrys where they had an Ark Party.'[76] They even shared an interest in controlling their weight: reporting to her mother-in-law that she was trying to get down to 11 stone, she added that, 'Stan has a weighing machine in his bathroom on which he places himself solemnly every unoccupied minute & I also visit it weekly so we keep in near touch to our weight & diet accordingly.'[77]

Lucy subordinated her own interests to her husband's needs. She was very disappointed, she wrote in her diary, that she had missed a speech by Stan in the House because she was 'at a wretched meeting about babies!'[78] When she went to the first night of a performance of 'Elijah', a fundraising event for the Birthday Trust, she wished she could have been with Stan, who 'wound up the India Debate in the H. Of C. – My heart was there'.[79]

Mrs Baldwin's unqualified backing of Stanley in his political life may be contrasted with Margot Asquith's lack of helpfulness as the second wife of the Liberal politician Herbert Henry Asquith, whom she married in 1894 and who was Prime Minister between 1908 and 1916. She did nothing to support the war effort and made no attempt to hide her extravagance, which probably contributed in some way to his fall from power in 1916. Vita Sackville-West took even less interest in the political life of her husband Harold Nicolson when he stood as a Conservative candidate for Leicester in the 1935 General Election. He asked Vita to accompany him on a campaigning visit, explaining that the electorate expected to see his wife and would otherwise think they were divorced, but she replied, 'I do genuinely think that an isolated appearance at Leicester would be worse than none, because of its inconsistency'. She added, 'it would also lead to bazaars and things *after* the Election, if you get in.'[80] Harold was 'puzzled and disappointed and rather cross' at her attitude, saying that 'it does ignore my need and difficulties'.[81] It is likely that Vita's lack of interest, which was proportionate to the very real help given to Stanley by Lucy, contributed to Harold's failure in political life.[82] Another happy marriage in the public eye was that of Clementine and Winston Churchill, which their daughter Mary Soames describes as a 'loving and heroic partnership'.[83] 'His cause was her cause', wrote Violet Bonham Carter, 'his enemies were her enemies, though (to her credit) his friends were not invariably her friends.'[84] Churchill always relied on the support of women, especially Clemmie and Violet Bonham Carter. When Violet, the daughter of Asquith, announced her plan to train as a nurse at the start of the 1914–18 war, he gave her a lecture on 'the duties of women' to those at the 'apex' of responsibility for the war. 'No, my dear,' he told her, 'you must remain here at your father's side – and mine . . . We who are directing these immense and complicated operations . . . need every comfort, care and cosseting . . . *We* are your duty. This is your war-station.'[85]

Mr Baldwin's enemies were quick to attack his wife's involvement in his political life. Lord Derby complained to Neville Chamberlain that 'The worst of Baldwin is his leadership. His policy is good: he makes, as a rule, very excellent speeches, but after that he fails as a leader. He has no hold on his party . . . *Between ourselves, I think Mrs Baldwin has done him incalculable harm.* She may be quite right to spare him as a general rule, but surely she ought to let him know some of the criticisms which I know she hears herself but which she keeps from him. The worst thing for a man like that is to be allowed to live in a fool's paradise.'[86]

But Baldwin benefited enormously from the support of his wife. The image of 'man and wife' went everywhere with him, even to a meeting on 8 March 1928 to celebrate the Equal Franchise Bill. Vera Brittain writes in *Honourable Estate*, a novel that is carefully set in the historical reality of the time, that 'the audience rose to its feet with a roar, and Mr Baldwin, solid, square-headed and affable, came in with his wife'. The couple presented a singular but genuine illustration of the old adage that 'behind every great man is a good woman' – an image that emerges from Leo Amery's description of the run up to the election of 1924, when the speeches of the party leaders were broadcast over the wireless for the first time. While MacDonald ('spoiling his effects by over-emphasis and by turning from side to side') and Asquith were unable to turn this opportunity to their advantage, 'Baldwin, with Mrs Baldwin knitting beside him, addressed himself, in quiet, confidential tones, to man and wife sitting by the fireside. He proved himself an admirable broadcaster, and his broadcast largely swung the election.'[87] This image of a happy and peaceful marriage was a valuable political asset to the Conservative Party after 1928, when it was necessary to appeal to the newly enlarged female electorate. But it was also an asset to the pain-relief campaign, since it associated the tradition and solidity of the Conservative Party with the new idea of avoiding pain in labour.

The only real obstacle to Mrs Baldwin's campaign was created by the medical profession. On the whole, general practitioners opposed the idea of midwives using gas and air and the British Medical Association (BMA) passed a resolution to this effect at its 1939 annual meeting. This resolution had no official bearing on the work of midwives, since the Central Midwives Board, not the BMA, was the statutory body, but it angered many of those who supported the analgesia campaign. Shortly after the BMA meeting, the Independent MP Eleanor Rathbone referred in Parliament to 'the selfish attitude of a certain portion of the medical profession who expressed their views the other day'[88] and a letter to the Trust said that it was only because of the 'inarticulacy ... of thousands of working class women', that the strength of the resentment against the 'recent decision of the BMA has not been realised'.[89] At this time, argues Frank Honigsbaum, an historian of British medicine, the GP was being squeezed out of midwifery by a pincer movement: pressure from obstetricians trying to consolidate their role as experts and pressure from midwives, 'who, aided by the revolutionary Minnitt machine and the backing they received from public health officers under the 1936 Midwives Act, took over an ever-increasing share of home confinements'.[90] During the debate that preceded the passing of the resolution at the 1939 meeting of the BMA, a number of doctors said they 'wanted to stop midwives controlling the midwifery of the country'.[91] The GPs' struggle to maintain a central role in childbirth failed. By the end of the Second World War, only about one out of three GPs still practised midwifery.[92] However, their efforts to sabotage the use of analgesia by midwives was more successful. According to *Maternity in Great Britain*, the report of an important and national birth survey in 1946, the negative attitude of GPs was 'the deciding factor' in the delay to develop and provide analgesia for childbirth.[93]

Mrs Baldwin's dream of bringing pain relief to *all* women, regardless of income, was still a distant dream by the end of the Second World War. There had been some measure of success: whereas in 1930, only one hospital in Britain (Queen Charlotte's Hospital in London) had routinely offered pain relief to mothers in 'normal' labour, by 1936 few voluntary hospitals did not; and many municipal hospitals, too, which were largely attended by working-class mothers, had adopted the policy of providing relief to every mother in labour. The Chairman of the House Committee at the City of London Maternity Hospital wrote a letter to *The Times* in 1937 to express his appreciation of Mrs Baldwin's work. 'When I first joined the committee of this hospital in 1929,' he said, 'analgesics for normal maternity cases in the wards were almost unknown.' But now, he added, 'their use is ordinary routine and they are availed of in practically 100 per cent of cases, and what is true of this hospital is true virtually for all similar hospitals'. This remarkable change in so short a time, he observed, was 'due to the inspiration and the tireless efforts and encouragement of Mrs Stanley Baldwin'. Virginia Woolf quoted from this letter in *Three Guineas*. 'Since chloroform was first administered to Queen Victoria on the birth of Prince Leopold in April 1853,' she added, ' "normal maternity cases in the wards" have had to wait for seventy-six years and the advocacy of a Prime Minister's wife to obtain this relief.'[94]

Many women did not benefit from this advance, however. Forty-six per cent of mothers in England delivered at home in 1946 and only 20 per cent of these were given any sort of pain relief; of the mothers who were attended by midwives, the figure was as low as 8 per cent, reported *Maternity in Great Britain*. The most common analgesic was chloroform, which was used in 14 per cent of domiciliary confinements. Only one in five practising midwives in 1946 was qualified to administer gas and air, which was used in a mere 5 per cent of home births. Moreover, the use of gas and air was practically limited to England, where 7 per cent received it compared with only one mother out of 433 women in Wales and *none* in Scotland.[95]

But the campaign to educate public opinion and to produce a change in attitude had been a triumphant success. The 1946 national birth survey found that the most commonly stated reason for dissatisfaction with treatment during labour was the lack of analgesia.[96] In 1946, for the first time, the Women's Cooperative Guild, the women's arm of the working-class Cooperative Movement, called for pain relief to be made available for normal labour;[97] then, the following year, it demanded that all midwives be trained and equipped to provide it.[98] The anaesthetics campaign had been so successful that it had already generated a reaction – the concept of 'natural' childbirth. This strategy for birth was advocated by Grantley Dick-Read in his books *Natural Childbirth* (1933) and *Childbirth Without Fear* (1942), which argued that, by the controlled elimination of fear, the need for analgesic drugs could be avoided. But most women did not want to avoid these drugs – they wanted to have them. A building labourer's wife, who delivered her baby at home with the assistance of a midwife, said that, 'Something should be given. I was tired out before I started. People with plenty of money don't have to suffer pain.'[99] A Mass Observation report in 1945 quoted one woman as asking, 'Rich people don't suffer, why should we?' Another complained, 'if you have money you can have the best anaesthetics and everything. That's not right is it?'[100] The disparity between rich and poor in the provision of pain relief had not, after all, been removed. A letter to the *Lady* complained that, 'this is not democracy. One of the most cruel class divisions yet remaining in this country is that rich mothers need not suffer in childbirth as though we were still in the Stone Age, while poorer ones far too often do.'[101]

This unequal provision slowly disappeared following the Second World War, as a result of the health service established by the National Health Act. Although it took some time to develop the resources to deliver a universal service, full responsibility was now taken by the state for the delivery of adequate and safe methods of pain relief to all mothers who required it. Mrs Baldwin had taken a leading role in a revolution that not only transformed the experience of childbirth, but narrowed the gulf between the lives and the expectations of poor women and rich women. She had used her influence for the benefit of all women, including those less fortunate than herself. In her honour, a gas-and-air machine was named 'The Lucy Baldwin Apparatus' by British Oxygen in 1959.

Lady Baldwin died in 1945. But her campaigning work continued to exert an influence on national life. Four years later, a Private Member's Bill for Analgesia in Childbirth was introduced in the House of Commons by Peter Thorneycroft, a Conservative MP.[102] Mrs Baldwin would have been delighted if she had still been alive – that a Conservative MP brought in a Bill aiming to make analgesia in labour a statutory right. The Bill produced a furore: Labour MPs accused Thorneycroft of party politics and said the Bill was unnecessary, since its contents were covered by the NHS; while Conservative MPs said that the legislation for providing analgesia in childbirth was only permissive and ought to be made into a duty. Aneurin Bevan, the Minister of Health, angrily accused Thorneycroft of aiming to exploit 'human pain as a political stunt' and the *Sketch* took this opportunity to produce the following verse:

> Getting Aneurin Bevan
> Into Heaven
> Won't be any easier
> Even with analgesia.[103]

Several files at the Public Record Office are brimming with letters begging Bevan to push through Thorneycroft's Bill, from individuals and from organizations ranging from the Midland Federation of Housewives and the Union of Catholic Mothers to the Women's Section of Islington Borough Communist Party. A telegram from Streatham Hill in South London urged him, 'Appeal your personal intervention save Analgesia Bill stop Pain more important than any policy.'[104] Thorneycroft pointed out, 'Mothers do not suffer pain according to the party to which they belong ... They all suffer the same pain, and they all demand the same relief.'[105] This was the very argument that Mrs Baldwin had put forward in the 1930s.

Bevan may well have been suspicious of the analgesia campaign's historic association with Mrs Baldwin and therefore with the Conservative Party – an association that was highlighted during Commons debate by a reference to her 'pioneer' work.[106] But in any case, as everybody involved was well aware, it would have been impossible for Bevan in the early years of the NHS to ensure that all women were offered analgesia.[107] Eventually the matter was resolved by a proposal from Labour of some additional clauses to the NHS (Amendment) Bill, which would strengthen legislation covering pain relief in labour. This managed to defuse the power of Thorneycroft's Bill and to give the message that Bevan's ministry was working hard to deliver obstetric analgesia under the NHS.[108] Thorneycroft's Bill finally died when it was defeated on its third reading by 108 votes to 44, five months after its introduction.[109]

The Bill was heavily covered in the press while it was passing through its various stages and it may well have damaged Bevan's reputation in the eyes of some of the female electorate. One woman who described herself as a socialist warned Bevan of

the perfect chance it will give the Tories to get at millions of women if you do not pass the Bill. Absolutely millions of them who are too busy to take an interest in politics but will certainly not remain indifferent over a Bill like this. It is bad enough that the thing has been put forward by a Tory ... We cannot afford *not* to pass the Bill, everything will count now.[110]

Another Labour supporter was afraid that, 'the indifference to the suffering of about half the electorate may seriously prejudice many voters against the Labour Party'.[111] Maybe the analgesia issue contributed in some way, however small, to the reduction in Labour's majority in 1950. If so, then the association between obstetric analgesia and the Conservative Party, which had been created by Mrs Baldwin's passionate campaign, can be seen to have lingered on beyond her death.

3

'A BRITISH RACE PATRIOT'
Violet, Viscountess Milner

Violet, Lady Milner, 1872–1958, was born Violet Georgina Maxse, the youngest of the five children of Admiral Frederick Augustus Maxse and his wife Cecilia, the daughter of Colonel James Steel (Indian Army). Her parents separated when she was small and the five Maxse children spent part of their time in the country with their father, a hero of the Crimean War, and part in London with their mother. Both parents introduced Violet to a network of gifted politicians, artists and writers, and she took an interest in politics and culture from her earliest years. She became fluent in French and was well read in French literature.

In 1894 she married Lord Edward Cecil, a distinguished soldier and the fourth son of Lord Salisbury, who was Conservative party leader and prime minister in 1885–6, 1886–92 and 1895–1902. This marriage brought Violet into the circles of the greatest in the land. In 1899 during the Boer War Lady Edward accompanied her husband to South Africa, where he took a leading role in the defence of Mafeking against the Boers. Violet and Edward had two children: George, who was killed on active service in France in 1914; and Helen, who in 1921 married Alexander (Alec) Lord Hardinge, who succeeded his father as Second Baron Hardinge of Penshurst in 1944 and was private secretary to George V, Edward VIII and George VI. After their return from South Africa, Lady Edward and Lord Edward Cecil grew estranged from each other and led virtually separate lives until his death in 1918.

In 1921 Lady Edward married Alfred Lord Milner, whom she had met in South Africa during his period of office as British proconsul between 1897 and 1905. Lord Milner had been a member of the war

*cabinet during the First World War and was secretary of state for
war in 1918–19; he was secretary for the colonies between 1919 and
1921. They shared a powerful sense of duty to the British Empire. His
death followed four years after their marriage and Lady Milner grieved
bitterly, devoting herself to the management of his papers and
affairs. In 1932, at the age of sixty, she began a period of sixteen years
as the editor of the* National Review, *which had previously been edited
by her brother, Leo Maxse. Lady Milner used the* National *to address
the political issues of the day and to put forward her own views;
according to her obituary in* The Times, *she made the* National *'one
of the hardest-hitting periodicals in Britain'.*[1] She died at the age of
eighty-six.

Violet Milner was an exponent of strong imperial views. As the un-
married Violet Georgina Maxse, the daughter of an admiral, then as
Lady Edward Cecil, and finally as Viscountess Milner, she sought to
disseminate these views as widely and as effectively as possible. For
her, the idea of Empire amounted to a kind of religious faith, which
she shared with her beloved second husband, Alfred Milner, the British
statesman who was British High Commissioner in South Africa during
the Boer War of 1899–1902. Milner developed a theoretical account
of his imperialist faith, which he called 'Key to my position' and which
Lady Milner found in his papers after his death and published in *The
Times* as ' "Credo". Lord Milner's Faith'. It contained a clear statement
of his – and her – imperial vision:

I am a British (indeed primarily an English) Nationalist. If I am also an
Imperialist it is because the destiny of the English race, owing to its insular
position and long supremacy at sea, has been to strike fresh roots in distant
parts of the world. My patriotism knows no geographical but only racial
limits. I am an Imperialist and not a little Englander, because I am a British
Race Patriot ... It is not the soil of England, dear as it is to me, which is
essential to arouse my patriotism, but the speech, the tradition, the spiritual
heritage, the principles, the aspirations of the British race. They do not cease
to be *mine* because they are transplanted.

Imperialism should become the faith of the whole nation, believed Milner.[2] It was a sacred duty, which is powerfully conveyed in *Stalky & Co.*, a school story first published in 1899 by the Milners' friend Rudyard Kipling (who was a cousin of Stanley Baldwin). When a visiting speaker to the school gives an account of the 'fair fame of their glorious native land' and then waves a large calico Union Jack before the boys, they are appalled. Seventy-five per cent of them are sons of officers in the services and for them, the waving of the flag in this way 'was no part of the scheme of their lives; the Head had never alluded to it; their fathers had not declared it unto them. It was a matter shut up, sacred and apart.'[3] For them, suggests Kipling, imperialism was a duty so deeply felt that it was offensive to have it made explicit in this crude and jingoistic way.

Today, the memory of British imperialism provokes a shudder of distaste among many people and it seems incomprehensible now that so many companies and institutions between the wars were given names like 'Imperial Airways' and 'Empire Cinema'. Then, too, some people were ambivalent about the idea of Empire, especially within the Labour Party, but for many it was accepted as natural and right and as Britain's civilizing mission to the world – a mission of benevolence that was justified by the superiority of the British race and British institutions. When the Duchess of Atholl referred to 'the tremendous responsibilities resting on this country as the Motherland of a world-wide Empire', she was describing a duty that was widely felt.[4] The British public were proud of the British Empire Exhibition at Wembley Park, which was opened by King George V in 1924 and which boasted a magnificent Palace of India and a Malaya Building, with domes and minarets. There was a national consensus that, as Baldwin stated in his Empire Day Message in 1925, the British Empire was good for everybody, colonisers and colonized:

The Empires of old were created by military conquest and sustained by military domination. They were empires of subject races governed by martial power. Our empire is so different from those that we must give the word Empire a new meaning or use instead of it the title British Commonwealth of Nations.[5]

Key to this idea of Empire, of course, was pride in being British. 'There are two things of which I am intensely proud,' commented Lucy Baldwin. 'One is being born British. The other is being the wife of Stanley Baldwin.'[6]

Lady Milner's early years were heavily imbued with the imperial creed. Her family was closely associated with the *National Review*, a right-wing monthly periodical. For almost forty years, it was the one-man show of her brother Leo Maxse, who was 'A British Imperialist bound only to the British Empire; a Tory of the type called a Die-Hard', according to G. K. Chesterton in a fond obituary.[7] Violet was brought up to take politics seriously. Educated largely by governesses, she was 'one of the very few remaining *grandes dames* of English society, survivors of an earlier age . . . [and] steeped in politics' according to Patrick Donner, who was a director of the *National* from 1933 to 1947. 'There was no aspect of domestic politics,' added Donner, 'with which she was not familiar, but where foreign affairs were concerned, she was an expert.'[8] Fluent in French, she spent two years studying painting in Paris and knew many leading French politicians, notably her lifetime friend, the statesman Georges Clemenceau. Violet Markham observed after her death that she had 'known everyone who counted'.[9]

Violet Milner kept a personal diary, in which she devoted considerable space to political issues. In 1926, when the Trade Union Congress (TUC) ended the General Strike with its unconditional surrender, for example, she observed drily that Baldwin's reaction on the wireless 'struck the exact note – semi sob-stuff and wholly non-committal – that [was] likely to be effective'.[10] The business of reading and writing was a serious matter for Lady Milner, especially in relation to politics. Her overwhelming concern during the General Strike was the absence of newspapers: she reported in her diary that she 'bought two crystal wireless sets – one for my own and one for the maids' use', and was very pleased to see 'a very thin *Times*' on the following day.[11] She discusses the rivalry between the Government's temporary news organ, the *British Gazette*, and the TUC's riposte, the *British Worker* ('Nothing else was printed, not even Hansard'),[12] and was pleased to see the Paris edition of the *Daily Mail* on sale two days later. When the strike was over, Lady Milner was concerned that *The Times* were still 'out' in London and she wrote in her diary that the editor, Geoffrey Dawson, who was a friend, did not know when the newspaper's 'own Bolshies will return!'[13]

Given the importance that Lady Milner attached to the written word, it was perhaps inevitable that her own contribution to the imperial mission would lie this way. She made strategic decisions about the publication and distribution of both her husbands' papers after their respective deaths and then, when her brother Leo Maxse died, she took over the editorship of the *National*, regarding this as her 'pious duty', in the words of her obituary in *The Times*.[14] In this way, she became a midwife for the ideas and reputations of the three most important men in her life: her brother Leo, her first husband Edward Cecil and, most importantly, Alfred Milner. Her attempts to influence political thought did not properly begin until her second widowhood, but her earlier life provided a preparation for this work – the experience, the material and the contacts she was later to need. Leo Maxse's participation in the imperial idea was wholly intellectual (as hers proved to be also), but both her husbands were involved in a practical and active way in the imperial mission. Lord Milner, indeed, acquired a great reputation as an imperial statesman, equalled only by that of Joseph Chamberlain, who was colonial secretary during the Boer War.

Although the Maxse family was connected with the peerage through the barony of Berkeley, Violet's family background was upper-middle class rather than aristocratic. She did not really enter the highest echelons of society and politics until she was twenty-two, when she married Lord Edward Cecil, son of the Third Marquess of Salisbury, in 1894. This brought her into one of England's great Conservative families and the world of Hatfield House in Hertfordshire, its family seat, which was a significant political centre. The importance of Hatfield is explained by Lord David Cecil in his book *The Cecils of Hatfield House*:

[It is] complex partly because it is both public and private. It was designed to be the house of a great nobleman, when great nobles ruled the country. This means it has something of the palace about it, with its grand staircase and huge ornate rooms intended for state occasions and semi-public gatherings. All the same, the impression it leaves is not that of a palace; it is also a family home with the characteristics of a family home.'[15]

Joining the Cecil family must have been exhilarating for Lady Milner, given her keen interest in politics. One year after her marriage, her father-in-law became Prime Minister for a third time, staying in power until 1902. Edward himself was a distinguished soldier and was decorated with the DSO for services in Egypt and Sudan on the same day in 1898 as Violet's brother, Sir Ivor Maxse. He played an active part in Britain's rule of the Empire: he was aide-de-camp to Lord Kitchener during the conquest of the Sudan in 1896–8; agent-general of the Sudan government and director of intelligence at Cairo in 1903; under-secretary of war and subsequently under-secretary of finance to the Egyptian Government in 1906; and financial adviser to the Egyptian government between 1912 and 1918.

Violet had first met Edward in early 1894, on a visit to Dublin Castle, where he was serving as ADC to the commander-in-chief of the British army in Ireland. She wrote to her mother on 18 February that 'the only one I feel really at home with is Lord Edward Cecil. He doesn't go to balls, worse luck, but he's been to call three times and I shall meet him tonight at a dinner the Guards are giving for the Viceroy.' Less than a month later, on 13 March, she joyfully reported that, 'I am going to marry Edward Cecil. We settled this last night.'[16] The Cecil family were less delighted with the news. They feared that Violet, as a woman from a more artistic and literary background than Edward, would be bored by the life of Hatfield. Lord Salisbury even went so far as to warn Violet that 'Hatfield is Gaza, the capital of Philistia.'[17] An even more worrying concern for Edward's parents was her religious background – or rather, her lack of it, since her father was a professed atheist. They themselves were very high Christians and earnestly hoped that she too would accept the Christian faith. They put considerable pressure on her to do so, even sending her for instruction by the future Bishop of London. 'I spent some hours with him,' wrote Violet, 'and I was not asked to go again.'[18] Her atheism caused Edward great distress. In her later marriage to Milner, though, it became a common bond: their religious faith was not the Christian gospel, but the values he set out in his imperialist 'Credo'.

Violet accompanied Edward to South Africa in 1899, after he received orders to help Colonel Baden-Powell raise two regiments of soldiers for the defence of Bechuanaland and Matabeleland against the Boers. When she and Edward landed at Cape Town, they stayed at Government House with the British high commissioner, Sir Alfred Milner – who was to become her second husband after Edward's death. Lord Edward Cecil was highly praised for his role in the Boer War, especially for his role in preparing the town of Mafeking against the threat of siege. He ordered four times more food and ammunition for the town than had been officially allowed and because of this, the town was able to resist the eventual long siege; the eventual relief of Mafeking was celebrated by Britain as a national victory, with rejoicing all over the country. While Edward was in Mafeking, Violet stayed at Groote Schuur, Cecil Rhodes's estate near Cape Town. From here she carried out relief work for refugees and sought to improve conditions in hospitals by supplying the wounded with comforts like toothbrushes and slippers.

After leaving South Africa, Edward and Violet grew apart and although they remained married (Edward's religious beliefs would have allowed nothing else), they effectively led separate lives. When he went to Egypt in 1901 as under-secretary and established himself in Cairo, she did not make her home there, and visited Egypt only once or twice; instead, she stayed in England at Great Wigsell, their family home near Hawkhurst in Sussex. He remained in Egypt for the rest of his working life until 1917 and their only regular contact was during his month or so of annual leave in England. However, they corresponded regularly and letters from Edward to Violet reveal his continuing affection for her. 'Dearest Love', he wrote in the summer of 1900, 'the world is still rather grey. I do seem to lose all interest in things when you are away. I don't think you know what a support and inspirer you are to me.'[19] They both suffered a terrible blow when their son George was killed in 1914, in the early days of the war, while on active service in France. 'I try to be brave', wrote Lady Edward to her husband, 'and don't mend very well.'[20] Their other child was the future wife of the second Lord Hardinge of Penshurst.

But the key factor in the breakdown of the Cecil marriage is likely to have been the intimate friendship between Lady Edward and Milner, which developed when they first met in 1898 in South Africa. They started a regular correspondence almost straight away: the first extant letter from Lord Milner to Violet is dated as early as 1898, the year of this first meeting. In all the letters to her that have survived, he writes in a frank and confidential manner, telling her for example about the uneasy relations between himself and Kitchener, the soldier and statesman who was commander-in-chief of the British army in South Africa between 1900 and 1902. During the 1916 government crisis, she was kept informed by Lord Milner on matters of state. If they also wrote letters of love, these were probably destroyed at the time or weeded out later. Some sense of the early years of their relationship emerges from a letter to Lady Edward from Mrs Louise Dawkins, a mutual friend. Written from Simla on 19 October 1899, it appears to be a reply to a request from Lady Edward for some information about Milner. Mrs Dawkins informs her – but indirectly, in relation to some shared acquaintance – that 'Milner succumbs very easily to feminine charms but I also know that he is equally good at wriggling out of the fair sex's hands when he wants to' (this may have been a gentle warning to Violet to be careful with her feelings). However, she assures her that 'Milner does attach great importance to your opinion'.[21] The serious and intellectual Lady Edward was certainly different from some of Milner's earlier objects of affection, such as Elinor Glyn, the romantic novelist.

A letter still exists which was written by Milner to Violet on 5 August 1917 (and therefore just over a year before Lord Edward's death) and which – in a section that has been clearly crossed out but is still legible – provides evidence that they had an 'understanding'. In this crossed-out section, Milner tells Violet:

Of course, I have always felt that sooner or later you would have to free yourself from 'impossible' conditions, and I am always shaping my own plans with that in mind. Every year makes it easier, as once [Helen] is launched on her own life – and if she only gets healthier, this should be possible in a few years – there is no more reason, only either of us should mind anything [sic].[22]

The '"impossible" conditions' mentioned by Milner almost certainly refer to Violet's marriage to Lord Edward.

Increasingly, Lady Edward took on imperial duties. One of these was the 1820 Memorial Settlers' Association, an organization which worked in conjunction with the Overseas Settlement Department of the Dominions Office. It promised 'A Full and Free Life in Prosperous South Africa' in its advertisements, such as this one in the *National Review*:

An ideal land for the retired man. Living and labour are cheap; taxes are low; sport inexpensive; excellent educational facilities and good prospects for the rising generation.

For the young man with modern capital who wants to farm, training and expert advice are free.

Lady Edward also became Vice-Chairman of the Overseas Settlement of British Women. In a way, she became an extension of Milner's 'kindergarten', a group of brilliant young men that he recruited to work with him in South Africa when he was British high commissioner. These included John Buchan, the future novelist and governor-general of Canada, who was his private secretary in 1901, Bob Brand, Lionel Curtis and Geoffrey Dawson. Milner trained these men in the arts of imperial administration and they worked with him in his efforts to rebuild South Africa after the Boer War. John Buchan was later to recall that when Milner invited him to come to South Africa in 1901, he was 'the most controversial figure in the Empire, applauded by many as the strong man in the crisis, bitterly criticised by others as bearing the chief responsibility for the war'.[23] Buchan admired Milner enormously. According to his son William, he revered him 'as much for his gentleness and courtesy as for his high visionary aims and superb practical ability'. All the members of the kindergarten revered both Joseph Chamberlain and Milner, believing in their vision of an imperial federation, where Britain would be a dominant force within a closely bonded empire. When Milner returned home from South Africa, he sought to initiate a rebirth of the imperial mission and the kindergarten set up the *Round Table* magazine, in order to influence the opinion of the public about the importance of the Empire. Edward Grigg became editor of the *Round Table* and was effectively a member of the kindergarten, although he had not been part of the group in South Africa. Like Lady Edward, all these men were interested in journalism. Milner himself had once been a journalist, working as deputy editor on the *Pall Mall Gazette* from 1883–6. Sir Edward Grigg was imperial editor at *The Times* before the 1914–18 war and Geoffrey Dawson became the newspaper's editor between the wars.

In 1918 Lord Edward Cecil died, at the age of fifty-one. Three years after his death, his widow published a collection of sketches he had written at various times during his eighteen years of service in Egypt, which he had sent home to amuse his family in Britain. He had stipulated, though, that this writing was 'for family consumption only as I could only live in a cellar under an assumed name if some people saw it'.[24] It is not difficult to see why he made this request: published as *The Leisure of an Egyptian Official*, these sketches give an insulting picture of Egypt, Egyptians and Egyptian life. According to Cecil, Egypt had produced 'countless servants, watchmen, grooms, and cooks', but 'no single man of eminence, or even partial eminence'; they are 'without that something', he added, 'which enables some Negroes even to rise to eminence among their fellow-men.' Cecil's accounts of daily life are intended to illustrate this supposed stupidity of the Egyptian: in the sketch 'Getting Up and Breakfasting', for example, a tram line in front of Lord Edward's abode is so badly designed that unless the driver slows down sufficiently, the car goes off the line. 'As no Egyptian even profits by experience, as when it is cold he cannot think at all,' comments Cecil, 'the early tram runs off the line five days in seven.'[25]

The Leisure of an Egyptian Official did nothing to help Anglo-Egyptian relations. Moreover, it was out of touch with the spirit of the time. Egyptians, according to Cecil, were 'people literally without a history'. But this was not the belief of the British public: just two years later, following the discovery at Luxor of the unrifled tomb of the Pharaoh Tutankhamen, they were infected with a massive enthusiasm for Egyptian history. 'Ancient Egypt suddenly became the vogue,' wrote Robert Graves and Alan Hodge. All over Britain,

replicas of the jewellery found in the Tomb, and hieroglyphic embroideries copied from its walls, were worn on dresses; lotus-flower, serpent, and scarab ornaments in vivid colours appeared on hats. Sandy tints were popular, and gowns began to fall stiffly in the Egyptian style. Even the new model Singer sewing-machine of that year went Pharaonic, and it was seriously proposed that the Underground extension from Morden to Edgware, then under construction, should be called Tootancamden, because it passed through Tooting and Camden Town.[26]

New buildings, too, drew on the heritage of Egypt: Adelaide House, which was built at the end of London Bridge in 1924–5, was given ancient Egyptian details. Evidently, Lady Milner had misjudged the feeling of the public. But her decision to publish *The Leisure of an Egyptian Official* was consistent with her world view, because it shows a people weakened by the withdrawal of British administration. The Preface to the Fifth Edition, written in 1929, explains to the reader that 'The book helps us to understand something of the general work of the men of our race in the outer world' and warns against trusting the 'Oriental rulers who succeed the English'. These are problems, advises the author of the Preface, which 'each generation of Englishmen has to learn how to understand . . . if England is to keep her place in the world'.[27] The overwhelming message of the book is the superiority of the British and the British Empire.

The publication took place eight months after her marriage to Milner and surprise has been expressed that he let her go ahead. He himself, as colonial secretary in the Lloyd George coalition government, had conducted long negotiations with the Nationalist leaders in Cairo and had reported in favour of virtual independence for Egypt (although the Cabinet rejected his recommendation). In his book *England in Egypt*, first published in 1892, he had described Egypt as an intriguing and extraordinary 'Land of Paradox'.[28] His tone is one of respect, albeit for a country that is decidedly foreign and not British.[29]

Lady Edward Cecil became Lady Milner three years after Edward's death and twenty-seven years after her first marriage; she was now forty-nine and Lord Milner, who resigned from his post as colonial secretary sixteen days before the wedding, was sixty-seven. In the period between Edward's death and this second marriage, Milner plied her with practical advice on how to organize her affairs.[30] But occasionally, a more passionate emotion bursts through the business-like prose of his letters:[31] in the margin of the last page of a letter written in January 1920 from Cairo, he declares, 'What a joy it will be to see you again!'[32] Their wedding was quiet. Geoffrey Dawson was one of the few people to be told about the wedding beforehand; Lord Milner, he wrote later, 'rather shyly imparted to me as a dead secret his arrangements for being married on Saturday'. Dawson was surprised by the news, as he had always regarded Lord Milner as a confirmed bachelor who wished to devote all his energies to the imperial mission.[33] But Lord and Lady Milner appear to have been immensely compatible: 'I wish you were here', wrote Milner to his wife from Sturry Court, their home in Kent, 'and that I could look forward to a quiet evening with you.'[34] Misunderstandings were swiftly sorted out and on one occasion Milner wrote from the male sanctuary of his club, the Athenaeum: 'My Beloved, I was so sorry for the contretemps this morning – *all my* fault, I *admit!*'[35]

Milner died in 1925, just four years after their marriage. 'It's all so dreadful', wrote Violet in her diary some months later, 'without *him*.'[36] In February 1926, she wrote that it was

exactly a year since my darling Alfred and I left the Cape. I have all day had this like a pain at my heart. It is 9 months to a day since he died – in this very room. I don't know how each day passes by in its solitude and grief. The contrast between the heavenly companionship of the past and the desolation of the present seems too great even to understand. It can only be endured.[37]

'This time last year he was alone in this room,' she wrote in dismay shortly before the first anniversary of his death. 'He wrote his diary for the last time. God help me!'[38] But she determined to take up the baton of his imperial work. Leo Amery recorded in his diary that when he visited Sturry 'to have the last look at my old chief', he found Lady Milner 'calm, unemotional and businesslike' and wanting to discuss practical matters, such as the appointment of additional trustees to the Rhodes Trust (an organization that awarded Rhodes scholarships at Oxford University to outstanding students from the Commonwealth and the USA). Another pressing issue was Milner's plan for Edward Grigg to go to Kenya as governor.[39] Most other women at such a time, observed Leo Amery, would have been 'afraid to face anybody'.[40]

On 8 January 1926 she wrote in her diary that she went to visit her friend Clemenceau, and had a long talk with him about life, about sorrow, about myself and my loss. I told him of my conversation with—, who said, 'do you believe in a future life?' 'No.' 'Did Lord Milner?' 'No.' and how he afterward said that my disbelief had consolidated his own faith in further existence after death.

Clemenceau caught me by both shoulders, we were standing up, and said, '*Voilà la différence entre L'Emotivité et la Raisonnement.*'

This visit 'did me good', added Lady Milner, 'this call to effort and to truth!' Truth for her was the championing of Milner's reputation and his imperial creed.

The historian A. M. Gollin has suggested in his book, *Proconsul in Politics: A Study of Lord Milner in Opposition and in Power*, that she contributed very largely to the view of Milner that has persisted ever since. This portrayal has been described as the *Religio Milneriana*, a term initially – and contemptuously – used in the early 1900s by Sir Henry Campbell-Bannerman, then leader of the Liberal Party; according to his biographer, Campbell-Bannerman 'attributed a large part of his difficulties with his colleagues and especially those of them who were Balliol men to what he characteristically called the *Religio Milneriana* ... this blind belief in a Balliol hero he regarded as a psychological infirmity of the Oxford mind'.[41] Campbell-Bannerman found his task complicated by the influence Milner exerted upon one section of the Liberal Party – the Liberal Imperialists generally and Asquith, Grey and Haldane in particular, who resented any criticism of Milner. To overturn these struggles within the Liberal Party, Campbell-Bannerman set about undermining the prestige of the high commissioner for South Africa and had achieved considerable success by 1905–6.

This *Religio Milneriana* was restored after Milner's death by his wife and the kindergarten, who were now much older and in positions of influence. 'In their rapture', commented Gollin, 'they were responsible for the creation and propagation of a number of myths about Milner, praising every one of his actions.'[42] Violet's first effort at glorification was the publication on 27 July 1925 of his 'Credo' – which she had found in her husband's papers – in *The Times* and the *National Review*; it was also reprinted as a pamphlet that was sold for a penny, bearing the statement that it was 'now published, by Lady

Milner's permission'. She fully understood the historical importance of the mass of documents he had left behind and she set about distributing them in a strategic manner. Engaging Cecil Headlam in the role of editor, she produced two volumes of *The Milner Papers: South Africa*, which were published in 1931 and 1933. She kept a tight control over this work and there are many references in her diaries to her own role within it: on 29–30 March 1933, for example, she worked on the papers continuously; and on 28 June 1933, she had 'been at it all day with the Milner papers'. In 1929 she handed over to the Public Record Office, the British national archive, various documents relating to the Doullens Agreement of 1918, which had arranged for the coordination of all the Allied Armies on the Western Front under the command of General Foch (and which was the prelude to the Allied victory). These papers were of great value to the nation because Milner, as secretary for war in 1918, had represented the British government at the signing of the agreement. Additional Milner papers were given to New College in Oxford. Lady Milner became regarded as an expert on Milner – not so much as his wife and widow, but as an authority in her own right. She wrote in her diary in March 1932 that after lunch, 'Mr Baldwin came to ask me for any books or speeches of Alfred's that would help *him* to make speeches at Ottawa. He talked with considerable frankness about the Government. He stayed some time.'[43]

She distributed his property, most of which had been left to her, in a way that was calculated to bring honour to his name and his imperial mission. Sturry Court, near Canterbury, was given to the King's School, one of the major public schools for boys. The Junior School moved to this site in 1919 and it was renamed Milner Court. Five Milner memorial scholarships were created at the school, open to the sons of men serving in the civil services of India and the colonies, or 'who reside in those distant parts of the empire where adequate educational facilities are not available'; in addition, three memorial leaving exhibitions were set up, open to those seeking 'to prepare themselves for a career in the Empire overseas'. Lady Milner's generosity was complemented by a gift from the Trustees of the Public Memorial to Lord Milner, a group of his friends and admirers, who purchased seventy acres of adjoining land for the school to use. These gifts were marked by a ceremony at the school on 18 July 1928, when

Lady Milner laid the foundation stone. Another cause for celebration was the opening for public use of the Milner Memorial Ground, an acre of turfed and planted land nearby, which had been bought by the donors of the Milner Memorial Fund. Leo Amery gave a speech, in which he said that Lord Milner had been a great servant of his country and of the British Empire and that 'when the history of our lives came to be written few names would occupy a higher place'.[44]

After her husband's death, Lady Milner took on various kinds of public service. She became a member of the Blanesborough Committee on Unemployment Insurance and with characteristic thoroughness she visited numbers of Labour Exchanges between 1925 and 1927 as a way of understanding the issues involved. 'We had a *tremendous tussle* lasting nearly the whole time, over the rates of benefit', she recorded in her diary, adding with some satisfaction that 'the Committee *has not divided* and there is some hope of a united report'.[45] At committee meetings she became friendly with the Labour MP Margaret Bondfield, another member, who was to become the Minister of Labour in 1929. She developed great respect for Miss Bondfield, despite the sharp difference in their political views. After a meeting in 1926, she 'brought Miss Bondfield back to lunch with me. A very interesting vital woman.'[46]

In 1932, seven years after Milner's death and when Lady Milner was sixty years of age, she embarked upon her great work – her 16-year editorship of the *National Review*. Although this new role started as she was moving towards the autumn of her life, she had always been involved in some way with the *National* (or *Nat*, as it was often called). Their father, Admiral Maxse, had bought the periodical for her brother Leo Maxse in 1893 from Alfred Austin, who had already established its character as a Unionist and Imperial publication. Leo maintained and developed this character and the cover of the *National* was primrose, the colour of the flower associated with Disraeli because Queen Victoria had sent a wreath of primroses to his funeral. Leo attained great influence in the role of editor, largely as a result of his line on the Dreyfus case in France and his warnings of German bellicosity before 1914. Although one Liberal periodical, *The Nation*, described the *National* as representing the 'tea-table splutter of the golf-house and the club-room',[47] its circulation figures just before the 1914–18 war approached 20,000; this was comparable to that of the largest-selling weekly, the *Spectator*.[48] The *National* found a 'ready readership among those who fancied themselves the natural governors of late Victorian and Edwardian Britain'[49] and it was also the kind of high Tory journal to be found, along with the *Fortnightly Review*, in the officers' mess, among sporting weeklies and illustrated magazines.[50]

Leo Maxse fell ill in 1929 and Violet started to take part in the management of the journal by making editorial decisions, contributing articles and revising proofs. In the edition of September 1930, she referred to herself as 'Acting Editor' and as 'the amateur who stumbled into his chair'; she thanked the supporters of the *National* for their kindness as she was conscious, she said, 'of having frequently made howlers'. Because the future of the journal seemed uncertain, the Maxse family converted it into a private company and created a board of management dominated by themselves, with Violet Milner and her brother, Sir Ivor Maxse, as key figures. The object of this change was 'to ensure the permanency of the *Review* on its present lines, and to prevent it from falling, at any future time, into the hands of owners who might wish to alter its robust outlook on national questions'.[51]

Leo's illness made Violet feel 'very, very low'[52] and she was devastated by his eventual death in 1932. 'At 10.30 the night nurse called me and I stayed with Leo *until he died* at 1.30', she wrote, adding, 'My darling brother.'[53] She now took over his role as writer and editor, but made it clear to everyone that she was doing so on his behalf: that she had taken up the baton of his work, as she had done for Milner after his death. This idea was reinforced by the fact that when Leo was editor, the front cover always bore the words 'Edited by L. J. Maxse', set out clearly and directly under the title of the journal – but when Violet took over, the cover made no reference to her editorial role. But in any case, this would have been a sensible approach for a periodical like the *National* during the interwar period, when women were not generally regarded as capable of political and intellectual analysis in the way that men were supposed to be (and many men felt like H. H. Asquith, who was 'not even sure' that he liked 'highly educated females', as he told his wife Margot[54]). Of course, Lady Milner was ideal for this job. 'They asked me to undertake the Editorship of the *National*', she wrote in her diary, adding that someone else would do 'all the *non*-political work'.[55]

The structure of the periodical remained more or less the same under Violet's reign as it had been under her brother Leo's. The essence and core of each number were the forty or so pages of editorial, called the 'Episodes of the Month', which had been written entirely by Leo – and were now written entirely by Violet. Her diaries are full of references to work on the 'Eps': 'Writing Eps, I have no heart for them now Leo is not there, and it is no longer *his National*', she wrote in early 1932.[56] 'I have had a slow steady drive at Eps', she wrote a week later, 'correcting and writing all day.'[57] Sometimes she found it arduous – 'Work at *Eps* collar [that is, boring] work. I write without any spark now.'[58] But her attitude was a professional one and she always managed to get the 'Episodes' ready in time. She welcomed criticism and was grateful to Patrick Donner when he 'criticised my Eps very usefully'.[59] The information she put into the 'Episodes' was obtained from sources at the highest level, whether at home or abroad. Donner, who lunched almost weekly with Lady Milner at her London home in Manchester Square, commented that, 'Everyone of note, sooner or later, found their way there, from the Prime Minister of Australia to Mr Dawson of *The Times*.'[60] She was a kind of political hostess, but not in the manner of Lady Londonderry: she did not preside over showy and lavish receptions, but over discreet and refined luncheons.

Even though Lady Milner was now putting so much of her writing energy into the *National*, she continued to comment in her diary on political affairs, such as recent developments regarding the revival of Joseph Chamberlain's controversial scheme for tariff reform (the idea of imperial preference, according to which all foreign imports would be taxed by Britain and the Dominions, while imperial products would be admitted duty-free). Having learned that a resolution had been brought before the House of Commons 'adopting 10% Tariff on everything but meat, bacon, wheat and grain, and giving free entry to Colonies and Dominions', she commented with satisfaction that, 'This is the biggest thing that has happened since armistice day and a true turn of the tide.'[61] But, in fact, the future of the Empire was starting to look somewhat bleak. There was a crisis in India, the 'jewel in the crown' of the British Empire, because the Indian Congress was demanding independence and was following Gandhi in a policy of 'civil disobedience'. Attempts at a solution were complicated by conflicts within the Conservative party over proposals leading to the 1935 Government of India Act. In Egypt and East Africa, too, there was strong opposition to British rule. All these matters were aired in the *National*. On a February day in 1933, Lady Milner 'egged away at Eps all the morning. *Subject India*'.[62]

She introduced a number of innovations to the *National* and in 1937 it absorbed the *English Review*. She introduced a literary side to the publication, which involved a signed 'Literary Article' and a series of anonymous 'Book Reviews'. A typical edition of the *National* under Lady Milner's editorship contained book reviews, correspondence, and articles on a broad range of subjects. In just one edition, for example, this range included: 'Geneva and Nanking', 'The Colorado Beetle', 'British Sea Powers and Indian Home Rule', 'Winter Sports at Home', 'Is the House of Lords Noble?', 'Mr Baldwin *versus* the Empire', 'Some Jews and Others', 'Flying in the Eighteenth Century', 'Germanism and Anti-Semitism', 'European Civilisation and African Reactions', 'Communists Turn Capitalists', 'The British Guiana Constitution', and 'Ellen Terry'. The style is always clear, factual, unadorned and to the point, whatever its subject – the virtues of imperial preference and tariff reform, or the weather forecast in the regular 'Rain Guide for the British Islands'.[63]

Lady Milner's writing style in the 'Episodes' was more restrained than her brother's, although both Maxses had a reputation for strongly held opinions. Leo Amery referred to this characteristic in his diary on November 1906, in connection with a meeting that was held 'to see what could be done to organise the sound people in the Liberal party to keep the Government in order on Imperial questions'; Leo Maxse and Lady Edward were 'extreme as usual', he reported, 'and we really did more practical business after they left.'[64] Violet was far more willing than Leo to engage in debate and to convince through argument, although she was by all accounts a most formidable woman. Donner's memoir recalls a weekend party at Great Wigsell, when one of her guests was awed into a most unenviable position:

Lady Milner, Diana Mayne, Alan Lennox-Boyd and I had started lunch when our hostess was called away to the telephone. Something had gone very wrong with the soup, which tasted most peculiar. Alan, seizing the opportunity, called the dog and put his plate on the floor. The dog lapped up about a quarter of it and then decided that he didn't like it either. Alan had just time to pick up the plate and put it back in front of him as Lady Milner returned. She sat down and said, in her most authoritative voice, 'Alan, you haven't finished your soup. Please do so while we wait.'

Alan's face was a study, but he finished the soup.[65]

The *National Review* was an ideal medium for spreading the Milner gospel and most editions contain at least one piece about Milner's life and work. The edition for July to December 1933, for example, contains an article by James M. Rendel called 'Lord Milner in South Africa', as well as an excerpt from 'The Milner Papers' that was edited by Headlam and another piece entitled 'The Milner Papers' that had been 'serialised by the Viscountess Milner'. In January 1931 the imperial statesman George Ambrose Lloyd wrote her a letter, listing the three kinds of public in need of 'our propaganda'. First, he said, there were the 'Conservatives who liked their views propounded in terms of the "Nat". They have not as yet learnt from anyone to be ashamed of the Imperial spirit.' Second, there was the kind of Conservative which 'likes another language than the "Nat" . . . [and which] needs confirming in its views'. And finally, there were the readers that were 'free thinking'. Just as the Fabian Society lured thousands into Socialism by clever propaganda, he argued, 'so we need some clever and disguised propaganda to lead free thinkers into Conservatism'.[66] Like the Milners, Lord Lloyd was a diehard defender of the Empire, and had been Governor of Bombay and High Commissioner for Egypt. However, Lady Milner would not have regarded the *National* as any form of propaganda; rather, she saw it as an organ of 'true' opinion.

Very quickly after taking over the role of editor, Lady Milner began warning her readers against the dangers to Britain of German nationalism. As early as March 1933, her 'Episodes of the Month' were commenting that Germany was 'a bad neighbour and a tricky customer to have dealings with'. She argued that whether or not Germany became Fascist was not the point: what *did* matter, she said, was Germany's behaviour as a neighbour. She called for massive rearmament and preparation for war, recommending to her readers that they lay in stocks of food 'as far as their cupboards will hold them'.[67] The chief concern, she stressed, 'should be to see that we have an army and a navy [that is] adequate . . . and then we need not be anxious about Herr Hitler or any other Herr.'[68] Her warnings became more and more urgent and started to dominate each publication of the *National*. She tried hard to inform her readers as fully as possibly on Nazi policy, by publishing extracts from *Mein Kampf* (not the 'emasculated' version that had been prepared for British readers by the Nazi propaganda machine, but the 'unexpurgated version of this official Bible of political blood-lust'[69]) and from the speeches of Hitler, Goering and Goebbels. No one who read the *National* could claim to be ignorant of what was going on in Germany and her criticism of Neville Chamberlain's attempt at appeasement was unrelenting. Many readers of the *National* were grateful that she was prepared to take on this responsibility and wrote to express their appreciation. 'All that has happened in the Rhineland', wrote Brigadier General John Hartman Morgan as early as 1936, 'confirms the vision and foresight of everything you have written in the *National Review* during the last few years.'[70] The imperial mission was never forgotten, however. 'Each part of the Empire', wrote Lady Milner in January 1939, 'should know exactly what task it has to perform to save the heritage of all.' To this end, she added,

we should keep our immense home markets for our Empire as far as possible. This is as important a measure of defence for us as it is for the strength of the Empire itself . . . Now then, Mr Chamberlain, is not this programme after your great father's heart? Suppose you have a try at carrying it out?[71]

Lady Milner's warnings were based on a careful analysis of the political situation in Europe, although her great sorrow at the loss of her son George in the 1914–18 war is likely to have shaped the tone of her expression. She believed that there were important lessons to be drawn from the mistakes of the earlier war, especially the evil caused by delay in rearmament. 'To most people in England', she observed in

1934, 'the War came as an overwhelming surprise. They had so often been told that war was "unthinkable" that they had ceased to think about it. When it came – suddenly, it seemed to those who had believed the statements of political leaders – the nation stood up to meet it and to face the appalling losses which had been brought upon it by the lack of foresight of Cabinets and Parliaments.'[72] The same message was being pressed by Winston Churchill, who was directing a vigorous anti-appeasement campaign. It may seem odd that she did not ally herself with Churchill, but in fact she had loathed him ever since he made a bitter attack on Lord Milner in his capacity as under-secretary of state for the colonies. Two of her great strengths, however, were fairness and an ability to subordinate personal feelings to the needs of a larger purpose. Consequently, after years of railing against Churchill in the *National Review*, she finally – in August 1939 – acknowledged the importance of his work for national defence:

For three or four years Mr Churchill has done national work which is beyond praise. He has steadily and eloquently warned the country of the danger ahead. He has gingered up one set of ministers after another and forced them to do their duty. It is no small thing to have played the part of Demosthenes in our State during these critical years.[73]

When war was finally declared on Germany on 3 September 1939, Lady Milner wrote in her diary, 'War has begun. Germany attacked Poland at 5 a.m.' She added, in a sad reference to the death of her son George, 'It is 25 years since my boy was killed.'[74] Lady Milner's opposition to appeasement was her greatest triumph as editor of the *National Review*. Ed Murrow, who covered the war in Europe for America as director of the American broadcasting company, CBS, later said that in his opinion, she had summed up a spirit of determined resistance to Germany more than anybody else in Britain.[75]

In 1948, when she was seventy-four, Violet announced her plans to retire from the *National*. She received many letters of congratulation on her achievements as editor. 'It was a strong force', wrote Iverach McDonald, then assistant editor of *The Times*; 'one of the real links of Empire.'[76] The role of editor was taken over by Sir Edward Grigg, who had been appointed Governor of Kenya Colony at Milner's suggestion. When he in turn retired in 1954, it was taken over by his son, John Grigg, until 1960, when the *National Review* was finally closed down – it had become impossible to keep a monthly periodical going, especially one that rested on opinion rather than news. After her retirement, Lady Milner set about writing *My Picture Gallery 1886–1901*, a memoir of her life as a girl and young woman and her reminiscences of the people she had known in Victorian days. She appears to have given up trying to influence the minds of her readers: 'I do not write with any idea of teaching anything', she wrote in the Preface, 'but I have a longing to show others the people I have admired and the scenes among which I have lived.'[77]

In a way, she had nothing left to teach: because the imperial gospel, which had been the mission of her life, was shown to be no longer relevant after the Second World War. In his 'Credo', Milner had expressed the hope that negative feelings about the Empire would soon disappear and that 'all Britons, alike in the Motherland or overseas, will be Imperialists, that it will be the happier fate of those who come after us to create that state which it has been our duty to preserve for them the possibility of creating'.[78] But this was a vain hope. Just a few years after the publication of *My Picture Gallery* in 1951, the Suez crisis crucially exposed Britain's weakness as an imperial power. In 1960, Harold Macmillan's 'wind of change' speech in Cape Town acknowledged the inevitability of African independence. Milner's 'Credo' had become an outdated faith.

4

'TO THE WOMANHOOD OF DARK AFRICA'
Joan, The Hon. Lady Grigg

Joan Grigg, 1897–1987, was born Joan Alice Katherine Dickson-Poynder. She was the only child of Sir John Dickson-Poynder, Sixth Baronet and First Lord Islington, and Anne Beauclerk Dundas, the last Dundas of Dundas to be born in Dundas Castle near Edinburgh. Joan had a happy childhood in London and Wiltshire. Governess-educated, she grew up well read and was fluent in French. She was also a great beauty. During the 1914–18 war, when only nineteen, she volunteered as a nurse in the Voluntary Aid Detachment (VAD). She worked first at a Red Cross Hospital in Canterbury and was transferred in 1917 to a Red Cross Hospital at Rouen in France, where she tended sick and wounded soldiers from the Front. At the end of the war she was working with the French army.

The immediate postwar period found her partly enjoying all the balls and house parties that were open to her, but also partly hungering for a more useful and worthwhile existence. She was 'an idealist looking for an opportunity',[1] which came to her when she married Sir Edward William Macleay Grigg, another idealist, who was seventeen years her senior. They met at Cliveden, the home of Nancy and Waldorf Astor, who were close family friends. Joan and Edward had three children: John, Annabel and Anthony. Sir Edward had a varied career, starting as a Times *journalist before the First World War (in which he won the DSO and Military Cross) and ending in 1944–5 as Minister Resident in the Middle East in the last phase of Churchill's wartime government. During the 1930s he was one of the MPs who opposed appeasement. He was created Baron Altrincham in 1945.*

Two years after their marriage, Sir Edward was appointed Governor of Kenya Colony and the Griggs lived in Nairobi between 1925 and 1930. Lady Grigg was not content simply to go through the motions of being the Governor's wife, however. Appalled by the lack of medical care for women, she created the Lady Grigg Welfare League to provide nursing and maternity services for all races. The story of the League is given in this chapter. According to the Dictionary of National Biography, *Lady Grigg's work for maternal welfare in Kenya 'enhanced the distinction of her husband's administration'.*[2] *After Kenya, Joan Grigg continued to do public service, but never again had the scope that had been available to her in East Africa. When she accompanied her husband to the Middle East and was living in Cairo, the same sort of opportunity beckoned. But her time there was too short. After 1945, she became indignant that the East African Women's League was for whites only and she started an East African Women's Society that was multi-racial.*

Joan Grigg was twenty-eight years old when she and her husband reached Mombasa by boat on 2 October 1925. They had travelled from Britain to Kenya so that Sir Edward could take up his new post as Governor of this British colony. They took the train from Mombasa to Nairobi, the capital, and arrived there, three days later, to be greeted by a massive welcoming reception. 'The whole town was out – Indians, white people and thousands and thousands of natives of every sort of tribe', wrote Joan enthusiastically to her mother back in England. They were met at the station by officials and then 'drove in an open motor along a road lined with huge crowds to the chief Square of the town, which was packed, with a platform in the middle. The whole place was highly decorated and the roofs of the houses crowded with people.' They climbed the platform and took part in a formal ceremony to mark the start of the new governorship. 'Ned took the oath', reported Joan, 'and I was given flowers by the children and then endless addresses were read and presented by Indians, missionaries and representatives from every section of the community. The natives of Africa were represented by a sad old man with huge ear lobes and ostrich feathers on his head. Ned and I looked very nice I think', added Joan, 'as he wore a scarlet uniform and I wore my bright blue "Jeanne

Lanvin" dress so with the white uniforms of the Staff we looked just like the flag.'[3]

The Griggs were at once delighted with Kenya: the people, the climate and the natural beauty. 'It is so deliciously hot', wrote Joan to her parents in the second month of their new life. On a visit to the coastal city of Mombasa, she said, she rushed down

into the sea at 6 o'clock in the morning – the sea is like warm milk . . . and all the air is scented with oleanders. It is a lovely place, a low shore of bright orange and red cliffs with clusters of coconut trees and bright green grass – then the mango trees with their shiny leaves, bright green that never changes – baobab trees, huge and broad and brown, but soft like cardboard . . . and banana trees with leaves large enough to make into a dress.[4]

In another letter home, she told her parents that they 'would love the nights here – they are so warm and the crickets and the frogs make such a row; the world seems full of mystery, and lurking, wild life.'[5]

But Joan quickly realized that underneath this surface of delight and mystery, there was a high level of poverty and suffering, especially among the African population. 'Oh darling', she wrote to her mother shortly after their arrival, 'the amount of things to be done in this country is overwhelming.'[6] In particular, the level of health was very low. The colonial medical services for the African population were rudimentary and it was not until 1926 that the first general medical dispensaries, with just one or two rooms, started to be set up for the rural areas.[7] John Carman, a doctor who went to Kenya in 1926 as a Medical Officer, described the dismal state of the few native hospitals in urban areas: 'The bucket latrines were innocent of the least attempt at fly-proofing . . .The theatre did boast its own water supply, but it is a tribute to the resistance of the African organism to pathogenic bacteria, that there was not more post-operative sepsis.' No wonder that 'Western medicine had not become very popular and there were many empty beds in the wards'.[8] Lady Grigg was appalled by the sufferings of the Kenyan people. 'Yesterday morning I visited a surgery for natives, and saw the most terrible cases of yaws [a skin disease] and syphilis,' she wrote to her mother shortly after her arrival, adding, 'it is frightfully prevalent amongst them.'[9]

Kenya's role as a colony of Britain dated from 1896, when Britain constituted this territory as the East African Protectorate. In 1920, the Protectorate became Kenya Colony, which it remained until its independence in 1963. There was opposition to the colonial administration throughout this period, culminating in the 'Mau Mau' rebellion of the 1950s. When Lady Grigg arrived in Kenya Colony in 1925, each racial group was administered separately, with Africans – the great majority of the Kenyan population – at the very bottom of the hierarchy. There were many African tribes, the largest being the Kavirondo and the Kikuyu, with different customs and languages, who were generally lumped together in the single category of 'natives' by the colonial administration. Absolute preference was given to the 'Europeans' (as the white settlers chose to call themselves), who had started to settle in Kenya after the building of the railway towards the end of the nineteenth century. By 1920 a massive area of the fertile 'White Highlands' were reserved for European farms, while 'Native Reserves' had been established for the African population. The whites found abundant labour to run their farms and households, since many Africans were desperately poor. Many of the settlers were from the upper classes of Britain, who had been keen to escape the rising rate of income tax and death duties and were also lured by the prospect of a more adventurous life in beautiful surroundings.

There was a dramatic contrast between the wealth of the settler Europeans and the poverty of the Africans. When the Colonial Secretary, Leo Amery, visited Kenya in 1927, he was dismayed by the conditions suffered by the African population: 'We have simply treated them as some sort of game reserve,' he said, in which 'precious little' had been done for the natives.[10] The average income of an African family was less than five Kenyan pounds a year, according to Norman Leys in his book, *A Last Chance in Kenya*, which was published in 1931 by Leonard and Virginia Woolf's Hogarth Press. This critical account of the British administration of Kenya noted that out of this five pounds each family had to pay 28 Kenya shillings in cash to the Government, on average, and other taxes in addition; the chief tax was the hut and poll tax of 12 shillings, which every male of sixteen and over had to pay on his own behalf and also on behalf of dependants who lived in huts of their own, such as an aged mother.[11] Africans had to submit to measures of control that were similar to those being developed at the time in South Africa, in the name of 'separate-development'. One of these measures was the Native Registration Act, which required all adult males to carry a pass bearing a thumbprint – a *kipande*. In 1923 (before the Griggs arrived), there was a general strike in Kenya, when farm and plantation workers were supported by servants in European households in their protest against unfair labour laws. When one of the strike leaders was imprisoned, large numbers of people protested and 150 Kenyans were shot down by the police in Nairobi.

Ultimate power in the colony rested with the Governor, who was answerable to London. Beneath this tier of power was the Kenyan legislature, but only Europeans had the right to vote. Tensions often developed between the settler community and the British government, which was concerned that the settlers did not care about the welfare of the native population. These tensions reached a peak in 1923, when Britain started to discuss plans for extending the franchise to the Indian community, descended from Indians who had been brought in by the British to build the railway in the last decades of the nineteenth century. The settlers rallied to stop the plan, under the vigorous leadership of Lord Delamere, a large landowner and leader of the elected members in the Kenyan parliament. Edward Grigg regarded Kenya as an important area of white settlement and believed that the economic prosperity of Kenya depended on the contribution of the white community. Just before his departure from Kenya in 1930, he gave a speech concluding with the heartfelt wish that 'all of you here that represent the British race should keep up the standards of your civilization and see that your children maintain them too.'[12] Joan, on the other hand, did not believe there was any future in Kenya for large-scale white settlement. This was one of the few issues on which she and her husband dis-agreed.[13]

The Griggs tackled the challenges of Kenya together. '*We* have this stupendous Governors' Conference to face at the end of January. The Governors of Uganda, Tanganyika, the Soudan and Nigeria [are coming],' wrote Joan to her mother near the end of 1925.[14] Like Mrs Baldwin, she supported her husband's work with enthusiasm. 'Ned made his second speech in the Legislative Council yesterday and it was very very successful.' she wrote to her mother in December 1925, adding, 'I think *we* have got all *our* schemes through.'[15] For his part, he worried that while his own life was full of interest and challenge, 'Life at Government House was often bleak and lonely for her.'[16] But she had plenty to do as the Governor's wife. 'The incessant social side of Government House life,' she complained to her mother, 'is sometimes terribly trying.'

One of the Griggs's shared tasks was the business of setting standards for the white community: a 'white man's conduct in Dark Africa must be equal to his pretensions as a leader of civilization', believed Sir Edward. This was difficult at times. For example, the men – even the farmers living up-country, who were generally old-fashioned in their style of life – had a habit of wearing pyjamas at dinner. While the food was good and skilfully served and the women were punctiliously dressed, wrote Sir Edward, 'the men dined in dressing gowns of figured silk covering pyjamas in which they afterwards went to bed'. He was determined to stop the practice but 'it caused me a great deal of embarrassment', he explained in his memoir, 'since it is not easy even for Governors to lay down the law in other people's houses.'[17]

An additional worry was the small group of rich and rackety whites known as the Happy Valley set. Joan had been prepared for their decadent behaviour before leaving Britain by Queen Mary, who had warned her about an

irresponsible group in Kenya which disregarded all convention and restraint, especially that of the marriage tie. They were not numerous, and they were in no way representative of the settler community, which was hardworking and rather old-fashioned in its conventions ... but they attracted much more attention, particularly in the picture papers which specialise in showing the well-to-do in their sillier moments.[18]

In the playground of the fertile White Highlands outside Nairobi, the Happy Valley crowd indulged in orgies of heavy drink and adultery (their notoriety reached its peak with the murder of the womanizing

Lord Erroll in the early 1940s, a decade after the Griggs had left).
Lady Idina Gordon, who married Lord Erroll, was at the centre of this
crowd and was only satisfied, it was claimed, if *all* her guests had
swapped partners by nightfall. One of her favourite games involved
'blowing a feather' across a sheet held out by the guests around a table;
when the feather landed on the sheet, she would announce who was
to sleep with whom. Lady Grigg visited her home on one occasion and
was 'shocked to find Idina's clothes and pearls scattered across the
floor, the dogs unfed and the servants gone. It was considered that
Idina carried on shamelessly in front of Africans.'[19] Lady Grigg put
Idina on her blacklist.

Very often, wives of British diplomats abroad have found it difficult
enough simply to keep up with the demands of proconsular life, let
alone take on additional responsibilities.[20] But Joan Grigg was made
of sterner stuff. She had already coped with the challenge of caring for
soldiers wounded in the trenches during the 1914–18 war, as a Red
Cross nurse working for the Voluntary Aid Detachment. In 1917, at
the age of 20, she had gone to a Red Cross hospital at Rouen in France
to care for soldiers brought directly from the Front. She was faced
daily with the sight of dead, dying and mutilated bodies, a sight that
was described in *Testament of Youth* by Vera Brittain, who was also
in the VAD:

The enemy within shelling distance – refugee Sisters crowding in with nerves all
awry – bright moonlight, and aeroplanes carrying machine-guns – ambulance
trains jolting noisily into the siding, all day, all night – gassed men on stretch-
ers, clawing the air – dying men, reeking with mud and foul green-stained
bandages, shrieking and writhing in a grotesque travesty of manhood – dead
men with fixed, empty eyes and shiny, yellow faces . . .[21]

Some of the men nursed by Joan continued to correspond with her
after the war.[22]

Joan Grigg was driven by a strong social conscience, which had been
nurtured by her family background. An only child, she had grown up
in an atmosphere where public service was regarded as a duty. Her
mother, Lady Islington – though better known in the fashionable world
as a brilliant mimic and wit – had founded day nurseries in the East

End of London. Her father, a Conservative MP who had crossed the floor to become a Liberal on the issue of free trade versus tariff reform, had been Governor-General of New Zealand and had distinguished himself both in politics and philanthropy. He was under-secretary for the colonies from 1914 to 1915 and under-secretary for India from 1915 to 1918. 'You would *never* be dull here', wrote Joan in a letter to her parents, explaining that 'the days slip by so fast – and they simply bristle with all the problems you have put so much of your life's work into.'[23] She was determined to do something useful for the people of Kenya. Her first plan was to take over responsibility for a children's home that had been set up by Lady Northey, a previous governor's wife. She thought it was badly run – 'the most miserable place inadequate and dirty and without one picture' or any attempt to make it attractive. 'I am going to reform the whole place,' she decided.[24] 'Oh Mums, I *do* wish you were here to help me with this children's home,' she wrote to her mother, explaining that, 'there is absolutely nowhere here for mothers to send ailing babies . . . I have called a committee meeting and I am going to try to reform the whole thing.'[25] She invited all the chief members of the Lady Northey home committee to Government House for tea and then arranged a series of meetings to discuss plans for the future. But they were disappointingly unresponsive. 'I should like to behead a lot of these women' she wrote.[26] By November, she was 'losing patience with the whole affair'[27] and, by December, she had given up: 'I now feel quite indifferent as to whether they accept my plan or not', she announced, 'because I would much rather have my own show.'[28]

Her 'own show' was much more ambitious than a children's home: she decided to create a network of centres to deliver nursing and maternity care for women. As a new mother herself, she was keenly aware of the dangers and physical hardships of childbirth, which were causing great concern in Britain at this time. In 1915 the Women's Cooperative Guild had published *Maternity*, a volume of letters by working-class mothers describing the difficulties of pregnancy and birth in the homes of the poor; the book had massive appeal and was sold out almost immediately. It spearheaded a maternity movement, which was given massive impetus by the steady rise of the maternal death rate. Yet another influence on Joan may have been her admiration for Lady Minto's work for maternity care in India, in her role as Vicereine (she would have known about this work because her mother and Lady Minto were friends). 'I am making a great struggle to start a nurses association out here, like Lady Minto's in India,' wrote Lady Grigg at the beginning of 1926, adding modestly, 'only of course on a tiny scale.'[29] Lady Minto was one of several Vicereines who had sought to do useful work for women and children in India, following the precedent set by Lady Dufferin in 1884. Asked by Queen Victoria to take an interest in the condition of women in India, Lady Dufferin had set up the National Association for Supplying Medical Aid to the Women of India.[30]

Joan Grigg organized a central council called the Lady Grigg Welfare League. It represented all races, which would administer three combined enterprises – 'maternity hospitals and training schools for Africans in Nairobi and Mombasa; a maternity hospital, school for midwives and infant welfare clinic for Indians; and a hostel in Nairobi for training nurses to serve the European community.'[31] The symbol of the council was a blue bird: Joan was very fond of the blue birds she found in Kenya and concluded one of her letters home by saying: 'There are such lovely birds, bright blue – like the birds of happiness.'[32] This enthusiasm permeated her attitude towards everything, including her sense of imperial duty. Whereas Violet Milner engaged with imperialism as an intellectual, her own approach was practical and down-to-earth. 'This is women's side of Empire-building!' she exclaimed in a description of her League.[33]

On a visit to Britain in the spring of 1927, she solicited contributions from the readers of *The Times*: the greatest need, she explained carefully in a letter to the Editor, was for a centre in Nairobi that would look after African mothers and children and train African midwives. She also asked for money to establish an association of trained nurses for Europeans, but as a project of secondary importance. Plans for an Indian scheme, she said, were already well supported by the Aga Khan. Donations quickly started coming in, including a cheque for £25 from Queen Mary, which was accompanied by wishes for 'every success in your efforts'. The Queen's donation was made public in a letter from her treasurer to *The Times*, which indicated her support for the work of the League as a whole. This was heartening. But the overall response bitterly disappointed Lady Grigg, because nearly all the money – over £3,000, the equivalent of about £100,000 today[34] – was specially earmarked by the donors for the European Nurses Association and Maternity Home. Very little was sent in for the African centre, even though Lady Grigg had emphasized that 'the young native women are so helpful and so eager for enlightenment from women of our own, higher civilisation'.[35]

Joan Grigg's concern for the maternal welfare of African women was seen as unnecessary by many whites, both in Britain and in Kenya, who believed that 'native' women gave birth without difficulty. 'One often hears the opinion, vouchsafed by people who should know better,' wrote a midwife in the *Nursing Times* in 1934, 'that women of coloured races have what is called "an easy time" during childbirth, and therefore present none of the interesting difficulties of midwifery practice.' Drawing on her own experience in India and Africa, the author of this article argued that the truth of the matter was 'far otherwise'.[36] A doctor working for the Lady Grigg Welfare League in Nairobi made the same point. 'The popular impression not only in Europe, but amongst quite a number of our oldest residents in this Colony,' he said,

is that the native women bear their children with the greatest ease. A comparison is sometimes drawn between the rare mishaps among the animal world and the native. The impression is that the native woman is seen tilling the soil one day, that night she bears her child and the next morning is again seen tilling the field but this time bearing the child upon her back.

But he had seen many women dying in labour, he added, sometimes undelivered after suffering for days. 'The native woman, whether Kikuyu, Kavirondo or whatever other tribe inhabits Kenya,' he insisted, 'needs trained assistance just as much as the European.'[37]

It was always difficult to raise money for the Welfare League. Sir Edward had difficulty in persuading his Executive Council to provide financial support[38] and so the chief subscribers were voluntary, such as the Beit Trust, Sir Robert Horne, the Aga Khan, the British Red Cross and the Church Missionary Society. Fundraising was essential and Lady Grigg organized a successful fête at Government House in

Nairobi, 'in aid of Maternity and Child Welfare work for all races in the Colony and Protectorate'. Some of the work for the fête was done by Karen Blixen, the novelist who wrote fiction under the name of Isak Dinesen; she was living in Kenya at the time and was a good friend of Lady Grigg. Karen Blixen had gone to East Africa at the beginning of 1913, in order to marry her cousin, Baron Blor von Blixen Finecke and they farmed coffee at the foot of the Ngong Hills outside Nairobi. The marriage ended in divorce and Karen – who was known as 'Tania' by her friends – became an intimate friend of Denys Finch-Hatton, a hunter, the younger brother of the Earl of Winchilsea. It was largely Finch-Hatton's hunting safaris that established expeditions to Kenya as a romantic adventure for the rich. In 1931 Finch-Hatton was killed in a flying accident and Karen, grief-stricken, returned to Denmark; she drew on her experience of life in Kenya to write *Out of Africa*, which was published in 1937. Tania and Joan had different opinions about the condition of women's lives in Kenya: Tania took a romantic view of tribal life and women's place within it, while Joan believed that it meant virtual slavery for women. But despite these differences, Joan loved her company: 'I have just come back from the most delicious day and night with Tania Blixen,' she wrote on 30 March 1928; Tania, in her turn, often visited 'Joanie' at Government House.

Her help with the fête was given grudgingly, however. 'I probably won't get much written today,' she told her mother in a letter on 1 August 1926, 'as I have a lot of preparations to make for Lady Grigg's *confounded Fête tomorrow*; among other things they have asked me to make roasted almonds for their tea pavilion.' As far as she was concerned, 'the whole festival seems pretty crazy and so barbaric that in a hundred years' time I think such phenomena will seem utterly incomprehensible; of course it is in aid of a good cause to which any profits will go, but with such enormous costs – not to speak of the trouble – I think direct begging would be much more profitable.'[39] In the event, the fête raised the considerable sum of £3,000 (now about £100,000).[40] 'It was one of the most exhausting things I have ever experienced,' complained Baroness Blixen, adding that 'what cheered me on the most was the cocktail bar'.[41]

Doctor John Carman also helped out with the fête. The money raised, he said, was used to set up four clinics for African children –

three in the African locations and one in the African railway quarters (assuming that Dr Carman remembered these details correctly, three of these clinics would have operated outside the workings of the Lady Grigg Welfare League). Lady Grigg declared a wish to visit the clinics and it was his job as Medical Officer, he recalled, to receive her. At each clinic, he was presented to her – and then, after showing her round, he dashed off to the next clinic to welcome her once more. But each time, she looked inquiringly at him as if she had never seen him before and waited for him to be introduced. In this way, he said resentfully, the ' "Great Lady" had forgotten the humble doctor' three times.[42] Carman believed that she looked down on him because he was not an important figure – but she was not particularly good at remembering faces and probably did not expect to see him again. By the standards of the day she was not a pompous character, but her elevated social status made some people feel uneasy.

The racial divisions in Kenya were transported wholesale into the structure of the Lady Grigg Welfare League, which had separate sections for the African, Indian and European communities. The African section provided a basic set of services, while the level of service delivered to Europeans approximated to the nursing care enjoyed by better-off families in Britain. Each section of the Welfare League had its own committee and there were no Africans on any of these committees – not even on the committee for the African section. The 'Management Committee' of the European branch was entirely composed of Europeans, most of whom were married women; it was chaired by Gladys, Lady Delamere. The Indian section had a 'Management Committee' of both men and women, some Indians and some Europeans, as well as a 'Ladies' Committee' dominated by Europeans. In the African section, there was an 'African Committee (Management)', made up of Europeans, mostly men, and a large 'Ladies' Committee' that was also entirely European and was headed by the Ladies Grigg and Delamere.

The racial distribution of the League's nursing staff was consistent with the committee structure: blacks cared for blacks under the supervision of a white matron; and whites cared for whites. There was some movement of staff between the various branches of the League and in 1933, a white woman called Miss Sherlaw who had been working in the European branch took up the appointment of matron at the Indian Maternity Home. However, no African or Indian nurses worked in the European Branch and no African nurses worked in the Indian section (though presumably Africans did the menial work in all branches of the League).[43] Accommodation proposed for the African section in 1930 made a distinction between the needs of European staff ('4 Bedrooms, Sitting room, Dining Room') and those of African staff ('8 Cubicles for Senior Nurses, 1 for each, Large Dormitory for Junior Nurses and Probationers, to accommodate about 8 girls. Lecture and Dining Hall').[44]

The first branch of the Welfare League was a Child Welfare Home for Arabs and Africans in Mombasa, a large city on the coast of Kenya that was inhabited by several communities of people. 'The natives here are very mixed,' wrote Lady Grigg to her mother, 'and some parts of the town are like bits of Cairo – Arabs, Indians, Swahili, Somali. They wear bright coloured wrappings here.'[45] She chose a site for the Home 'in a market square, shaded by mango trees and opposite the new war memorial', she noted in May 1926. 'I saw a deputation of Indians this morning', she added, 'and got them to promise to put up a welfare centre and maternity hospital up to 5000 pounds. One Indian's eyes filled with tears and he said I will do anything to help you over this because my mother died here having a baby owing to neglect. So I think this hospital ought to save a lot of lives before long.'[46] The Home opened on 16 August 1926 and in October the first baby was born. The following year, Lady Grigg wrote with delight that

the first baby born in the hospital came to see me yesterday. It was Arab – its mother of 16 and its grandmother came with it – both so pretty with polished toe nails and bright coloured saris and each with an amulet round the neck, the baby was absolutely clean and very fat and well.[47]

Large numbers of out-patients started to attend for medical treatment; soon, several hundreds of out-patients were being dealt with each month.

It was possible to start work so quickly at the Mombasa home because a Dr Cook, a British missionary doctor in Uganda, offered to lend two Buganda nurses to help out. He had already organized medical training for women in Kampala, the capital city of Uganda, and was keen to support the development of maternity care in Kenya. Uganda was far ahead of Kenya in its programme of maternity care provision and midwifery training. By 1929, Dr Shiels, the under-secretary of state for the colonies, was able to report to the House of Commons that in the previous year, there were 41 maternity centres in the Uganda Protectorate. 'Four new maternity centres,' he said, 'were in the course of construction. There were 93 native midwives on the official midwives roll on 1st January, 1929. In 1928 the average number of student midwives in training by the Church Missionary Society was 24 and 15 passed the qualifying examination during the year.' In addition, he added, the average number of students at another mission was 21 and three natives had qualified.[48] Uganda was a country with a very different history and set of problems from those found in Kenya. None the less, it offered an instructive example of maternity care provision in East Africa. Joan Grigg, who was evidently in communication with Dr Cook, is likely to have drawn some lessons from her knowledge of the work in Uganda.

Having set up the Mombasa Home, Lady Grigg turned to the other branches of her Welfare League. The African Maternity and Child Welfare Hospital and Training Centre was opened at Pumwani, Nairobi, on 1 August 1927. At the start, it was thought necessary to treat cases of general sickness as well as those of mothers and children, so that the native population would accept and use the institution.[49] This proved successful and in its first two years, the Centre cared for a large and rapidly growing number of women and children, without charging any fees. The European staff consisted of a matron and two nursing sisters and there were eleven native girls in training. The Children's Sick Ward, as well as a dispensary, was in the 'Carnegie Building', which was erected with money from the Carnegie Corporation. During 1929, over 200 children were admitted to the sick ward, suffering from complaints including bronchial and lobar pneumonia, malaria, hookworm, bilharzia, tapeworm, bad ears and eyes, dysentery, tetanus, lameness, abscesses, rickets and malnutrition. One child admitted to the Sick Ward 'had been ill for a week with diarrhoea and dysentery, and during the night passed thirty round-worms. After nine days the child was discharged well.'[50]

In 1929, 309 patients were admitted to the Maternity Wing and there were 221 births and 5 maternal deaths; many of these cases came to the hospital after five or six days in labour. A typical case was that of a woman who had 'been in labour for nine days. She had been badly circumcised and died from a ruptured uterus almost immediately.' In another case, 'stillborn twins born, the mother – who had been badly circumcised – died'. One woman who was 'brought in from a village for an operation which was necessary owing to bad circumcision' gave birth to a child, but it 'subsequently developed Lobar Pneumonia and Meningitis and died'. The effects of female circumcision were a routine cause of difficult childbirth; according to a doctor working at the Pumwani Centre, only 66 of the first 200 women to visit the clinic came from uncircumcised tribes.[51]

Female circumcision (or, as it is generally termed today, female genital mutilation), which is performed in many countries of the world, ranges from amputation of the clitoris to the excision of the clitoris and inner lips and, in extreme cases, the removal of the outer labia as well; the cutting is done with razor blades, pieces of glass or a knife, usually by the older women of the community. It has an ancient history in many tribes in Kenya as an initiation rite to mark the onset of a girl's puberty; there are special songs and dances, which teach the girl the duties she will need to perform as a wife and mother. Complications are likely to occur, which include haemorrhaging, urinary tract and menstrual problems, blood poisoning and difficulties with sexual inter- course. If the wound becomes septic, it may leave anything from massive cartilaginous plaque involving the front of the vulva and urethra, to ragged scarred areas involving the pubic area and vulva generally. This scar tissue is inelastic and the vaginal orifice may be contracted to a resistant ring of little more than an inch in diameter, with no power of dilatation. This can make it impossible for a woman to deliver normally, so that giving birth can be life-threatening and there is a high risk of intracranial injuries to the baby during birth. Incisions on either side of the vulva, and very often a third incision in the middle (an extremely painful procedure without anaesthesia), are almost invariably necessary to accommodate the birth. At the end of the twentieth century, millions of girls in the world are circumcised each year, although the practice has been designated a major human rights violation by the World Health Organisation (WHO). It was outlawed in Kenya by President Moi in 1982, after fourteen girls in one district died from associated infections.

Clitoridectomy had been raised as an issue in Kenya several years before the arrival of the Griggs; in the early 1920s, during the governorship of Sir Robert Coryndon, Grigg's predecessor, the Church of Scotland Missionary Society had made demands for it to be stopped.[52] The Chief Native Commissioner consequently sent a circular letter to all senior commissioners in August 1926, requesting that the local native councils should be approached in the matter and be directed that it was the desire of the British government that, 'in the interests alike of humanity, of eugenics and of the increase of population', the milder form of the operation should be reverted to.[53] The government made little headway with this, however, and, in 1929, the church demanded that all followers who wished their children to attend schools should pledge themselves against having their girls undergo circumcision. This ban was lifted when a petition was sent by the Kenyan people to the missions.

Concerned people in Britain took up the cause. The Duchess of Atholl and Eleanor Rathbone set up for the purpose an unofficial and all-party 'Committee for the Protection of Coloured Women in the Crown Colonies', which led to pressure on Sir Edward to end the practice in Kenya. Although the custom was almost universal in Africa and the Middle East, his memoir explains, 'The House concentrated upon Kenya, with the result that I was urged to make the practice illegal in Kenya, as *suttee* had been made illegal in India.'[54] He himself 'shared to the full Parliament's detestation of the practice', but regarded the matter as complex and feared that any attempt at abolition would be disastrous. All of his Provincial Commissioners warned that 'every family which observed the law would suffer by a catastrophic fall in the bride-price of its marriageable young women'.[55] A further headache for Sir Edward was that opposition to circumcision was interpreted by many Kenyans as yet one more example of the British repression of African national life. Indeed, Jomo Kenyatta, the president of the Kikuyu Central Association who was visiting Britain (and who was later to become the first president of the republic of Kenya), defended circumcision as a sacred rite that was essential to

Kikuyu society, in the course of an inquiry in London. In *Facing Mount Kenya* (1938), he devoted a whole chapter to the defence of clitoridectomy.[56] Grigg advised Downing Street not to use force to stop circumcision, but to take a slower approach through education.[57]

Training midwives was regarded as an absolute priority by Lady Grigg's League and the first seven probationers in midwifery at the Pumwani passed their examination in 1929. It was hoped, stated the Centre's annual report, that most of the midwives, once trained, would 'be sent to the native reserves to work amongst the tribes, under the supervision of the nearest doctor, nurse or Government Hospital'. There was concern, though, that most of the applicants came from Nairobi or nearby and would be unwilling to go into the reserves after training. The committee was therefore 'very anxious that girls should be received direct from the various tribes'. However, most of these girls would be unable to read and write or to speak Ki-Swahili, the common language of Kenya, so it was decided to offer instruction in all these subjects. An additional language problem was that midwifery lessons needed to be given in the language of the trainees, not in English. 'When persons were engaged overseas for duty amongst the native races of Kenya', observed the Centre's report, 'some time must elapse before they are sufficiently acquainted with the native language.' An interim solution was supplied by the Missionary Alliance Council, which allowed a Miss J. Carr, who spoke Swahili, to visit the hospital once a week from Kabete to lecture to the probationers. Another solution was the translation into Swahili of a series of lectures written by the matron.[58]

The commitment to train natives to work as midwives who would replace attendants within the community was based on a belief that traditional midwifery was barbaric and dangerous to health. Such an approach to midwifery in the developing world is not uncommon in the West today. It is regarded by some as a form of cultural imperialism and efforts have been made by the World Health Organization and other international organizations to recognize and to acknowledge the value of traditional birth attendants (TBAs). But at least in the 1920s and 1930s, contempt for TBAs was equally in evidence in Britain. One of the main thrusts of the British Midwives Act of 1936, which established a salaried service of professionally trained midwives, was to abolish the practice of maternity nursing by 'handywomen'. These unqualified attendants were especially missed by poor mothers, who had relied on their help with child care, making fires, and washing and cooking for the family, the kind of work that was not provided by a qualified midwife. Handywomen were often blamed for the high rate of maternal mortality, but there was no direct evidence that they were an important cause of the problem.[59]

The Lady Grigg Indian Maternity and Child Welfare Hospital and Training Centre was set up in an Indian-designated area of Nairobi, because the Indian, European and African communities lived separately from each other. According to its 1929 report, some patients travelled long distances to give birth in the hospital and some cases had to be turned away. Altogether, there were 126 admissions and 119 babies were born; there were no maternal deaths, but eight babies died. The first Indian midwife passed her certificate of competence in 1929 and another passed the year after. However, the Centre was experiencing great difficulty obtaining Indian girls for training as midwives, because of 'the prejudice which at present exists against taking up Midwifery'. Patients were charged a fee, but arrangements were made for women in financial need. This met one of the Centre's key goals: 'The provision of accommodation, not only for women whose husbands were in a position to meet the full charges of the Hospital, but for the poorer section of the community.'[60]

The European branch of the Lady Grigg Welfare League was faced with a much lower level of need than the African and Indian branches, since white families were much better-off. It set up a more general Nursing Association, with a remit to employ nurses who would care for the general medical needs of white families throughout Kenya, including the more remote districts; in 1933, 260 requests were made for a nurse from the Association. A headquarters was set up and named the MacMillan Memorial Nurses' Institute, in honour of Lady MacMillan, who supported the League both financially and by sitting on its committees. She had come to Kenya with her American husband soon after the Boer War, but was prematurely widowed; she stayed on, devoting her wealth and time to good works. In its first year the Nursing Association employed about ten nursing sisters, who were selected with the help of the Society for the Overseas Settlement of

British Women (of which Lady Milner was Vice-Chairman), which carried out the interviewing and selection in Britain. Two of the first batch of senior sisters returned in 1931 for second tours of duty. To help with payment for the nurses' fees, families were encouraged to join a special insurance scheme organized by the League, but few chose to do so. In the early 1930s, the Nursing Association was forced by the worldwide economic depression to cut services. Settler families had less money to pay for a nurse and the shipping lines withdrew the free passages from Britain for new sisters, which they had donated in the first few years.

The Lady Grigg centres were soon well established and were visited by dignitaries from Britain. One of the Mombasa Home's visitors was the Prince of Wales (who later became King Edward VIII in 1936, before abdicating to marry Mrs Simpson). He made an official visit to Kenya in 1928 and Lady Grigg took him round: 'We visit my maternity hospital and he enjoys poking into the native huts.' The Prince enjoyed the rest of his visit, too, following it up with another – but unofficial – visit in 1929, when the Griggs were still in Kenya. They all went to a camp outside Nairobi that had been specially arranged by Lord Delamere, so that the Prince could see a lion hunt. 'The Prince entertained us in princely fashion,' recalled Sir Edward. 'It was very hot . . . our sundowners were cooled with ice from a fixture new for Kenya safaris, an ice machine.'[61] A regular visitor to the Pumwani Centre in Nairobi was Baroness Blixen. In June 1928 she wrote to her aunt:

I have such a horror of everything to do with childbirth; the other day, when I went with Lady Grigg to her Native Maternity Home, I went in to see a very young native woman, with such a sweet face, taken into the "labour room," – they said that she would have her baby in half an hour.

Karen Blixen's squeamish attitude towards childbirth may be contrasted with the down-to-earth approach of Lady Grigg. 'Of course in some ways it is so natural', wrote Blixen, 'but I think it is an awful method and could wish they could discover another one, – think how nice it would be if one could sit on an egg . . .'[62]

At the Mombasa Home, the first centre set up by the League, the first nurses from Buganda were replaced by two Swahili-speaking probationer nurses, one from Zanzibar. A distinguished benefactor from the Mombasa community, Sir Ali bin Salim, donated a piece of land for a dedicated clinic and the building was ready for occupation in March 1929.[63] A journalist visiting the new building in 1929 reported that

... There are two wards which are the acme of comfort, one for Arabs and the other for African women. The sister in charge is assisted by three native girls, one of whom is exceedingly well trained ...

Each baby is supplied with a separate cot, and although there is no operating theatre and only the really necessary equipment at present, the wards are beautiful, comfortable and airy.

He added, 'The patients usually remain in the Home for about ten days, unless there are complications or the bed is urgently needed' (this custom of staying in bed for ten days after birth was consistent with practice in Britain). Mombasa now 'boasts a flourishing institution second to none in this or any other country,' enthused the *Coast*, a newspaper read by the white community of Mombasa.[64]

In 1930, after five years of duty as Governor, Sir Edward and Joan Grigg left Kenya and returned to Britain. They were racked with dysentery and Sir Edward was smarting from criticism by the recently elected Labour government of his tenure as Governor. However, Joan's work in Kenya continued to thrive. 'Your great work', wrote a friend who had visited the home in Mombasa, 'has materialised beyond all dreams! . . . the mothers all looked so happy and comfortable with the babes in their neat cots covered with mosquito netting and your little blue blankets over them!'[65] The 1933 report of the Native Affairs Department stated that 'the Lady Grigg Welfare Hostel at Pumwani is proving its great value. It is becoming daily more popular and its work more widely known and appreciated.'[66] In the following year the Department reported that 'the work of the Lady Grigg Welfare League prospered during the year. At the African Maternity Centre at Mombasa 181 labour cases were taken during the year, and at the African Centre in Nairobi, 303 labour cases were taken while 13 African midwives were in training, of whom three qualified.' A few years ago, added the report, it was a rare occurrence for a maternity case to be brought to hospital – but now,

all over the Colony women come to our hospitals before labour has commenced and only a lack of beds stands in the way of the establishment of a very extensive indoor maternity service, and only the lack of a sufficiently large number of women of adequate education to be trained, and the lack of facilities to train them, if they were available, stand in the way of the establishment of an adequate home midwifery service.

The very success of the League was identified as an obstacle. 'It is greatly to be regretted', complained the report, 'that to no inconsiderable extent the increasing popularity of the centres militates against increased house visiting.'[67]

However, it is impossible to quantify the value and achievements of the Lady Grigg Welfare League, since no data were available on the levels of mortality or morbidity either before or after it was set up. African women nearly always gave birth at home in their communities, without the involvement of the medical authorities; and in any case, little attempt was made to collect data on the health of the African population. A doctor working at the Pumwani clinic wrote an article about the first 200 maternity cases so as to 'throw some light', he said, 'upon the state of maternity among some of the Kenya tribes' and to put some facts before the Kenya Branch of the British Medical Association.[68] The need to produce information as basic and as preliminary as this reveals how little was actually known. Even two and half decades after Lady Grigg's arrival in Kenya, efforts were only just being started to collect data on health, by the newly created East African Medical Survey. The Colonial Office reported in 1950 that a first step had been made 'on the collecting of vital statistics: over 5,000 maternity histories obtained from native women have been analysed by the East African Statistical Department'; it added, though, that, 'The accuracy of the data leaves much to be desired.' The report did not offer any conclusions on maternal health. In relation to infant health, it found a mortality rate of 20 per cent, which is equal to two deaths out of every ten infants in their first 12 months[69] and indicates a very low level of health.

Whatever the clinics did or did not achieve regarding actual levels of health, it is clear they produced a radical change in attitudes towards clinical midwifery. At first, there was widespread scepticism, not least among the white settlers. 'When Lady Grigg first mooted the proposal of a Welfare Home in Mombasa for African, Indian and Arab women,' observed the Coast Guardian in 1936, '...those who knew their Mombasa laughed heavily (behind Lady Grigg's back) and told the joke over their sundowners.'[70] African communities, too, had their doubts: 'It is only the younger of the African women', wrote the journalist who visited the Mombasa home, 'who take advantage of this first-class treatment at present. The older women will have little or nothing to do with it, being very conservative.' He added, though, that 'The number of patients is already obviously increasing – as the young African women love the Home and the comforts for which it stands.'[71] In 1931, about 100 native chiefs from various districts were shown over the Pumwani hospital and 'appeared much impressed with what they saw'.[72] Even the Fort Hall Local Native Council, which had initially said that the Pumwani would be of no use to anyone, started making an annual grant and sent a young woman to be trained, with plans to send others. Fort Hall is far from Nairobi, especially without motor transport, so this was a firm statement of support for the work of the League. The problem of how to establish adequate maternity services in Kenya, stated the 1934 report of the Native Affairs Department, was 'no longer a psychological one but one of economics alone'.[73]

In just four years, Lady Grigg had laid the foundation of a maternity service that not only served the needs of women in need in Nairobi and Mombasa, but also trained midwives to care for mothers in the outlying areas. In recognition of this achievement, Sir Edward Grigg dedicated Kenya's Opportunity, his memoir of Kenya, 'To My Wife whose Welfare League for all Races in Kenya opened a New Life to the Womanhood of Dark Africa'.[74] Apart from her efforts, virtually nothing was done by the British administration to improve the health of Kenyan mothers. In December 1929 in the House of Commons, the under-secretary of state for the colonies, Dr Shiels, was asked by the Duchess of Atholl MP what steps were being taken to train native midwives in Kenya. 'The Lady Grigg Child Welfare League has

maternity homes and child welfare centres in Nairobi and Mombasa,'
he replied, adding, 'The training in midwifery of Indian and native
women is undertaken at these centres.'[75] If Lady Grigg had not created
her Welfare League, Shiels would have had no choice but to answer,
'No steps have been taken.'

Today, the Pumwani Maternity Hospital in Nairobi is one of the
largest maternity hospitals in Africa. The original building still exists
and is the school of midwifery at the centre of the hospital. The training
of midwives continues to be given top priority and its history is
remembered. 'This is the oldest school for training of midwives in this
country,' observed the Medical Officer of Health for Nairobi in 1975,
adding that 'the first batch was trained in the early 1930s'.[76]

5

'THE RED DUCHESS'
The Duchess of Atholl

Katharine, Duchess of Atholl 1874–1960, was born Katharine Marjory Ramsay, in Edinburgh. She was the eldest daughter of the second marriage of her father, Sir James Ramsay, Tenth Baronet of Bamff, a historian, to Charlotte Fanning Stewart, whose parents were killed in the Indian Mutiny. Kitty, as she was generally known, was a scholar and a musician and studied at the Royal College of Music in London. In 1899 she gave up her studies to marry John George Stewart-Murray, Marquess of Tullibardine, the eldest son of the Seventh Duke of Atholl, known as Bardie; he succeeded to the title in 1917. They had no children, which was a bitter disappointment to Kitty. In the 1914–18 war she was involved in the organization of the VAD. When Bardie was sent to Gallipoli in 1915, she went to Alexandria to be near him and when the British troops were evacuated to Egypt, she helped to care for them in Cairo. She was a prominent figure in Scottish social service and local government and her public service was recognized in 1918 in the form of the DBE.

Kitty opposed the movement for female suffrage. At the suggestion of Lloyd George, however, she stood for election to the House of Commons in 1923 as Conservative candidate for Kinross and West Perthshire. She was successful and became the first Scottish, and first Conservative, woman minister, as Parliamentary Secretary at the Board of Education from 1924 to 1929. In this way, despite her earlier opposition to votes for women, she acted as a pioneer for women in parliamentary politics. Very quickly the House realized that underneath Kitty's demure and small exterior lay a spirit that was determined to fight cruelty and injustice. In 1929 she embarked on a campaign against the circumcision of women in Kenya. She supported Winston Churchill's opposition to the Government's proposals for a new constitution for India and on this issue she gave up the party whip. She returned to the fold when Mussolini invaded Abyssinia. The outbreak of the Spanish Civil War in 1936 brought her into conflict once more with her party and finally lost her the party whip. Horrified by the rise of Fascism in Spain, she spoke openly against British support for a non-intervention treaty and argued that it effectively gave aid to Franco. Her efforts to help the demo-cratically elected Spanish Republican government are the subject of this chapter.

Kitty finally resigned her seat in 1938 on the party's policy of appeasement; she sought re-election as an Independent candidate, but without success. After the Second World War, she focused her interest on the fates of Poland, Czechoslovakia and Hungary and campaigned against the horrors of Stalinism. She continued her struggle against injustice until her death at the age of eighty-six.

In 1923 the *National Review* published in full the Duchess of Atholl's maiden speech in the House of Commons.[1] This was a natural step for a Tory periodical like the *National*, since the Duchess was a Conservative MP with imperialist convictions. But in the middle of the following decade, the Scottish Duchess deserted her rightwing colleagues to support the side of the Republicans in the Spanish Civil War. This shift was met with astonishment. Members of Parliament could hardly believe their ears when the patrician Duchess – who was sixty-two years of age and had been an MP for thirteen years – first delivered a stinging attack on the Franco regime in 1936. What was especially remarkable about her support for the Republicans – which led to nicknames like 'The Red Duchess' and 'Red Kitty' – was the previously dark blue colour of her Conservatism. For she was not simply a Conservative, but had been an outspoken leader of the diehards in their opposition to the Government of India Bill. There was 'nothing in recent Parliament history', commented the *Spectator*, 'to compare with the evolution' of the Duchess from rightwing Con-servative to a rebel on behalf of Republican Spain.[2]

The Spanish Civil War began in July 1936, when General Francisco

Franco led a military uprising against Spain's legally elected Republican government. The war quickly assumed international importance, because it was widely regarded as a fight for democracy and freedom and also because Franco was heavily backed with military aid from Fascist Italy and Nazi Germany. 'Never since the French Revolution', wrote Robert Graves and Alan Hodge in their social history of interwar Britain, 'had there been a foreign question that so divided intelligent British opinion as this.'[3] For the most part, allegiances in Britain were predictable: Conservatives, aristocrats, businessmen and Roman Catholics generally supported the rebel cause; while middle-class intellectuals (the 'Parlour Pinks' of an article in the *National Review*)[4], working-class Marxists and many of the unemployed united to support the struggle of the Republicans, a popular front of communists, socialists, liberals and anarchists. But one allegiance had not been at all predictable – that of her Grace, the Duchess of Atholl.

But for the Duchess herself, this evolution made perfect sense. It was the inevitable outcome of her analysis of the political situation in Europe, following Italy's invasion of Abyssinia in 1935 and Hitler's occupation of the demilitarized Rhineland the year after. These acts of aggression led her to the grim conclusion that Germany was now the greatest risk to peace, even more than Soviet Russia. On 5 November 1936 she made her first speech on foreign affairs in the Commons, stressing the importance of British obligations towards smaller nations like Czechoslovakia, Yugoslavia and Romania. Then, in February 1937, she visited these countries with the Independent MP Eleanor Rathbone and Lady Layton, a Liberal who was active in the campaign for Family Allowances. 'The great lesson of our trip', wrote the Duchess, was 'the danger faced by Europe as a whole. Half the continent, it seemed to our party, was trembling in the balance between dictatorship and democracy.'[5] The Spanish Civil War seemed to exemplify this balance – or the trembling, at any rate. Moreover, a victory by Franco would create a client state of Germany and Italy that would threaten Gibraltar and British imperial interests in the Mediterranean.

Of particular concern to Kitty (as she was known by friends and family) was the Non-Intervention Agreement organized by Britain and France, which prevented the possibility of fair play for the democratically elected government of Spain. This treaty, which stated that all nations should abstain from sending weapons, manpower or food to either side, was signed by 27 countries, including Germany and Italy. A Non-Intervention Committee was set up in London but its proceedings were a farce, quickly degenerating into procedural wrangles and mutual recriminations. Italy and Germany cheated right from the beginning, with Italy sending whole divisions to Franco, numbering some 100,000 men altogether. In addition, Franco was given valuable aid by American companies such as Ford, Studebaker, General Motors, Dupont and Texaco, as well as by British businesses. Rio Tinto Zinc supplied foreign exchange to the rebels at an excessively favourable rate, to which Kitty objected in one of her first questions on the Spanish war in the House of Commons.[6] In effect, the British government was supporting the Nationalists but giving the impression of neutrality under the cloak of the Non-Intervention Agreement.

Meanwhile, the legal government of Spain was prevented by the Agreement from buying weapons or food and other necessities in the world market. In October, Russia sent some assistance to the Spanish government, but its help was on a much smaller scale than the fascist aid to the rebels (though it did mean a general increase in the influence of the communists, helping to prepare the ground for a communist-led government in 1937). The League of Nations offered no help of any substance, beyond making alternative arrangements for the housing of the Prado art collections. In Kitty's view, allowing the Spanish government to be defeated in this way was tantamount to taking sides.

On the one hand, the conflict had its roots in the social, political and religious history of Spain – one of the poorest and most backward of European countries, with a feudal system of landownership, a dominant Roman Catholic church (which backed the generals), a decadent aristocracy, and a powerful army. But on the other hand, it was a very real enactment of the struggle against fascism and emphasized the division of Europe, said Harold Nicolson, between left and right – 'Which way do we go?' he asked.[7] This question became an irresistible cause for the Left Wing of the thirties. Writers and artists all over the world supported the Spanish government, ranging from the sculptor Eric Gill to the composer

Benjamin Britten, the singer Paul Robeson, the film stars Charles
Chaplin and Marlene Dietrich, and the novelist Ernest Hemingway.
In Spain itself, there were few artists and intellectuals who were not
pro-Republican. Of these, Pablo Picasso and the poet Federico Garcia
Lorca were the most well known outside the country and there was
international outrage when Lorca was sentenced to death and then
shot by the Nationalists.

Many foreign supporters of Republican Spain risked and lost their
lives on its behalf. Over 40,000 young people from fifty countries went
to Spain to fight for the Republic in the International Brigade: they
went into battle, gave medical aid, drove ambulances, and took part
in propaganda work. On Franco's side, there were only 1,000 foreign
volunteers. About 2,000 of the Republican Brigaders were British and
of these, one-quarter – 500 – died at the front; Virginia Woolf's
nephew Julian Bell went as an ambulance driver and was killed in
1937, while she was writing *Three Guineas*. One member of the British
Battalion who survived was the poet W. H. Auden, who also worked
as an ambulance driver. In his poem 'Spain 1937', which he gave to
Nancy Cunard to publish and which is generally regarded as one of
the finest poems to have come out of the Spanish Civil War, Auden
conveys the magnetic pull of the war that drew him and other
foreigners to Spain:

> To-day the deliberate increase in the chance of death,
> The conscious acceptance of guilt in the necessary murder;
> To-day the expending of powers
> On the flat ephemeral pamphlet and the boring meeting.
>
> To-day the makeshift consolations: the sacred cigarette,
> The cards in the candlelit barn, and the scraping concern,
> The masculine jokes; to-day the
> Fumbled and unsatisfactory embrace before hurting.

For many Brigaders, joining forces with the Republicans was a political
imperative. The poet John Cornford, for example, went to the front
to

Raise the red flag triumphantly
For Communism and for liberty.[8]

For this cause, he died. But although Cornford was a socialist intellectual, he was from an upper middle-class background and was seen as a member of the Establishment: his father was a Professor of Classics, his mother was a poet, and he was known to be a brilliant student. His death was devastating to many people in Britain: it was reminiscent of the deaths of the war poets in the Great War and seemed to herald yet another wave of mass killings. One woman who was a student at Oxford at the time recalls that when she heard of his death, 'We knew then that another major war was inevitable.'[9] Jessica Mitford, the sixth daughter of Lord and Lady Redesdale, was one of the few British women to go to Spain, in order to work as a journalist with her cousin and lover Esmond Romilly. Within a few days of his arrival in Spain, wrote Jessica later, Esmond and sixteen other Englishmen were sent to the Madrid front:

There they were in almost continuous action, living the muddy, bloody, confused life of foot-soldiers. A week before Christmas, in a single disastrous battle, all but two of the English group were wiped out. Esmond and the other survivor, ill with dysentery and battle fatigue, were sent back to England, entrusted with the heartbreaking task of visiting the relatives of the dead.[10]

Many others supported the Republic at home in Britain: collecting money, helping refugees, organizing popular protests and demonstrations, and putting pressure on governments. The Medical Aid Committee, for example, collected books for wounded soldiers and the 'Co-op' sold sixpenny milk tokens for starving Spaniards. The Duchess of Atholl, in her turn, put pressure on the government to stop the farce of Non-Intervention and to take steps to protect the legal Spanish government. Eleanor Rathbone took the same view and they both argued this case to the House of Commons, whenever the opportunity arose. For Rathbone, as an Independent MP, supporting the Spanish government was a fairly straightforward matter: she was free of party priorities and was able to follow her conscience as she chose.

But for Kitty, defying the party orthodoxy on Spain produced real difficulties. She was virtually alone among her Conservative colleagues – with the exception of Captain J. R. J. Macnamara, Major Jack Hills and Vyvian Adams, all backbenchers – to object to the treaty. Churchill, her old ally on India, supported non-intervention, although he also said that the British government must not be seen to be assisting the fascists. This is at least one area in which Kitty was hampered by being an elected MP: if she had not sought direct political power but had simply relied on her social status and connections, she would have been free of these constraints.

The Duchess had always been anxious to make the right moral decision in any situation and to stand by it. It was typical of her character that as a student at the Royal College of Music, she had refused a prestigious scholarship because she had no need of the money; instead, she arranged for it to be given to a young student in need – Samuel Coleridge-Taylor, who later became a famous composer. 'A nicer woman never lived,' commented Patrick Donner, a fellow Conservative MP who shared her views on India although none of those on Spain; he added that 'her sincerity was never in question' (and that she 'dressed incredibly badly').[11] The Duchess's motivation was consistently sincere and disinterested. Her involvement in the campaign against the Government of India Bill, which proposed giving the Indian provinces control of their own internal affairs, illustrates this well. For whereas Winston Churchill's opposition to the Bill was at least partly a strategy to topple Baldwin from the leadership of the Conservative party in order to pursue his own political ambitions, the Duchess's position developed entirely out of her concern for the needs of the Indian people and her faith in the benefits of British imperialism. 'Certainly few members of Parliament take their duties so seriously', wrote the Labour MP Ellen Wilkinson. The Duchess 'has toiled along wet towing paths and stumbled over rubbish boats' to see the conditions suffered by the people living in boats on the canals of England, added Miss Wilkinson, in a reference to her campaign to improve the education of the bargees' children when she was at the Board of Education.[12]

She refused to take action on any issue until she was certain of her facts, even on the question of the age of consent for girls in India (which was thirteen before the Child Marriage Act of 1930). She regarded the raising of this age as a matter of the greatest urgency, but still declined to add her name to a letter of protest to *The Times* before reflecting thoroughly on its implications. 'I should like to have had more time', she told Miss Rathbone, who had sent it to her, 'to take counsel with people who know more about India as to the probable effect of such a letter on a subject in which racial and religious feeling is so much involved, than I do, before signing a letter dealing with a subject of such delicacy.'[13] This fastidious approach was gently mocked by some of her parliamentary colleagues. Miss Wilkinson reported that when Kitty was a government delegate to the League of Nations, 'she was nicknamed the Duchess of Not-At-All, so completely did her mind seem to be closed to the changes that were there being urged'. Perhaps, speculated Wilkinson, 'this is the quality of her mind, which is pre-Raphaelite in its careful accuracy of detail'.[14]

Kitty wanted as many people as possible to have an accurate grasp of important facts. To this end, she wrote *Women and Politics* in 1931. It was conceived as a dutiful response to the full enfranchisement of women in 1928 – to 'meet what I believe to be a desire on the part of many women to add to their background of political knowledge'. Promising to describe 'our present taxation in some detail, in order to give a background of knowledge', as well as a full coverage of other key topics, the book is thorough and systematic but hardly engrossing.[15] She never deviated from this earnest style, either in her writings or her speeches. It was nicely contrasted by Donner with the more frivolous behaviour of Diana Churchill, Winston's daughter, in his account of a speech by Kitty on the question of India:

The scene in the crowded . . . Town Hall was, in its way, unforgettable. The Duchess spoke first and soon became immersed in the horrors of Hindu temple prostitution. Diana Churchill, who had travelled up with me, sat on the edge of the platform, silk-stockinged legs dangling over the side. A chair could have been found for her, but this she declined. She liked sitting on the floor and seldom failed to do so on her occasional and unannounced visits to my flat. She was an extrovert, totally unselfconscious and, before the rivetted gaze of our audience, painted her nails bright scarlet with care and concentration. 'We must not shirk, however repulsive and horrible, the detailed investigation of the

1. 'The gorgeous company of the "Haves"' Edith Londonderry in 1932 at a fête in Reims, France, unveiling a statue of Dom Perignon, the Benedictine monk who first put the sparkle into champagne.

2. 'An Upper Class ... who still wield a certain influence behind the scenes' Lady Londonderry resplendent in diamonds and ermine.

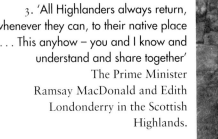

3. 'All Highlanders always return, whenever they can, to their native place ... This anyhow – you and I know and understand and share together' The Prime Minister Ramsay MacDonald and Edith Londonderry in the Scottish Highlands.

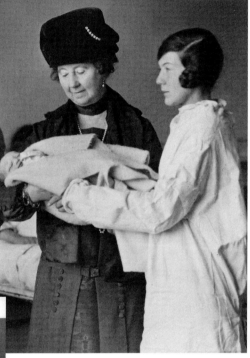

4. 'I feel that I am Stan's "Trainer" for the Arena' Lucy Baldwin stands by her husband Stanley (middle) as he talks to Neville Chamberlain (June 1937).

5. 'I am especially interested in making anaesthetics available in normal cases of childbirth' Mrs Baldwin at Queen Charlotte's Hospital, London, with a newly born baby (1930).

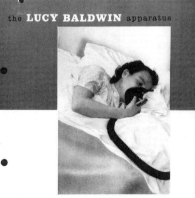

the **LUCY BALDWIN** apparatus

fornitrous oxide/oxygen analgesia in obstetrics

THE BRITISH OXYGEN COMPANY LIMITED

6. 'A great and glorious victory over pain and suffering' 'The Lucy Baldwin Apparatus', so named in memory of Mrs Baldwin by British Oxygen in 1959.

7. 'One of the few remaining *grandes dames* of English society, survivors of an earlier age' Violet Milner in her early fifties, shortly after her marriage to Alfred Milner in 1921.

8. 'The destiny of the English race ... has been to strike fresh roots in distant parts of the world' Violet Milner, who was then Lady Edward Cecil (centre), on the verandah of Cecil Rhodes's mansion in South Africa, while her husband was on active service in the Boer War of 1899–1902. Seated next to Lady Edward is Alfred Milner, the British High Commissioner, whom she married over twenty years later.

9. 'We have just got back from Safari ... it was lovely – we camped in a green valley beside the Gouya River' Joan Grigg on safari in Kenya in 1930.

10. 'This is women's side of Empire-building!' Lady Grigg visits a mother and her children at their home in rural Kenya, 1928.

11. 'The native woman ... needs trained assistance just as much as the European' Lady Grigg gives a speech at a ceremony to open the Indian Maternity Home in Nairobi, Kenya.

The TATLER

Vol. XLIV. No. 1221. London, November 19, 1924 | POSTAGE: Ireland, ½d.; Canada and Newfoundland, 2d.; Foreign, 3d. | Price One Shilling

THE DUCHESS OF ATHOLL

Who is the only woman in the new Government, and has been appointed Parliamentary Secretary for the Board of Education. This photograph was the first one taken of her Grace in her office at the Ministry of Education. The Duchess of Atholl is the daughter of Sir James Ramsay, Bart., by his second marriage. She was married to the Duke of Atholl in 1899

12. 'We have still to make . . . the nation realize what women can contribute to the work of Parliament' The Duchess of Atholl MP gives a speech in Perth, Scotland, with her husband seated behind her (1924).

13. 'The Duchess of Atholl is the only woman in the new Government' The cover of *The Tatler*, 19 November 1924.

A PENGUIN SPECIAL

PENGUIN SPECIAL

Duchess of Atholl, M.P.

DUCHESS OF ATHOLL

SEARCHLIGHT ON SPAIN

SEARCHLIGHT ON SPAIN

2nd impression within a week!

A TOTAL OF 100,000 copies

6^d　6^d

14a. 'The cheers of the children and some 150 teachers ... were something never to be forgotten' The first contingent of 4,000 child refugees from Spain arrive in Britain in 1937 because of the Duchess of Atholl's and the Basque Childrens Committee.

14b. 'The Duchess of Atholl's book will do more good for the Republican cause and it is [an] able and succinct statement of a case' *Searchlight on Spain* was published in 1938 as a 'Penguin Special'.

15. 'She inspired half the poets and the novelists of the Twenties' Nancy Cunard poses for a photograph by Cecil Beaton.

16. 'One of the most interesting of the newer small presses . . . issuing exquisite limited editions of modern writers' Nancy Cunard and her lover, Henry Crowder, working at the Hours Press in Paris, 1930.

HENRY
MUSIC
by

POEMS BY
RICHARD ALDINGTON   HENRY
HAROLD ACTON   CROWDER
NANCY CUNARD
WALTER LOWENFELS
SAMUEL BECKETT

17. 'Henry . . . became my teacher in all questions of colour that exist in America and was the primary cause of the compilation . . . of my large *Negro Anthology*' This volume of music by Henry Crowder was published by the Hours Press in 1930, with a cover designed by Man Ray.

18. 'She gave you a job and made you feel you were just the one to do it!' Stella, Marchioness of Reading, chairman and founder of the Women's Voluntary Service for Civil Defence (WVS).

19. 'Not patronage by the few, but personal service by the many' Lady Reading and the wife of the United States Ambassador in London look on as two WVS volunteers can fruit (1949).

20. (*below*) 'Tea at an hour's notice for any number between forty and four hundred has become a commonplace' Feeding Civil Defence workers from a WVS mobile canteen after an explosion in 1943.

21. (*above*) 'What a knack of dodging and cooking and managing' WVS volunteers making soup on the streets of Coventry after eleven hours of bombing by German aeroplanes in April 1941.

dreadful horrors that go on . . .' continued the Duchess, while Diana, oblivious to her surroundings, concentrated on making a good job of her nails.[16]

Leo Amery could hardly bear listening to the Duchess, who was dubbed 'The Begum of Blair', speak on India. The boredom of the audience during the India debate at the Conservative conference in October 1934, he commented with an amused irony, 'was intensified to fever pitch when the Duchess of Atholl got up and in her earnest monotonous way began reciting evidence of the diminution of efficiency under Indian ministers – one of them the fact that someone had been appointed a professor of gynaecology who had never done an abdominal resection. This got the audience into such a state that they clamoured for a vote . . .'[17]

Marginalized by her fellow Conservatives on the issue of Spain, Kitty was grateful to work with members of other parties. In January 1937, she took an active part in setting up an all-party National Joint Committee for Spanish Relief, of which she was Chairman and Eleanor Rathbone was Vice-Chairman; the Liberal MP Wilfred Roberts and the Communist Isabel Brown also took leadership roles. It met regularly in a committee room at the House of Commons during the next two years and its range of activities included the evacuation of Spanish children from bombed areas to safer ones. Meanwhile, Kitty and Eleanor worked closely with members of the Liberal and Labour parties to keep up a stream of questions in the House on the subject of Spain. These efforts were a valuable contribution to the struggle of the Republican government; indeed, the anonymous author (styling himself 'The Unknown Diplomat') of *Britain in Spain* argued that given the massive impact of the Non-Intervention Agreement, '*the key to the Spanish crisis is* neither in Rome nor in Berlin, not to speak of Burgos; it is *in London* [sic]'.[18]

Following her conscience rather than the party line, even to the point of working with individuals from the other parties, was not unusual for women in this period. There was a precedent for this kind of solidarity in the suffrage movement: for before 1928, however much women had been divided by social class and party difference, there had been a degree to which suffragists of all classes and political affiliations joined together in the single cause of the franchise. This unity was reflected at the parliamentary level: after Lady Astor's election as a Conservative MP, Ethel Snowden and Edith Picton-Turberville refused to stand against her as Labour candidates. 'I am a Labour woman,' said Ethel Snowden, 'but the work which Lady Astor is doing for women and children both in parliament and the country makes her services invaluable.'[19] Lady Astor and Mrs Wintringham, a Liberal and the second woman to take her seat as an MP, exchanged telegrams of mutual support at elections.

In fact, though, Kitty had taken no part in the suffrage movement – except to oppose it. In 1918, she had sought to block the motion to give women the vote at the age of twenty-one. She argued that it would be a mistake to give the franchise to women, who were not ready for it; in any case, she said, the average housewife and mother did not want the vote and mothers with large families had no time for political meetings. Then, in the early 1920s, Lloyd George suggested to her that she stand for Parliament, as he wanted to see more women of all parties in the House. She took the matter seriously and when King George V came on one of his visits to Blair Castle, the Atholls' magnificent family seat in Scotland, she asked him for his opinion. He advised her against such a plan, on the grounds that she would not be able to combine her social duties with life at Westminster. But the Duchess had no worries on that score, she said, because of the 'wonderful domestic gifts' of her husband, 'Bardie', who was the sort of man to remember to place a Koran at the bedside of King Feisal of Iraq when he visited the castle. Her mind was made up: she abandoned her previous doubts about women's role in politics and decided to stand for Parliament. In 1923, she was elected MP for Kinross and the West Division of Perthshire, holding this seat for fifteen years until 1938.

The very male culture of Westminster was not always comfortable territory for women. Following one of the Duchess's many interventions on Spain in the House, a senior official in the Foreign Office noted in a minute that he felt 'rather sorry for the *Duke* of Atholl'.[20] The House itself went to very little trouble to welcome women in the 1930s, recalled the Labour MP Edith Summerskill later. There was only one room for women members, she said, with an adjoining smaller room containing an iron Victorian wash-stand with a tin basin:

The Duchess of Atholl, looking a little like a Victorian governess would, on changing her frock, present her back to the half-open door to enable her maid, standing in the corridor, to fasten the numerous small buttons which only the maid's practised hand could manipulate.[21]

But the Duchess never allowed her marginal position as a woman to prevent her from working for the causes in which she believed and she hammered home her message on Spain with a persistence that many of her parliamentary colleagues found wearing. If anything, she became all the more determined to draw attention to areas that would otherwise remain neglected, such as the practice of female circumcision in Kenya. In 1929 she organized the setting-up of an all-party Committee for the Protection of Coloured Women, under the chairmanship of Josiah Wedgwood, a Labour MP; other members were Eleanor Rathbone, Edith Picton-Turberville, and the Conservative member R. A. Butler, who was secretary. The committee proposed that colonial governments should find out more about the practice of the custom and that ways should be found legally to protect any girl who wanted to avoid circumcision.

The 'Noble Lady the Member for Kinross' raised the issue of circumcision in the House of Commons on 11 December 1929. She provided a level of detail that was welcomed by some members but horrified others. 'The rite is nothing short of mutilation,' the Duchess told the House, adding that, 'It consists of the actual wholesale removal of parts connected with the organs of reproduction . . . the girl has a whistle put into her mouth so that her screams will not be heard.'[22] Two days later, on 13 December, the Duchess brought up the issue of circumcision again, asking the under-secretary of state for the colonies about the specific case 'of a young Kikuyu girl, in the Kiambu district of Kenya, who was recently compelled to undergo a form of operation forbidden by the Kiambu Native Council against her will'.[23] As a consequence of this campaign by Atholl and her committee, the secretary of state for the colonies asked Edward Grigg, the governor of Kenya, to furnish a full report on the subject. At no point was any attempt made to discover the point of view of Kenyan women.

Being an MP transformed Kitty's perspective on the role of women in society. She moved from the conviction that women's lives were unsuited to the public arena to a view that was virtually the opposite: that public and parliamentary life was flawed by its masculine character and would benefit from the application of women's values. 'I think we have still to make the House of Commons and the nation realize,' she argued, 'what women can contribute to the work of Parliament and to do this it seems to me, we have to use many of the qualities we find needed in our domestic life.'[24] Her views on marriage and the role of a wife also underwent a dramatic change. 'Forty years ago', she observed in 1958, 'the ideal wife was one who said "Amen" to her husband whenever he opened his mouth. Today that idea has been abandoned and we have instead an idea of comradeship, of partnership in life's happiness and difficulties alike which we recognise as much better.'[25] The Duchess was greatly supported in her political work by her husband Bardie, even though he was constantly troubled by financial worries. In her loyal book about their lives together, she described his patient kindness on the night before her maiden speech in the House of Commons, when he helped to build up her courage. His own concerns were centred on Scotland, where he took an active part in public life; he was also one of the founders of the National Trust for Scotland.

Their marriage appears to have been blessed with mutual respect and devotion but lacking in warmth and passion. In 1925, when Kitty was fifty-one, events related to her work at the Ministry of Education caused her to re-establish contact with a former admirer, Ted Butler, a classics master at Harrow who was now retired; he had married and was now a grandfather. They started to correspond and occasionally had the opportunity of meeting together. At the end of 1926, he wrote to thank her for a pencil she had sent him for his birthday:

My first writing with this beautiful pencil must be to you. I need not tell you how I shall prize it and how much it will mean to me. My birthday was the happiest one I have had for years. Exactly ten months have passed since a certain luncheon, and to me at any rate has been going from rock to rock. Bless you for it – Always your affectionate EMB.[26]

They remained in contact until Ted's death in 1952. This 'close, platonic friendship', comments Kitty's biographer Sheila Hetherington, 'must have given Kitty at last the warm reassurance which had eluded her in marriage.'[27] It is possible, too, that Kitty derived some fulfilment of her passionate nature from her involvement in the Spanish Civil War. There was a sense of romantic engagement in the commitment of Republicans and Brigaders alike, which was expressed in a flowering of poetry, fiction and art.

Possibly the chief disappointment in Kitty's marriage was their childlessness – for she believed that the capacity for motherhood was for women the 'basic fact of our physical existence'.[28] It may have been this gap in her life that led her to care so much about the refugee children of Spain and to work vigorously on their behalf. In April 1937, a successful Nationalist offensive against Bilbao created concern for the children in the city, which had little food and was subject to aerial bombardment. The National Joint Committee proposed bringing a number of them to Britain and once permission had eventually been obtained, it set up the Basque Children's Committee. With the hard work of the Duchess as chairman and Lady Layton as an energetic member, the committee managed to bring 4,000 Basque children to the United Kingdom. They had a dreadful journey: they were bombed while marching to board the ship and eleven children were killed. When they finally arrived in Britain, said Kitty, 'the cheers of the children and some 150 teachers . . . were something never to be forgotten'.[29] Shortly afterwards, Bilbao fell to the rebels, causing the children great distress. When conditions became safer many of them were returned to Spain, although 1,000 were still in Britain at the end of the Civil War.

In January 1937 Ellen Wilkinson proposed an all-women delegation to Spain. Kitty and Eleanor Rathbone agreed to go with her, on behalf of the National Joint Committee for Spanish Relief, and a fourth member of the party was Dame Rachel Crowdie, a leader of the nursing profession who had been a member of the League of Nations secretariat. Leaving Britain in April, they travelled overland to Toulouse and from there by air to Barcelona. It is hard to imagine Kitty's feelings when she entered the centre of Republican Spain, which was completely different from anything she had ever seen. 'Practically every building of any size had been seized by the workers and was draped with red flags or with the red and black flag of the anarchists', reported

George Orwell, who came to Barcelona as a Brigader just months before Kitty's arrival; 'every wall', he added, 'was scrawled with the hammer and sickle and with the initials of the revolutionary parties; almost every church had been gutted and its images burnt.'[30] The delegation of women were welcomed by the Republican Government and given every opportunity to see whatever they liked – hospitals, schools and prisons for political prisoners. They tried to visit insurgent territory, too, but too many obstacles were put in their way by the Nationalist government. The most interesting personality Kitty met was the Communist leader Dolores Ibarruri – fish pedlar, miner's widow and Member of Parliament – who was known everywhere as 'La Pasionaria'. Her eloquence and strength were invaluable to the Republican side from the very start of the war: when the government called on the people to rally to the defence of the republic, it was she who made the appeal over the Madrid radio.[31] The Duchess was initially reluctant to see her, but was persuaded to do so by Ellen Wilkinson. 'I have never ceased to be glad that I did so', she wrote later, recalling that Señora Ibarruri was 'beautiful, with rich colouring, large dark eyes, and black wavy hair. She swept into the room like a queen, yet she was a miner's daughter married to a miner – a woman who had had the sorrow of losing six out of eight children.' In Madrid, the outpost of Republican resistance under siege by Franco, Kitty was appalled by the suffering of the children. They were under constant attack from the air and from shell fire, as the rebels encircled the city and moved closer daily. Food and the necessities of life were scant. She made a broadcast from the Madrid wireless station, appealing to Britain for help for the children of the city. No part of Madrid was more than a mile or two from the front line and Kitty and her party had their first experience of the bombing when a shell exploded outside an hotel where they were eating lunch.

Increasingly Kitty was dubbed 'The Red Duchess'. On the one hand, Republican plans for social reform, such as social insurance, universal education, and the widespread establishment of health clinics (although many of these goals had to be abandoned because of the demands of war) were consistent with her own, humane, views of social justice. But on the other hand, she was not a 'red' in any way; in 1931, indeed, she wrote *The Conscription of a People* in order to expose the horror of labour conditions in Soviet Russia. Many aspects of life in Republican Spain, especially in Catalonia, the centre of political extremism, were sharply at odds with her own set of values. There was a movement to collectivize the land and factories and in the anarchist areas, the concept of ownership and of individual property had been rejected, along with money and other 'bourgeois' forms of society. And although it was found necessary to tolerate a mixed economy, the dream of destroying capitalism was fundamental to the goals of the Republic. Kitty, moreover, was uncritically loyal to a Britain that was rooted in capitalist values and the kind of social hierarchy that was denounced by the Republican government. She herself was at the top level of this hierarchy, as the daughter of a baronet and the wife of a duke, which is the highest rank that can be held outside royalty. One of the Duchess's critics accused her of hypocrisy, pointing out that 'the estates of the Duke of Atholl are larger than those of the biggest landowner of Spain'. Referring to the efforts of the Spanish government to redistribute land, he asked why she did not advocate 'the same remedy for the solution of the agrarian problem in Scotland and England?'[32]

In fact, the Atholls were hard up and unable to maintain the lifestyle which they might have been expected to enjoy, because the Duke had inherited a problem of deep indebtedness. For a time they let Blair Castle to an American and then, in 1928, they sold the best of the family jewellery and their London property in Eaton Place, moving to a smaller house in a less prestigious location. The Duke spent much of his time trying to think up various schemes that would stave off financial disaster and save the family estates. One of his pet projects was called 'Atholl Steel Houses', using surplus steel to build houses, which were in short supply. The first steel house was opened with a great fanfare by the Prime Minister, Stanley Baldwin, in 1925. But the project was a flop: despite the shortage of homes, people were understandably suspicious of living in metal houses, which were in any case hot in summer and cold in winter. The scale of the Atholls' financial difficulties was in quite a different league, of course, from that of most people who regarded themselves as hard up in the years of the Depression and Hunger Marches. However, the Duchess does not seem really to have grasped this difference. In *Women and Politics*, she makes the point that the rich of Britain were suffering as much as the poor from financial hardship, because they were losing their money and their homes (like herself and Bardie). 'Where English people make more use than formerly of London hotels or restaurants', she observed sadly, 'it is often because, owing to small domestic staffs, they do not find it easy to entertain guests at home'.[33]

She understood fully the gravity of the Spanish crisis as compared with her own minor difficulties, however. She returned from her visit to Spain fired with determination to put pressure on the British government to stop foreign aid to Franco. Her attitude to the Republic had undergone a profound shift. No longer was she simply concerned about the threat to peace posed by Franco and the moral deceit of the Non-Intervention Agreement. She was also, now, loyal to the Republican cause, because she had been so impressed by what she had seen in Spain. Shortly after her return she gave a speech at a National Emergency Conference convened at the Queen's Hall in London, under the auspices of an all-party group of MPs and the slogan of 'Save Spain – Save Peace'. There were 1,800 delegates, including representatives from Labour Party and trade union branches. Representatives of the South Wales and Durham miners called for a General Strike to secure for Spain the right to purchase arms.[34] This was unlikely company for a Conservative duchess. But by now, a typical English meeting in support of the Spanish Republic had set into a regular format that nearly always included the 'Red' Duchess of Atholl.

On 26 April 1937, two weeks after Kitty's return from Spain, the small Basque town of Guernica, of no military significance, was razed to the ground by German aircraft. Out of its 6,000 inhabitants, 1,654 people were killed and 889 wounded. A British journalist writing for the *London Mercury* (and using the Basque spelling of 'Gernika') reported that

It was about five-fifteen. For about two hours and a half flights of between three and twelve aeroplanes, types Heinkel 111 and Junker 52, bombed Gernika without mercy and with system. They chose their sectors in the town in orderly fashion, with opening points east of the Casa de Juntas and north of the Arms Factory ... Every twenty minutes fresh raiders came ... At seven-forty-five the last plane went away. One could hear now, through ears half-numbed by the engines of the heavy bombers and explosion of the heavy bombs, the nervous crackle of arson all over the town and the totter and the trembling collapse of roofs and walls. Gernika was finished, and . . . the total furnace that was Gernika began to play tricks of crimson colour with the night clouds.[35]

Germany denied responsibility but the evidence was indisputable. The Spanish painter Picasso portrayed the horror of the event on his immense canvas, *Guernica*, which was exhibited in the Spanish Pavilion in the Paris World Fair of 1937, drawing international attention to the plight of the Spanish people. But the brutality of the Nationalists continued relentlessly. Between 16 and 18 March 1938, day-and-night bombing of Barcelona by Italian planes killed 1,300 people and injured 2,000.

Kitty was now ready to risk her political career for the Loyalist cause. June 1938 saw the publication of *Searchlight on Spain*, a Penguin paperback that she had written in order to 'examine as objectively as possible the main points in the war itself around which controversy has gathered'. It was necessary to write the book, explained the Duchess, because the rebels had falsified the truth. 'The attempts made shortly after my return from Spain to deny that Guernica was destroyed by aerial bombing', she said, 'helped me to realise the lengths to which propaganda might go.' The book was a development of some notes she had made for a speech at a conference on Spain, which was held at the Conservative College at Ashridge (and at which the Duchess was the only speaker who was pro-Republican). The book gives an account of the historical background to the Spanish Civil War, especially the poverty of the peasants and the workers and the failure of the ruling class to respond to their most basic needs. The Duchess made it clear that she was writing on her own account only, out of a sense of personal duty, and was not speaking on behalf of any political group: 'The writing of this book is my own idea alone, born of the desire which I hope may be forgiven in the daughter of a historian, to try to get at the facts; and of my conviction that it is the duty of members of Parliament to do this.'[36]

An immediate best-seller, *Searchlight on Spain* sold out within a week and quickly ran into a second and then a third edition. Altogether, over 300,000 copies, priced sixpence, were sold, and the text was translated into French, German and Spanish. The public may have been intrigued by the idea of a duchess supporting a popular movement. As the Labour MP Sir Stafford Cripps pointed out in the House of Commons, statements of support for Spain would 'be more convincing to the public coming from her, than they would be coming from these [Labour] benches'.[37] A review in *The Times Literary Supplement* made the same point: comparing *Searchlight* to another book on Spain that was written in the more complicated language of Marxist terminology, it observed that: 'The Duchess of Atholl's book will do more good for the Republican cause and it is a more able and succinct statement of a case.'[38] One of the Duchess's opponents, Professor Charles Sarolea of the University of Edinburgh, regarded the book as such a serious threat to the Nationalists that he responded to it with *Daylight on Spain. The Answer to the Duchess of Atholl.* The 'sudden worldwide notoriety of the Duchess of Atholl', he said, 'is only a master stroke of Popular Front propaganda.'[39] Certainly the sudden appearance of *Searchlight on Spain* in bookshops all over Britain, as well as favourable reviews in respectable journals, can have done little to raise the Duchess's esteem in the eyes of the Conservative Party.

Searchlight on Spain was the fourth Penguin 'Special'. Penguin Books had started publishing as recently as 1936, with immediate success, and were now commissioning writers to do 'Specials'. These were 'books of urgent topical importance published at sixpence within as short a time as possible from the receipt of the manuscript', stated the back cover of *Searchlight*. Their subjects were chiefly international crises and the authors were expected to rush them off at top speed, so that they would be on the market when the crisis was at its height. *The Times Literary Supplement* was impressed. It described *Searchlight* as 'an unusual publishing feat. Nearly 346 pages of a new work are available for the price of sixpence. One does not of course get an index and the misprints are overfrequent, but it is very good money's worth.' But if Penguin was willing to make some mistakes, the Duchess was not and drew on numerous reliable authorities to support all her facts.

Kitty's style of writing about Spain may be contrasted with that of Nancy Cunard, who went to Spain to write as a freelance journalist for the *Manchester Guardian* and the American *Associated Negro*

Press. There is no doubt that Nancy made every effort to find out what was happening, travelling fearlessly as far as possible out of republican territory and into the battle zone. On one occasion, for example, she reported that the enemy was 'at 700 metres; Illescas is at 1600 metres. We run across the road, ducking, then sit talking with those in the trenches on the right for about 20 minutes. Bullets pass. NOISE. In the distance more and bigger noise, muted by distance.'[40] But Nancy accepted the Republican version of events uncritically and emotionally, showing no interest in the internal struggles on the government side or the more complex issues underpinning the war.[41] The Duchess of Atholl, on the other hand, was less emotional and more analytical in her approach. It was perhaps this style that led Harold Macmillan, who worked with her at different times, to say that she 'had a masculine mind'.[42]

In the spring months leading up to the publication of *Searchlight on Spain*, disagreements within the Conservative Party on issues of foreign policy, especially appeasement, were starting to gain momentum. In February 1938, Anthony Eden resigned as Foreign Secretary, because he was unhappy about the discussions with Mussolini which Neville Chamberlain, now Prime Minister, was about to open. On 28 April, the Duchess wrote to Chamberlain to complain that even though the conditions for a pact with Italy included an agreement that no more Italian troops would be sent to Spain, they were continuing to arrive. Because of this, she warned, she might have to resign the government whip. The Prime Minister's response was swift. He instructed that the whip should be withdrawn from her, on the grounds that any answer from him would fail to satisfy her. Their letters to each other appeared in *The Times* on 29 April 1938. This was unfortunate for Kitty, for it meant that her constituents were made immediately aware of this development. Her position in her constituency was already weak; throughout 1937–8, she had received offensive letters from members of her constituency association, many of whom were Catholics, and a series of Blackshirt meetings were held in her constituency at Crieff, at Aberfeldy and at Auchterarder.

In October 1938, Chamberlain went to Munich and signed over to Hitler the German-speaking areas of Czechoslovakia in exchange for peace. At this time Kitty was in North America, speaking at events to raise funds for Spanish refugee children. She was horrified by the news and as soon as she returned, she wrote to her constituents to explain that in her opinion, the Prime Minister had retreated from the principle of the Covenant of the League of Nations. She was not the only Conservative MP to protest: Duff Cooper resigned his seat and some thirty Conservatives, led by Churchill, abstained when the settlement came for a vote in the House of Commons. But the Duchess's constituents were furious. The powerful landed aristocracy in West Perthshire, in particular, regarded her stand as a betrayal of their shared class position. 'The situation is becoming difficult for those of us who are working for you', wrote a loyal supporter 'as so many people feel that your support of the Spanish Government is wrong.'[43] In November, Kitty's constituency association agreed by 273 votes to 167 to seek a new candidate at the next election, so she resigned her parliamentary seat. She decided to force a by-election in December, standing as an Independent and campaigning on foreign policy, in alliance with Churchill against Chamberlain's appeasement of Germany. She denounced the Munich settlement and the government's line on Spain, calling for collective security and rearmament. She was backed by the Liberal and Labour parties in her fight against the official Conservative candidate, a local laird. She was also supported by a galaxy of political and literary stars, including Eleanor Rathbone, Lady Violet Bonham Carter, Winston Churchill (who rang her up nearly every evening during the campaign) and J. M. Keynes. Dolores Ibarruri sent a telegram of support from Spain. But Kitty lost by 1,313 votes. She felt the defeat keenly, believing that it seriously diminished her power to influence the British position on Spain. 'I wish I could feel I was worthy in any way to be compared to the Spanish Republicans', she wrote in dismay to Lloyd George.[44]

Any hopes of a Republican victory in Spain had been dashed by the start of 1939. Forced to fight a rearguard action from the beginning, the Republican army had been seriously weakened by internal division, both militarily and politically. The extent of this division astonished Jessica Mitford when she first arrived in Spain and was taken to the front by the Basque Press Bureau. Each encampment of soldiers, she saw, had its own political identity: 'That's a Communist battalion over on the right . . . Now further on you can see a company of Anarchists

. . . Over to the left there is a battalion of the Basque Catholic Nationalist Party . . .' There were even four anthems:

Cafes were crowded with people listening to the news broadcasts, following
each of which the crowds would respectfully stand at silent attention for
the playing of not one, but four, anthems, symbolizing the United Front – the
Basque National Anthem, the Spanish anthem, the Internationale, and the
Anarchist hymn.[45]

This 'rag-tag army' – as the British Brigader and poet Louis MacNeice
described it in his poem *Autumn Journal* (1939) – was badly equipped
and underfed. 'For the last eighteen months of the war', wrote George
Orwell, 'the Republican armies must have been fighting almost without
cigarettes, and with precious little food.'[46] But the most impossible
obstacle was the massive aid provided by Mussolini and Hitler. By
January, at least five Italian divisions were forming the spearhead of
an advance by Franco on Catalonia, and Barcelona fell at the end of
the month. A solid phalanx of refugees streamed eastwards to France,
pursued by Italian aeroplanes. This was followed by some scattered
fighting and then the final surrender of Madrid, on 29 March 1939.

By now, Spain had been displaced by Czechoslovakia as an issue of
international concern. For on 15 March, while Spain was in the last
gasp of defeat, Hitler marched into Prague. In the eyes of the world,
Spain had shifted from being an important political and military issue,
to a minor humanitarian problem about the punitive behaviour of the
Franco regime and the internment of Spanish refugees in France. Later
that summer, the Duchess went to the south of France to visit some of
these refugees who had been promised a home by Mexico. She watched
the first boat leave. As the boat began to move, a little Republican flag
fluttered out of a cabin window. Then how the cheers rang out! Rarely
in her life had she been more moved, she observed in her memoir many
years later.[47]

In a letter written well after the Second World War, Nancy Mitford
expressed regret that the lives of the Duchess of Atholl and Nancy
Cunard had been so intensely affected by the Spanish conflict. 'Women
should never take up causes, that's what it is', she concluded.[48] If
anybody had grounds for such a view, it was Nancy Mitford – for the

various 'causes' of the more extreme Mitford sisters had provoked family conflict and tragedy. Diana had espoused fascism and was imprisoned during the war with her husband Sir Oswald Mosley, leader of the British Union of Fascists; Unity fell under the spell of Hitler and when Britain declared war, tried unsuccessfully to kill herself, ending up as an invalid; and Jessica became a Communist. Nancy herself wavered between two poles: having flirted with Fascism, she ended the thirties as a socialist, helping to find homes for Republican refugees from Spain.

But the Duchess was different from the Mitfords. She did not so much 'take up causes' as apply herself always – energetically and scrupulously – to the righting of wrongs, whatever the political colour of the victim or the tyrant. Though called 'The Red Duchess', she was nothing of the sort: she was simply doing what she felt to be morally necessary in the face of injustice. After the Second World War, when she was well into her seventies, she turned her attention to the problem of Communist brutality and the fates of Poland, Czechoslovakia and Hungary. This now brought her into association with right-wing elements and produced a new nickname – 'Fascist Beast'.[49]

6

'THE GIOCONDA OF THE AGE'
Nancy Cunard

Nancy Cunard, 1896–1965, was the only child of Lady Maud and Sir Bache Cunard, grandson of the founder of the shipping empire. She grew up at Nevill Holt, a vast house and estate in Leicestershire, where her father enjoyed country pursuits. Her mother, an American, was far more interested in the life of a stylish hostess in London and was a great patron of opera. Their incompatibility led to a parting of the ways. One of Emerald's lovers was the novelist George Moore, who was an important influence on Nancy's literary interests. In 1916, at the age of twenty, Nancy married Sidney Fairbairn, a young Guards officer, but they separated after twenty months.

Nancy rejected her parents' world and chose a Bohemian life. In 1920 she moved to France, living mostly in Paris, which became her home for most of the rest of her life. She was active in Left Bank politics and intellectual life and was the friend and lover of various artists and intellectuals, including the Dadaist poet Tristan Tzara and the Surrealist Louis Aragon. She became the style icon of the Twenties and was represented in a number of novels of the time. However, many people were scandalized by her many love affairs and unconventional behaviour. A published poet herself, in 1928 she decided to act as the patron of other writers and artists and set up The Hours Press in France. The press published many modernist writers, including Pound. In 1931 she closed down The Hours in order to produce her Negro Anthology, *a massive collection of black art and literature that was conceived as a plea for civil rights. Her interest in the injustice suffered by blacks was at least partly generated from her love affair with Henry Crowder, a black American jazz musician. It was unusual at this time for a white woman to have a relationship with a man who was black.*

Following the outbreak of the Civil War in Spain in 1936, Nancy went to Madrid as a freelance journalist. She returned to France to produce anti-fascist propaganda, which was supported by her many artist and intellectual friends. During the Second World War she worked for the Free French in London; after the war she returned to France and continued to struggle against injustice, such as the exploitation of Venetian gondoliers. However, her physical and mental health started to disintegrate. Following a series of violent and drunken episodes, she died alone in a French hospital in 1965.

While Spain became the centre of the struggle between dictatorship and democracy in the mid-1930s, Paris between the wars was the centre of the avant-garde. 'Intellectually', wrote the English aesthete Harold Acton, 'Paris was the capital of the world.'[1] Artists and writers looked critically at many of the old conventions and forged new ways of thinking about culture and politics, creating a fertile atmosphere that was a beacon to intellectuals from other countries. One of these was a young Englishwoman called Nancy Cunard, who moved to Paris in 1920 at the age of twenty-four. She was one of many foreigners to flock to Paris at this time: from Romania, the Dadaist poet Tristan Tzara and the sculptor Brancusi; from Spain, the artists Pablo Picasso and Joan Miró; from Germany, the painter Max Ernst; from Ireland, the novelist James Joyce and the dramatist and poet Samuel Beckett; from England, the novelist and painter Wyndham Lewis; and from the USA, the art collector Peggy Guggenheim and numerous writers including Ernest Hemingway, Gertrude Stein and Ezra Pound. Stein tried to explain the attraction of Paris to expatriates like herself in a book called *Paris France*. 'Each country is important at different times', she wrote, 'because the world in general needs a different imagination at different times and so there is the Paris France from 1900 to 1939, where everybody had to be to be free.'[2]

Nancy Cunard was the daughter of Sir Bache and Lady Cunard, prominent members of the British social elite. They were both very rich, as Sir Bache was the grandson of the founder of the Cunard shipping empire and Maud (who called herself Emerald from 1926) came from an affluent American background. Nancy grew up in a world of tasteful luxury and spent the first fifteen years of her life at Nevill Holt, a rambling ancient house in Leicestershire with an estate of some 13,000 acres. The Cunards were not blessed with the aristocratic breeding of the Londonderrys and the Atholls, but their means and their social and cultural refinement enabled them to function almost as equals in high society. Emerald was a fashionable hostess like Lady Londonderry, but with a speciality in the arts rather than politics. She was a great patron of opera, as well as the protectress of many intellectuals, artists and musicians, and it was probably she that Robert Graves and Alan Hodge had in mind when they wrote in their social history of interwar Britain that 'Mayfair was a sort of informal university: with hostesses for heads of colleges'.[3]

But Mayfair life was not for Nancy, who ached to be free of the conventions and expectations of the world in which she had been raised. When she 'came out' as a debutante in 1914, she hated the dress she had to wear, which was 'shell pink with a long train composed of chiffon or net rose petals fluttering separately'.[4] Trying in every way to forge a path that was independent of her mother, she soon developed her own unique style of dress. It was so markedly different from her mother's that Cecil Beaton, the well-known photographer of fashion and high-society celebrities, drew attention to the contrast in his *Book of Beauty* (1930). While Lady Cunard was 'deliciously pretty', he said, Nancy 'resembles a robot woman in a German film.' Her eyes, he added, were

exaggeratedly serpent-like and the effect is increased by her painting them heavily with a dark liquid pigment inside the sockets, as the Arab women do. Her appearance is very Egyptian, with Nefertiti's long upper lip and slightly pouting mouth, which she paints like a crimson scar across her face. Her hair is metal blonde, her cheek bones pronounced, her nose a little blunt and finely sensitive, her movements rhythmical.[5]

She was stunningly beautiful – slim and long-limbed, with a short bob of golden hair.

In 1916, at the age of twenty, Nancy married a young Guards officer called Sidney Fairbairn, who had been wounded at Gallipoli in 1915. He was entirely suitable as a husband for Nancy in terms of his social background, but his old-fashioned attitudes made them an ill-matched pair. After only 20 months she could no longer bear what she described later as 'eternal bridge in dull company'[6] and they separated. Then Nancy found a genuine object for her affections: one of Fairbairn's brother officers, Peter Broughton Adderley, came home briefly on leave and they fell passionately in love. But he soon returned to the Front, where he was killed just weeks before the end of the war. Nancy was devastated, like so many other women who lost their men between 1914 and 1918. It is impossible to know how different her life might have been without this loss: as it was, her sexual life became noticeably promiscuous and she never married again. She died childless; she could not become pregnant after 1920 in any case, as a result of some gynaecological disorder.[7] In this way, the usual means by which women of the time established a life of their own, away from their parents – men, marriage and children – failed to provide Nancy with a route of escape from the orbit of her mother. In this context, her move to Paris can be seen as a desperate step to achieve this separation. Many years later, in 1955, she read the diary she had kept in 1919 and remembered her feelings of determination to leave England: 'On January 7th 1920, I went to France – alone "for ever".'[8]

She did not go simply as an exile, however. She also went as a pilgrim, enthused with a genuine interest in new ideas about poetry and art. Paris had for a long time been closely associated in her mind with literary and artistic creativity, through the example set by her friend George Moore, the Irish novelist, who had gone to Paris as a young man in an unsuccessful bid to become a painter. Moore became a friend of Manet, Degas, Zola, Mallarmé and many other artists and writers. He was one of the first British and Irish expatriates to move to Paris for the specific purpose of living among fellow artists and it was he, suggests Acton, who started the enthusiasm for everything French among English intellectuals. The weekly essays of Clive Bell, a well-known art and literary critic, wrote Acton, 'were peppered with Parisian studio patter, running riot in the tradition started by George Moore ... English painters borrowed French eyeglasses for their landscapes, nudes and still lives. Our standards were increasingly Gallic.'[9] Nancy's original connection with Moore lay through her mother, whom he adored throughout his life. He had fallen in love with Emerald at first sight in 1894, the year in which his eighth book, *Esther Waters*, was published to great acclaim; this was before Emerald's marriage to Sir Bache and two years before Nancy's birth. His love for Emerald brought him immense suffering, since she grew tired of his amorous devotion and herself fell headlong in love with Thomas Beecham, the conductor (she parted from Sir Bache when Nancy was nineteen). Moore was extremely fond of Nancy and many people wondered if it were he, rather than Sir Bache, who was her father. 'Kiss Nancy for me and tell her I look forward to hearing from her and going for a walk with her' was a typical message for Nancy in one of his letters to Emerald.[10] As she grew older they discussed literature together and he encouraged her interest in writing poetry; 'She has got an exquisite ear for rhythm,' he told Emerald with pleasure.[11] Nancy described Moore as 'her first friend'[12] and in later life wrote a book about him called *G.M.: Memories of George Moore*.

Nancy's life in Paris started in left-bank hotels and rented flats. Then, in 1924, she moved into a flat of her own on the Île Saint-Louis, with a view of the Notre-Dame cathedral. She was now able to settle down to a *vie de Bohème* that was on her own terms, free of her mother's wishes and expectations. Nearby lived her childhood friend Iris Tree (the daughter of the Shakespearian actor, Sir Herbert Beerbohm Tree) and she quickly made new friends in Paris. In 1923 she met two American women who became lifelong friends: Janet Flanner, a journalist who worked for the *New Yorker* from 1925, and Solita Solano, who was a novelist. Like Nancy, they were modern women determined to establish independent lives for themselves.

She had not been long in Paris before she became the lover of Tristan Tzara, a key influence in the development of the artistic movement known as Dada. As a renowned rebel against established orthodoxies, he must have delighted Nancy. Through him, she met some of the most exciting thinkers of the time and in the mid-1920s she became involved with Surrealism, which evolved out of Dadaism into the newest avant-garde movement in Paris – 'whose aim was to create a revolution, both political and artistic, combining the visions of Freud, Marx, Sade and Lautréamont'.[13] Guided by André Breton, Louis Aragon and Paul Éluard, it was grounded in a belief in the supreme power of dreams and the spontaneous activity of the mind; according to André Breton in his *First Manifesto of Surrealism* (1924), reason had been made obsolete by the pre-eminence of dreams. This new idea held a powerful appeal for Nancy – as did Louis Aragon, one of the group's leaders. Aragon became her devoted lover and, at this stage of her life, she was immersed in the activities of the Surrealist group. It was a hectic time and Nancy's great friend, the author Norman Douglas, objected to the mad whirl he encountered when visiting her in Paris. Acton recalled an occasion when

Nancy was making arrangements to show a Surrealist film in London, which involved more confabulations in cafes than Norman was prepared to put up with. Rather grumpy, he was dragged along to visit André Breton. After one horrified look at the Dali dominating Breton's room – an intricately demoniac picture of William Tell in his underwear with a bright phallus protruding, and such details as the carcass of a donkey on a piano with a horse galloping over it – Uncle Norman said sharply: 'I can't stay here. That picture will spoil my dinner. See you later, I must get some fresh air at once'.

'Nobody could detain him', added Acton. 'He had come to Paris to enjoy Nancy's company, but there were limits.'[14]

The Surrealists were a very male group, who did not count a single woman artist or writer among their number. Nancy's role was that of Aragon's companion, just as Caresse Crosby was Salvador Dali's companion and Peggy Guggenheim came with Max Ernst. But Nancy, just like Caresse and Peggy, had as much right as most of the Surrealists to qualify as an intellectual. Even before her arrival in Paris, she was a published poet: her first poems appeared in 1916 in *Wheels*, the first of a series of six anthologies of verse that were edited by Osbert and Edith Sitwell, self-styled rebels against the conventions of the neo-Georgian poets. Nancy took an enthusiastic role in this first anthology and wrote seven of its poems, including 'Wheels', which gave its name to the whole series:

> I sometimes think that all our thoughts are wheels
> Rolling forever through the painted world . . .

Aldous Huxley contributed also, but in a spirit of disdain. The people organizing the anthology, he told his brother Julian, 'are a family called Sitwell, alias Shufflebottom . . . Their great object is to REBEL, which sounds quite charming; only one finds that the steps they are prepared to take, the lengths they will go, are so small as to be hardly perceptible to the naked eye.' In a letter to Lady Ottoline Morrell, Huxley described the anthology as a 'horrible production' and added that, 'The Wheelites take themselves so seriously: I never believed it possible.' Reviewers were irritated by the negative tone of the anthology: *The Times Literary Supplement* described it as 'dour and morose' and objected that the poets 'see nothing bright in the present, and no bright hopes in the future'.[15]

Nancy's first whole volume of poems, *Outlaws*, was published in 1921 and was reviewed in the *Observer* by George Moore, who mingled praise with gentle criticism.[16] A second volume, *Sublunary*, was published in 1923 and a further volume, *Poems (Two) 1925*, was published by the Aquila Press in 1930. Her best-known work was *Parallax*, a poem of nearly 600 lines, which was published by Leonard and Virginia Woolf's Hogarth Press in 1925. The poem centres on the thoughts and wanderings of a young poet moving between London, France and Italy, and asks:

> Think how friends grow old –
> Their diverse brains, hearts, faces, modify; . . .
> Am I the same?
> Or a vagrant, of other breed, gone further, lost –
> I am most surely at the beginning yet.
> If so, contemporaries, what have you done?

The shifts from place to place explore the possibility of different perspectives on the same view, an idea that is reflected in the poem's cover, a set of line drawings by Eugene McCown, an American Surrealist in Paris who was a friend of Nancy. Opinions about the quality of *Parallax* were mixed. The Woolfs must have been impressed, since they chose to publish it, and there were some enthusiastic reviews; but others judged it to be too heavily derived from T. S. Eliot's *The Waste Land*, which had been published three years before in 1922. The *New Statesman* produced a detailed comparison of the two poems that was not at all to Nancy's advantage.

The publication of *Parallax* was one of many products of a close relationship between the intellectual life of Paris and London for, as Harold Acton observed, 'Bloomsbury was only an extension of Montparnasse.'[17] In their account of interwar Britain, Graves and Hodge comment that

there was an established avant-garde colony centred at Bloomsbury around the Hogarth Press – Leonard and Virginia Woolf, Duncan Grant, and Vanessa Bell – and the Sitwells, symbols of ultra-modernism in the popular Press, had close affiliations with Paris but resided in London.[18]

Nancy did it the other way round: she resided in Paris, but had close affiliations with London, visiting regularly in the first five or six years of her life in Paris. She brought her Paris friends with her and John Banting, the English Surrealist painter, described the vivid impression she and her lover, Louis Aragon, made at a party in London in 1925.[19] Even when in London, she frequented a place that recalled her life in Paris – a restaurant called the Eiffel Tower, which was on Percy Street and was owned by a central European named Stulik. It owed its fame to the artist Augustus John, who had discovered the place twenty years before and turned it into a rendezvous for artists. Michael Arlen used the Eiffel Tower as a model for a restaurant called the Mont Agel in his novel *Piracy* (1922): 'On many nights', he wrote, 'will come the toughs and roughs and bravoes of the town, to press their ill-vapoured noses against the windows of the Mont Agel and watch the leading beauties toying with their food and their poets.'[20] Nancy wrote a poem in 1923 about it:

> I think the Tower shall go up to heaven
> One night in a flame of fire, about eleven
> I always saw our carnal spiritual home
> Blazing upon the sky symbolically . . .

If ever we go to heaven in a troop the Tower
must be our ladder,
Vertically
Climbing the ether with its swaying group.
God will delight to greet this embassy
Wherein is found no lack
Of wits and glamour, strong wines, new foods, fine looks,
strange-sounding languages of diverse men –
Stulik shall lead the pack
Until its great disintegration, when
God sets up deftly in a new Zodiac.[21]

In this early period of living in Paris and visiting London, Nancy became widely known as an icon of style. She was photographed by Cecil Beaton and Man Ray, painted by Kokoschka and Wyndham Lewis, and had become such a celebrity, said John Banting, that he 'priggishly avoided joining the hive around her'.[22] Her style was widely imitated, though not very well, remembers Daphne Fielding, who was a friend of Lady Cunard (and who later became Marchioness of Bath). 'Scores of lesser leopards slank along the corridors of expensive hotels,' writes Fielding, 'helmeted in cloche hats or turbans, their hair cut short, dyed gold and arranged in two strands (which Nancy herself called "beavers") curving over the cheekbones like twin scimitars.'[23] Like many of her Surrealist friends, Nancy admired African art and had started to wear carved wooden and ivory bracelets all the way up her arm. Her image 'inspired half the poets and novelists of the twenties', wrote Acton,[24] and she was recreated in novels by both Michael Arlen and Aldous Huxley. She appears as Myra Viveash in Huxley's *Antic Hay* (1923) and as Lucy Tantamount in *Point Counter Point* (1928): she is presented as a rich and upper-class woman with an overwhelming sexual power over men, who plays with her admirers but is dismissive of their feelings. But Huxley's portrayal had more to do with his own perception and feelings than with the real Nancy. He had fallen desperately in love with her, a passion that made him deeply unhappy. Nothing developed beyond a brief affair in 1922 and he spent most of his time waiting around miserably for a word from her. It almost wrecked his marriage to Maria, who finally insisted that he choose between Nancy and herself. Huxley was an influential writer, so his image of Nancy was powerful and long lasting. A similar image reached a larger and less intellectual public through the character of Iris Storm in Michael Arlen's *The Green Hat*, a successful novel that was also made into a play and film. Arlen had been Nancy's lover for a time and, like Huxley, was infatuated with her; she can be recognized as one of those 'young women of patrician and careless intelligence' described in *Piracy*, 'whom it is the pet mistake of bishops, diarists, press photographers and Americans, to take as representing the "state" of modern society'.[25]

It would certainly have been a mistake to regard Nancy as a representation of the 'state' of modern society. If she represented anything at this time, it was the spirit of the avant-garde in Paris, which arrived in London much later. 'The average time-lag in art fashions between France and educated England was about twelve years,' write Graves and Hodge,[26] adding that the case of Surrealism was no exception. The first Surrealist Exhibition arrived from Paris in England in 1936 and was met with mockery and jeers. The Surrealist group 'are truly decadent', said the novelist and playwright, J. B. Priestley. 'There are about too many effeminate or epicene young men, lisping and undulating. Too many young women without manners, balance, dignity . . .'[27] No doubt Priestley would have regarded Nancy's life as decadent. She drank heavily, had numerous open love affairs and flouted convention with relish; nearly all her friends were homosexual or bisexual and she herself slept with women as well as men. At a party where her close friend Brian Howard and three other men brought out their powder puffs, records Hugo Vickers in a biography of Cecil Beaton, at first Beaton resisted joining in. But in the end, when he found himself 'amongst a crowd that included the writer Raymond Mortimer (looking like a poodle) and Nancy Cunard with wooden bracelets up her arm, he too donned make-up'.[28]

When most people thought of Nancy Cunard, they saw only the image that had inspired numerous artists and writers. 'They saw her as the Gioconda of the Age', wrote her friend Harold Acton, 'but never as her electro-magnetic self.'[28] This 'self' lay well beneath her surface frivolity. One side of it was visible to the Woolfs: Virginia saw her as 'the little anxious flibbertigibbet with the startled honest eyes, & all the green stones hung about her', while Leonard referred to her 'air of vulnerability'.[30] She gave the appearance of being a Bright Young Thing but she was not one at all: she was a serious woman, who wanted to do something worthwhile. In this she was unlike Diana Manners, another style icon of the period who was much photographed and written about. They had grown up in the same circles and Diana and her mother, the Duchess of Rutland, had stayed with Emerald and Nancy in a palazzo in Venice in 1913. Diana was a special favourite of Lady Cunard, who would probably have liked Nancy to be more like her – the kind of young woman who was content to settle down as the wife of the Conservative politician Duff Cooper and to play at being a film star. Diana adored Emerald and recollected in the first volume of her autobiography that while staying at the 'Casa Cunard' in Venice, Lady Cunard became 'real in my eyes – real and unique – and who was to be loved and served by me until her life's end thirty-five years later and mourned to this day'.[31] Diana belonged to a group of friends calling itself the 'Corrupt Coterie', which was led by Raymond Asquith and claimed 'to be unafraid of words, unshocked by drink, and unashamed of "decadence" and gambling – Unlike-Other-People, I'm afraid'.[32] But the 'Coterie' were only amusing themselves with the idea of decadence: in reality, they enjoyed conventionally privileged and orthodox lives. Nancy liked Diana but they never became real friends.

After the publication of *Parallax*, Nancy started to lose interest in the business of writing poetry herself; instead, she looked for ways of nurturing other writers who merited support. This was possibly because the general response to her own work – favourable but not enthusiastic – made her question her ability to be anything more than a minor poet. But equally, she appears to have wanted to wield some kind of discernible influence on art and literature. She had been introduced to the pleasures of patronage at an early age by her mother, at a time when private patronage was a real force, wrote William Buchan, in the social life of the time: 'Society was still small enough . . . for anyone with a cool head and a sense of relationships to chart the interconnecting channels of influence, to know who "counted and who did not, when it come to promoting a political career, a symphony or a play".'[33] Lady Cunard had in fact supported some of the same artists who now lived in Paris and were Nancy's friends and Nancy had first met Ezra Pound at her mother's tea table in London in 1915, when he visited almost daily.[34] She met the American photographer Man Ray when her mother asked him in 1923 to come to Dieppe to photograph a French family with whom they were staying. Harold Acton, too, was one of Lady Cunard's interesting people.

But Nancy was determined to develop her own way of nurturing the artists she admired. Instead of inviting them to splendid social occasions and helping them financially, like her mother, she set up a printing press to publish their work. In late 1927, with some of the money that had been recently left to her by the death of her father, Nancy bought an old peasant house called Le Puits Carré at Réanville, in the heart of Normandy – but only fifty miles and one hour's train journey from Paris. She obtained a Mathieu press that was more than a hundred years old from Bill Bird, an American newspaperman who had used it to print his Three Mountains editions of Ezra Pound, Hemingway, Ford Madox Ford, William Carlos Williams and others. Bird helped her to assemble the press and provided her with an old and experienced printer, while Louis Aragon came down from Paris to help with the new enterprise. Nancy called it the Hours Press and formally started its work in 1928, when she was thirty-two; she later told its story in *These Were the Hours*. The first publication was a limited edition of *Peronnik the Fool*, which George Moore asked her to print – 'I would like to start off the press with a bang,' he said, encouragingly. Other early publications included *La Chasse au Snark*, Louis Aragon's translation of Lewis Carroll's *The Hunting of the Snark*.

By 1928, Nancy had lost interest in Aragon as a lover, who suspected in any case that she had been having an affair with Breton. Towards the end of his life, he wrote that he could

still hear, in that house with its cardboard walls where Nane [that is, Nancy] and I were already beginning to . . . quarrel, where I suddenly discovered jealousy . . . I can still hear André [Breton] laughing at the pages of the *Traite*, without knowing that that forced gaiety of mine already hid that of *Othello* which I was secretly reading and re-reading in the original English . . .[35]

Then Nancy met one of the most important people in her life – a black American called Henry Crowder. This meeting took place in Venice, on a visit to her cousin Edward, who took her to a supper dance at the Hotel Luna to hear Eddie South's Alabamians, a Negro jazz quartet. Impressed, she and Edward invited them to their table and she was intrigued by Henry, the pianist. They swiftly became friends, then lovers, and she took him back with her to Le Puits Carré in France. In despair, Aragon took an overdose of sleeping pills; he survived, but his affair with Nancy was over.

Nancy and Henry installed a piano in the house and, with much encouragement, Henry set to music some poems by Harold Acton, Richard Aldington, Samuel Beckett, Nancy herself and Walter Lowenfels; these songs were issued by the Hours Press as *Henry-Music* in December 1930, with a cover design by Man Ray. Henry helped with the work of the press. In 1929 Nancy and Henry moved the press to Paris, to a small shop on the rue Guenégaud, a narrow side street on the Left Bank, near the Seine. For a couple of months they were helped by Georges Sadoul, a young man who was later to become a well-known historian of the cinema. The Hours Press was close to the Galerie Surréaliste and on its walls hung paintings by Joan Miró, André Masson, George Malkine and Francis Picabia, all of whom came to visit. The shop had 'a hysterical atmosphere; the printing press seemed to work in paroxysms, and everything else seemed ready to lose control,' recalled Acton, whose book of poems, *This Chaos*, was published by the Hours (and was dedicated to Nancy). He saw with fond amusement that

fetishes from Easter Island and the Congo held rendezvous among freshly printed poems. 'What are we doing here?' they asked. 'Let's run away . . .' They refused to stay put. They disturbed conversation with their antics and distracted one's thoughts. Each contained a separate universe. One expected them to march out of the door and up the street, shouting slogans in a truculent procession.[36]

The shop was a sort of headquarters for intellectuals and artists to gather, much like the bookshop and library set up in Paris in 1919 by the American Sylvia Beach, at 12 rue de l'Odéon. These gathering places were much more relaxed than the more formal salons set up by expatriates in Paris, such as the gatherings organised by Gertrude Stein. Ernest Hemingway visited Beach's shop almost daily and used it as a place to collect his mail. 'On a cold windswept street', he wrote with fond affection, 'this was a warm, cheerful place with a big stove in winter, tables and shelves of books, new books in the window, and photographs on the wall of famous writers both dead and living.' Joyce came to the shop every day, he said, very late in the afternoon.[37] Both Sylvia Beach and Nancy Cunard were central members of the expatriate community but they also had French friends and took part in French life. So did many of Nancy's English friends, who – like her – had learnt to be fluent in French as an essential feature of their upper-class education. But this was not the case with most Americans, observes Noel Riley Fitch in his book about interwar Paris, *Sylvia Beach and the Lost Generation*. They did not bother learning the language of their temporary home, writes Fitch, and it was 'the rule rather than the exception that Americans living in Paris did not associate with the French.'[38]

The Hours was the first press to publish the work of Samuel Beckett, who had been in Paris since 1928 working for James Joyce, who needed help because of his poor eyesight. Beckett's poem *Whoroscope* won a £10 prize offered by the Hours for the best poem on 'Time' under 100 lines. Nancy wrote later that she and her friend Richard Aldington, the imagist poet and writer, had set up the competition but were disappointed by the quality of the entries. Then, only days before the closing date,

a miracle came to the Rue Guénegaud after closing time on the last night of the contest and was found by me the next morning where it had been slipped under the door: across the cover of a small folder was written *Whoroscope*; beneath was the name Samuel Beckett. His name meant nothing to either Aldington or myself. The poem, on the other hand, meant a very great deal, even on the first, feverish read-through. What remarkable lines, what images and analogies, what vivid colouring throughout; indeed, what technique! This long poem, mysterious, obscure in parts, centred around Descartes, was clearly by someone very intellectual and highly educated.

Whoroscope was published in the middle of summer in 1930. 'The honour of being the first to print him (with what pleasure I say this), comes to me', observed Nancy with satisfaction, 'for *Whoroscope* was his first separately published work.'[39]

Another triumph for the Hours was the publication of Ezra Pound's *XXX Cantos* in a single volume, which was the first printing of all thirty *Cantos* available at that date. Nancy shared the common fondness for Pound, who 'was the most generous writer I have ever known and the most disinterested,' wrote Ernest Hemingway. 'He helped poets, painters, sculptors and prose writers that he believed in and he would help anyone whether he believed in them or not if they were in trouble.'[40] In the winter of 1922–3, Hemingway suspected that Ezra was slipping away from his wife Dorothy in Rapallo, Italy, in order go to Calabria 'to pursue some horizontal pleasures with Nancy Cunard, that gaunt, pale, lovely inspiration of more than one writer in the Twenties'.[41] Later, Nancy was bitterly dismayed by Pound's support for fascism. She received a letter from him in the middle of the Ethiopian War telling her that 'the Abyssinians are BLACK JEWS'; she found this 'totally baffling' and took the view that 'His is, indeed, "a Case", an utterly insoluble one.'[42] Another of the intellectuals who was published by the Hours and who disappointed Nancy with his politics was the South African poet Roy Campbell, who fought as a soldier for the Spanish Nationalists.

Other Hours authors included Norman Douglas, Richard Alding-ton, Arthur Symons, Robert Graves, Laura Riding, and Brian Howard; and many of the book covers were created by Man Ray and Yves Tanguy, an American Surrealist who was born and grew up in Paris. The dominant style of the books was modernist and in the opinion of many reviewers, absurdly obscure. One such review in a 1931 edition of *The Times Literary Supplement* complains that the method used in four books of poetry (by Graves, Riding, Lowenfels and Cunard herself) published by the Hours Press 'compels the reader who is not prepared to put in a week's work in the solution of a cryptogram which may turn out to be insoluble, or who has not the power of discovering [their] meaning by some mysterious intuition, to take the poems as a series of fragments'. Miss Riding, adds this review, 'often seems to wander for the sake of wandering'.[43] This criticism is not likely to have bothered Nancy too much, since she had set out to publish work that was unconventional and innovative. In any case, even a bad review from the intellectual press confirmed that these publications deserved attention.

Early in 1931 the Hours Press published *The Revaluation of Obscenity* by Havelock Ellis, which investigated the difference between eroticism and pornography. This book would have been banned in England, like a number of other books written by English and American authors and published in Paris. These included *The Well of Loneliness* by the lesbian novelist Radclyffe Hall, *Ulysses* by James Joyce (which was published by Sylvia Beach in 1922, after a New York journal that published early serial instalments had been prosecuted for obscenity), *Sleeveless Errand* by Norah James, *Lady Chatterley's Lover* by D. H. Lawrence (*The Rainbow* was first published in England but was prosecuted), and *The Mint* by T. E. Lawrence. Nancy is mentioned in Aldous Huxley's correspondence as a possible publisher for *Lady Chatterley's Lover* in 1929,[44] but this did not go ahead.

Nancy Cunard's Hours Press was part of a flowering of English-speaking presses and publishers between the wars. Other small and private presses of the time included the Ovid Press, which was set up by John Rodker in 1919 and published T. S. Eliot and Pound; the Seizin Press, established by Laura Riding and Robert Graves in London in 1928 and then moved to Deya, Mallorca, in 1930; and the Nonesuch Press, which was set up by Vera and Francis Meynell and David Garnett in 1923. The Woolfs set up their Hogarth Press in 1925. Nancy later recalled that when she told them about her own plans for a press, they tried to discourage her, warning that, 'Your hands will always be covered with ink!'[45] (although when asked about this later, they said that they did not remember the occasion and doubted that they gave her any such advice[46]). In Paris, Sylvia Beach ran her Shakespeare and Company, which brought out *Ulysses*; Harry and Caresse Crosby started the Black Sun Press in 1927; and in 1928, Edward Titus started the Black Manikin Press.

These new presses were part of a massive wave of interest in publishing at the time, which also led to the appearance of Penguin Books in 1936. But they can also be seen as a reaction *against* the strand of publishing that was represented by Penguin, which aimed to make classics and new writings available to as many people as possible. Bound in paper covers, Penguins were sold cheaply at sixpence each, making the purchase of a book possible for the ordinary and educated middle classes. In just a few years, Penguins became a household word. 'The cheerful, orange-and-white covers of their fiction', wrote Graves and Hodge, 'were to be seen on every bookstall and at every newsagents . . . before three years had gone by one could scarcely find a bookshelf in Britain which did not contain at least half a dozen Penguins.'[47] When Lord Londonderry's *Ourselves and Germany* and the Duchess of Atholl's *Searchlight on Spain* were published by Penguin in the late 1930s, they were guaranteed a wide readership. Culture was becoming available to the masses: not only through cheap paperback books, but also through the mushroom growth of the wireless, which started in 1922 (about a million people owned radio sets in 1925 and nine million in 1939), and through films, which became 'talkies' in 1928. Some aesthetes were appalled by this popularization of culture and sought to establish criteria that would distinguish what was vulgar from what was 'proper' art; very often, 'proper' art was esoteric, difficult to understand and very expensive. Certainly this was true of publications by the Hours Press.

Although Nancy reacted against the conventions of her class, she was very much *of* her class. On the one hand, she had a taste for whatever seemed to her to be plain and simple: better a clay pot from the Dordogne, she said, than Sèvres.[48] Her cousin Victor used to say that she hated comfort and loved to live like a peasant – a 'fifteenth-century peasant *bien entendu*'.[49] But at the same time, she shared many of the basic attitudes of the elite – her friend Brian Howard, she said, 'had *beautiful breeding and taste* in art and culture of all sorts, in architecture, in dress, in food'.[50] Her friend Burkhart observed that her own 'breeding' was most obvious to an American like himself when he saw how other English people reacted to it: 'Not so much the tendency to servile flunkeyism among the older generation of waiters', he said, 'but among people of her class the instinctive and unconscious recognition of Nancy as "one of us".'[51] Her closest friends from England were nearly all from privileged backgrounds and were products of Eton and Oxford; fittingly, her friends Harold Acton and Brian Howard both appear in novels by Evelyn Waugh – Howard as Anthony

Blanche in *Brideshead Revisited* and Acton as Ambrose Silk in *Put Out More Flags*.

Nancy and the Hours Press published 24 books altogether, more than the 18 books published by the Seizin Press in its seven years and not so far off the 33 published by the Hogarth Press in its first seven years. The Hours was regarded as one of the best: 'Miss Nancy Cunard's Hours Press announces a number of new poems mainly by the modernists. All of them from this house are sure to be agreeably turned out in a large, plain format', wrote the *Observer* enthusiastically in 1929; and *Everyman* spoke of the Hours as 'one of the most interesting of the newer small presses ... issuing exquisite limited editions of modern writers'.[52] An important tribute to the Hours was paid by the American book-collector, Herbert L. Rothschild, who reproduced the first page of the fourth of Pound's *Cantos* in his *Contemporary Presses, a Survey* (1931). Nancy Cunard was taken far more seriously than aesthetes like the Sitwells, who cultivated several prominent writers (T. S. Eliot repaid their support by calling them 'Osbert and Edith *Shitwell*'[53]). Cecil Beaton referred mockingly to Edith Sitwell in his *Book of Beauty*:

That mysterious figure in the mediaeval brocades, with the rocks of amber around her neck, and the huge jewels on the long claw-like hands, is the cause of all the gossip, the nudging and furtive stares. 'She is Edith Sitwell, the poet,' the whisper, in awed tones, goes its round, and the gaping that follows is as though it were directed at an unearthly being, at some supernatural duck.[54]

In 1931 Nancy closed down the Hours Press. She had a new project – an encyclopaedic anthology of writings about black life, literature and history. The idea for this book was largely due to Henry, who 'introduced me', wrote Nancy later, 'to the astonishing complexities and agonies of the Negroes in the United States. He became my teacher in all the many questions of colour that exist in America and was the primary cause of the compilation ... of my large *Negro Anthology*'.[55] Nancy's concern about racial inequalities was not simply the result of her love for a man, however. She had by this time become a good friend of George Padmore, a Trinidadian activist against racial oppression who also lived in Paris. It was through Padmore that she took an interest in the case of nine black youths from Scottsboro, Alabama, who had been accused of assaulting two white prostitutes; and at Padmore's suggestion, she became the British organizer of funds to support the accused youths in 1931. But Henry was the soul behind the anthology itself and the final publication was dedicated to him. In April 1931 she distributed a circular as widely as possible, asking for 'contributions *from* Negros for inclusion ... I want outspoken criticism, comment and comparison *from* the Negro on the present day *civilisation* [sic]'. She asked for material to be sent to her at 5 rue Guénegaud, Paris, explaining that, 'This is the first time such a book has been compiled in this manner. It is primarily for the Colored people and is dedicated to one of them. I wish by their aid to make it as inclusive as possible'.[56]

Much of the research had to be done in the British Museum Reading Room, so Nancy and Crowder moved to London for this purpose. They soon discovered that there was less tolerance in England than in France for a black man living with a white woman. In Paris, blacks were accepted as a part of life: black American jazz musicians were hugely popular and in 1927 an all-black show called 'The Black Bird' opened at the Moulin Rouge. A particular favourite in Paris was the American dancer and singer Josephine Baker, who set up her own club – Chez Josephine – where she served soul food like chitlins and black-eyed peas. The English also enjoyed black music, but generally as a quaint diversion from the regular fare: Thomas Jones, who was deputy secretary of the cabinet at the time, described in his diary at Christmas 1927 a day of lavish entertainment at Cliveden where Lady Astor arranged for dancing to be followed by 'negro folk songs and spirituals with banjo accompaniment ... song after song'.[57] The racism encountered by Nancy and Henry in London was not overt and defined, like 'Jim Crow' in the USA, but was equally pervasive. It is well illustrated in *The Life and Death of Radclyffe Hall*, a biography of Radclyffe Hall that was written by her lesbian lover, Una, Lady Troubridge: Miss Hall drove her cousin Jane all over the States, writes Troubridge, with 'a revolver handy for *obstreperous negroes*. There was also an aggressive bull-terrier Charlie, as auxiliary protection ...'[58]

Nancy tried to prevent her mother from hearing about Henry, but this proved impossible. 'At a large lunch party in Her Ladyship's house', discovered Nancy later,

things are set rocking by one of those bombs that throughout her 'career' Margot Asquith, Lady Oxford, has been wont to hurl. No-one could fail to wish he had been at that lunch to see the effect of Lady Oxford's entry: 'Hello, Maud, what is it now – drink, drugs or niggers?'. . . Half of social London is immediately telephoned to: 'Is it *true* that my daughter knows a Negro?' etc., etc.[59]

Lady Cunard was appalled. She summoned Nancy and they had a savage quarrel, in which she threatened to have Henry deported. She had her daughter and lover followed by detectives and convinced Stulik, with whom they were staying above the Eiffel Tower restaurant, to send them away. After a while Nancy and Henry could bear the harassment no longer and fled to Austria, to stay with Brian Howard. Their visit was difficult, at least partly because Nancy had fallen passionately in love with Brian (a passion that was not returned), but also because she was overwrought generally – 'mercurially ill', according to Brian.[60]

While in this 'mercurial' state she wrote a pamphlet called *Black Man and White Ladyship, An Anniversary*, which she had privately printed in Toulouse in 1931. It was a bitter attack on her mother's objection to Henry, to which Emerald reacted by commenting that 'One can always forgive anyone who is ill'.[61] The pamphlet locates Emerald's objections not so much in racial, as in class, prejudice:

But, your Ladyship, you cannot kill or deport a person from England for being a Negro and mixing with white people. You may take a ticket to the cracker southern states of USA and assist at some of the choicer lynchings which are often announced in advance. You may add your purified-of-that-horrible-American-twang voice to the Yankee outbursts; America for white folks – segregation for the 12 million blacks we can't put up with – or do without . . .

No, with you it is the other old trouble – class.

Negroes, besides being black (that is, from jet to as white as yourself but not so pink), have not yet penetrated into London Society's 'consciousness'. You exclaim: they are not 'received'! (You would be surprised to know just how much they are 'received'.) They are not found in the Royal Red Book. Some big hostess give a lead and the trick is done!

For as yet only the hefty shadow of the Negro falls across the white assembly of High Society and spreads itself, it would seem, quite particularly and agonisingly over you.

Nancy took the view that the class basis of racism in England gave it a different character from racism in many other countries. For example, the Aga Khan was welcomed as a member of the Jockey Club in England, because his high social rank and wealth made his colour irrelevant, but he was turned down by the Kenya Jockey Club. In the late 1920s the British Governor of Kenya, Sir Edward Grigg, proposed that the Aga Khan be given honorary membership of the Club on one of his visits. He was astonished when this was briskly refused by the settler community, simply on the grounds of colour.

The final stages of research for the anthology were carried out in 1933 in the USA – which brought Nancy to her mother's native land. Once in the USA, Nancy and Henry were the victims of a racism that had little to do with class and everything to do with the colour of their skin. They stayed in a hotel in Harlem, a black neighbourhood of New York, at which Nancy was the first white woman guest: this, as well as the purpose of her visit, were regarded as a scandal by most of the white community. She received a number of obscene and unpleasant letters, including one from the Ku Klux Klan warning her to 'get out before we get you'. Her activities were widely covered by the American press, which made much of her upper-class background (though not always accurately: one of the headlines referred to 'Lady Cunard in Harlem'). Many of the articles about her associations with blacks were libellous and she promptly sued the proprietors of the *Empire News*, the *Sunday Chronicle* and the *Daily Dispatch*; her counsel observed that 'a woman has only got to do something unconventional for her to be made the target of scurrility'. The defendants quickly realized their mistake and offered an apology in court, as well as a substantial sum for damages and costs.[62]

The anthology finally appeared in 1934, when Nancy had reached the age of thirty-eight. One thousand copies were published by Wishart at her own expense and sold at a price of 42 shillings each. It is immense: an outsize folio of sorts, with 855 pages. There are seven sections and further sub-sections; the section on 'Africa', for example, has a sub-section on 'Negro Sculpture and Ethnology'. The book is packed with facts, such as data from the USA about 'coloured' people being denied the vote and statistics showing that expenditure on white education far exceeded that for Blacks. There are photographs, too, such as that of a bill for Negro slaves. 'It was necessary to make this book', states Nancy in the Foreword, 'and I think in this manner, an Anthology of some 150 voices of both races – for the recording of the struggles and achievements, the persecutions and the revolts against them, of the Negro peoples.' Black people are put firmly at the centre of the book, in which white people are presented as marginal – 'Reader! Bear in mind that those you read of here are Negro – when white, it is stated.'[63] A summary of the history of the black race is given and the book claims to depict 'the full violence of the oppression of the 14 million Negroes in *America* and the upsurge of their demands for mere justice, that is to say their full and equal rights alongside of their white fellow-citizens'.[64] Many of Nancy's friends contributed, including Ezra Pound, the American novelist Theodore Dreiser, George Padmore, Samuel Beckett and Langston Hughes, the black American writer who was a leading figure in the black renaissance.

Her attitude towards blacks may cause offence today because it was based on stereotypes that have been rejected. 'Everyone knows', she said, that 'the Negroes have a particular genius for music ... [the African] made music and unparalleled rhythm and some of the finest sculpture in the world. Nature gave him the best body amongst all the races.'[65] Similarly, she told the reader of her anthology, 'Reader, had you never heard of or seen any African sculpture I think the reproductions in this part would suggest to you that the Negro has a superb and individual sense of form and equal genius in his execution.' But Nancy was a woman of her time, when issues about race were perceived and described in different ways from those that hold today. In any case, she never overlooked an opportunity to fight against racism and its evil effects. When the death sentence was passed upon the

Scottsboro youths, she organized a series of inter-racial dances to raise funds for an appeal against the sentence. She also circulated an appeal for signed protests against the judgment: 'If you are against the lynching and terrorisation of the most oppressed race in the world', she urged, 'if you have any innate sense of justice, sign this protest and contribute towards the defence funds.' Replies came back promptly, from a number of prominent writers and intellectuals, including André Gide, Aragon, Breton, Beckett, Richard Church, the American composer George Antheil, Sinclair Lewis, Janet Flanner, and Dorothy and Ezra Pound.[66] Eventually the judgment was reversed by the American Supreme Court.

George Padmore regarded Nancy's work as a real contribution to racial equality and described her as 'remarkable' and 'extraordinary'.[67] At this time Padmore was a Communist, as was Louis Aragon, following a visit to the Soviet Union in 1930. Nancy herself put forward Communist views in her anthology. 'The more vital of the Negro race', she wrote, 'have realised that it is Communism alone which throws down the barriers of race as finally as it wipes out class distinctions. The Communist world-order is the solution of the race problem for the Negro.' To support her argument, she referred to the model of Soviet Russia, which she believed had solved the problem of racial difference (and which she was to visit in 1935). 'Up with an all-Communist Harlem in an all-Communist United States!' she exclaimed in a section entitled 'Harlem Reviewed'.[68] The Communist *Negro Worker* was excerpted heavily throughout the anthology, which criticized the National Association for the Advancement of Colored People (NAACP) and its leader, Du Bois, on the grounds that it had failed to recognize that the Negro question was fundamentally economic.

Henry Crowder returned to America once the anthology was completed and they never met again, despite making plans to do so. When she heard in 1955 that he was dead, she mourned deeply: 'Others have loved me more (?)', she wrote, 'and I, perhaps others. NO, probably not, for me, has this been true. In any case: Henry made me. I thank him.'[69] Perhaps one of the reasons for Henry's importance in Nancy's life was that he was impervious to the expectations of the world in which she herself had been raised. On one occasion she was amused to see him addressing envelopes in a way that disregarded the standard (for her) class-related conventions:

Addressing envelopes was also part of his work and I remember the start with which I first saw words like these: Sir Ralph Faggotson Esq.

It would have taken too long to explain the *why* of the correct way of addressing the aristocracy. All that was necessary was to make certain that no *Esq.* should henceforward follow a *Sir*, and in this Henry immediately concurred . . .[70]

As a man who was black, American, lower class and poor, he provided her with space to breathe – some neutral and reassuring territory in which she could be free from the suffocating attitudes of her mother and her class. It is possible that her work on the *Negro Anthology* was at least partially informed by a sense of gratitude to Henry. She continued to campaign against racial inequalities until the end of her life. In 1942, in the midst of the Second World War, she and Padmore wrote a long pamphlet about colonial affairs, entitled *The White Man's Duty*. It advocated a postwar future that was not tainted by racial prejudice and argued for the swift recognition of the rights of black people who were risking their lives to fight with the allies against fascism. By this time Padmore's Communist views had given way to Pan-Africanism and after Ghana's independence from Britain in 1957, he went to Accra to work for Nkrumah as Secretary for African Affairs. He died shortly afterwards in 1959.

Republican Spain was bound to claim Nancy's attention. Many of her friends in Paris rushed off to the Spanish front to join the International Brigade and she, now in her early forties, went to Spain to work as a freelance journalist. While in Madrid, she and John Banting went to visit Hemingway, who had also gone there to work as a reporter. Nancy recalled later that, 'A fine, strong drink was given the both of us – and I remember Hem taking off my boots and warming the cold feet. He was enchanting – such a sympathetic moment – from a non-Spaniard – was never my lot till then, nor yet again.' She had not known 'Hem' particularly well in Paris, but remembered 'the great, thumping, *so* pleasant mannered youth he was then, in 1923'.[71] In Madrid she also met the Chilean poet, Pablo Neruda, who believed that her influence as a publisher would better serve the Republican cause than her work as a journalist. He therefore advised her to return home to France and to produce anti-Fascist propaganda from there. Accordingly, she returned home to put the Mathieu press into use once more, to produce *Les Poètes du Monde Défendent le Peuple Espagnol*, a series of six leaflets of poems in English, French and Spanish. Many of her friends gave poems, including Tzara, Aragon, Langston Hughes, Brian Howard, as well as newer friends like Lorca and Neruda himself, who was now living in Paris and came down to Réanville to help Nancy. Brian Howard and John Banting also came to take part in the project and Brian introduced her in Paris to W. H. Auden, who had arrived from the Spanish front. He offered her his famous poem, 'Spain 1937', which was included in the fifth leaflet.

Yet another project to support the Republicans began in June 1937, when Nancy circulated a huge broadsheet entitled 'THE QUESTION' to a number of artists and intellectuals, asking them to state their views on the war: 'All we want is a message from you, a statement in not more than 6 lines. We ask you to phrase your answer on Spain, on Fascism, in this concise form.'[72] There were 145 replies, of which sixteen were neutral and only five (one of them from Evelyn Waugh) supported Franco. Those who sent statements of support for Republican Spain included Aragon, Auden, Jean Richard Bloch, Brian Howard, Heinrich Mann, Ivor Montagu, Pablo Neruda, Ramon Sender, Stephen Spender, and Tristan Tzara. Samuel Beckett's contribution was simply, 'UPTHEREPUBLIC!'[73] The collection was finally published by the *Left Review* in autumn 1937 as *Authors Take Sides*.

Once the Second World War began, Nancy lived in London in a bedsitting room, going out every evening to drink with Norman Douglas and Augustus John. Her disregard of the dangers of war was shared (though more comfortably) by her mother, who occupied two rooms at the Dorchester Hotel in London's West End, after her house had been burnt. But they did not see each other – the breach between them was permanent. Harold Acton observed that Nancy became more like her mother as she grew older: 'While she thought she was mimicking her mother's voice her own voice and idiom were almost identical, a staccato hovering over a phrase and a sudden drift elsewhere.' In spite of the rupture between them, he writes, 'each would ask me for news of the other in a seemingly casual way, as if I were a subconscious link between them'. He invited Nancy to dinner with some friends and describes how she

sprang towards us in her usual breathless manner, embraced us fervently amid sighs and exclamations, and leaned forward on her multiple bracelets to give vent to her frustrations; she who might have added lustre to the BBC or the Ministry of Information was drudging at a Free French organization, transcribing enemy broadcasts from Vichy.[74]

To Nancy's distress, her work for the Free French required her to monitor Pound's broadcasts from Italy. Predictably, her major contribution to the war effort was literary and centred on France: an anthology called *Poems for France. Written by British Poets on France Since the War*, which was published by La France Libre in 1944.

After the war, she returned to the life she had led before – living in France, reading and thinking, drinking with friends. She 'still dressed in her original style', noticed her old friend Iris Tree, when she came across Nancy in Venice wearing 'a turban of multi-coloured string netting wound round her head; a high fur collar framing her small pale face; her massive African bracelets of ebony and ivory clattering together on her now bony arms'.[75] She worked as hard as ever, writing biographies of Norman Douglas and George Moore. But life was becoming a struggle for Nancy: always fragile, her physical health was starting to deteriorate and she was thinner than ever. She was also less robust emotionally following the suicide in 1958 of her beloved friend, Brian Howard. She now slipped into episodes of excessive alcohol consumption and anti-social and paranoid behaviour. Then, shortly after arriving in London in April 1960, she was certified as insane and committed to an asylum for the mentally ill. This alarmed and worried her friends and also led to exaggerated reports of her behaviour by those who had never really forgiven her readiness to flout convention. When her cousin Victor Cunard fell ill, Nancy Mitford claimed in a letter to a friend that 'it was all brought on by the madness of N. Cunard – I mean by her going mad. She went to an hotel at 3 A.M. & when the night porter aged 90 showed her room she ordered him to sleep with her. She then set fire to a policeman. She is now in a bin whence she writes heartrending letters to poor Vic.'[76]

At first Nancy accepted her role as patient with resignation, even starting to put on some weight. But she then became terrified that she would be incarcerated for ever and begged her old friend Louis Aragon, who was now one of France's leading literary figures, to arrange her release. He spoke out on her behalf in a long leading article on the front page of *Les Lettres Françaises*, recalling all the achievements of The Hours Press and her support for the Republicans in the Spanish Civil War. Eventually she was released and she returned to France. But she was unable to achieve an emotional and physical stability, slipping as before into states of collapse, which became increasingly incoherent and violent. In 1965 she died, following a bizarre incident in which she set fire to all her letters and papers in the middle of the floor of a hotel room in the Latin Quarter of Paris. She was little more than a skeleton: 29 kilograms, estimated Raymond Michelet; and as little as 26, according to George Sadoul.[77] Her death was a 'tragic mess', wrote one of her friends, and her funeral was a sad and miserable farewell: 'Funeral 3rd class, grim, protestant, cold, 6 people.' A single wreath had a big broad red ribbon with gold lettering, saying 'Love from your Cousins' – who had never seen her.[78] But Nancy had written her own epitaph, long before, in the autobiographical summary she produced for her anthology, *Poets for France*. This epitaph effectively rejects her English connections and claims France as her natural home:

Poet and journalist. Founded and ran The Hours Press in Normandy and Paris, 1928–32. Worked for the Associated Negro Press of the US and was reporter in Spain on the Republican side during the Spanish War. Lives permanently in France, travels much . . . a convinced believer in French and Spanish spirit and culture.[79]

7

'NOT WHY WE CAN'T BUT HOW WE CAN'
Stella, Marchioness of Reading

Stella Isaacs, Marchioness of Reading, 1894–1971, was born Stella Charnaud in Constantinople. Her father, Charles Charnaud, was descended from French Huguenots and worked as director of the tobacco monopoly of the Ottoman Empire. Stella was his third daughter and the eldest child of his second wife, Milbah Johnson, who came from Lincolnshire. Unable to go to school because of ill health, possibly a curvature of the spine, Stella was educated by private tutors in the family home at Moda, on the Asian side of the Bosporus.

Shortly before the 1914–18 war the family returned to England, where Stella trained as a secretary in London. During the war she worked in the British Red Cross Society. In 1925 she went to India to work for Alice, the first wife of Rufus Isaacs, Viceroy of India between 1921 and 1925. He was created Marquess of Reading on his return. As a Liberal MP, Isaacs became in 1912 the first Jew to be made a member of the Cabinet; he was for a short time Foreign Secretary in Ramsay MacDonald's National Government of 1931. After the Readings' return from India in 1925, Stella worked as his private secretary. Alice Reading died in 1930. In the following year, when he was seventy years old, Lord Reading married Stella, who was thirty-seven. As the second Lady Reading, Stella devoted her time to public service and was Chairman of the Personal Service League in the 1930s. Lord Reading died just four years after their marriage, in 1935. They had no children.

Stella Reading is best known for her life's work: the leadership of the Women's Voluntary Service for Civil Defence (WVS). Created in 1938, the WVS became the largest of all voluntary organizations and its membership exceeded a million women by 1942. After the war it adapted to the needs of peacetime and became the Women's Royal Voluntary Service in 1966. Stella made time for other public duties, too. For over thirty years she was vice-chairman of the Imperial Relations Trust and after the war she served as a governor of the BBC and was its vice-chairman until 1951. She chaired the advisory council on Commonwealth immigrants to Britain for the Home Office in the 1960s and she was the first woman member of the National Savings Committee. There was always some kind of needlework in her hands during her brief moments of leisure and she was expert at tapestry; she was also an enthusiastic gardener at her country home in Sussex.

Stella was appointed Dame of the British Empire in 1941 and then raised to Dame Grand Cross in 1944. In 1958, she was created a life peeress and took the title of Baroness Swanborough – the first woman life peer to take her seat in the House of Lords. Following her death in 1971 at the age of seventy-seven, a service was held at Westminster Abbey to commemorate her life and work.

By 1938, the year of the Munich crisis, the possibility of another war with Germany seemed horribly real. The British government hurriedly made plans for home defence, finally heeding Lady Milner's warning: 'Our job is to look after ourselves, and to have sufficient force to prevent the next sudden German attack on civilization.'[1] Bombs had been dropped from Zeppelins and other enemy aircraft during the 1914–18 war and, for the first time in British history, there was a real danger of extensive air attacks against the civilian population. There was also a threat of poison gas, which had been used on the Western Front in the 1914–18 war and, then by the Italians against Abyssinia in 1936. It was evident that the Air Raid Precautions services (ARP) alone would not be adequate for the massive task ahead. But since every able-bodied member of the public would have to register for war service, it was not at first clear who would be available to do this work. There was only one untapped source of labour: the large number of women who were exempt from registration for war service because they were needed at home to care for children or other dependants or because they were too old. There were also women who were exempt because they were employed to do essential work. It was all these women, realized the Home Secretary, Sir Samuel Hoare, who would have to shoulder the vital job of organizing and protecting the national community.[2]

This was a formidable challenge, because there was no precedent for the mobilization of women staying at home. Unsure about how best to move forward, Hoare tried to think of a woman who would be capable of taking over the plan and developing it on a national scale. The obvious choice was Stella, Marchioness of Reading, who had already demonstrated impressive signs of leadership as Chairman of the Personal Service League. He made urgent efforts to contact her in April 1938. 'It seemed rather a bother at the time', she recalled long afterwards, because 'I was planning to leave to visit a friend in Bulgaria later in the week and I was nowhere near ready'.[3] She told him that she was planning to go abroad for a month, but he insisted that she return to Britain within fourteen days, with some kind of answer. As she sped across Europe on the Orient Express, the importance of the job she had been asked to fill gradually dawned on her. She developed plans for a strategy to carry it out and returned on the fifteenth day, with a proposal for the Women's Voluntary Service for Civil Defence.[4] In this way, at forty-four years of age, she embarked on the major work of her life.

Stella was the widow of Rufus Isaacs, the First Marquess of Reading, whose death just three years before had caused her terrible grief and distress. Her own background had been comparatively humble: she had grown up in a middle class family in Constantinople (which is Istanbul today), as the daughter of the director of the state tobacco monopoly of the Ottoman Empire. The family returned to England shortly before the 1914–18 war and experienced financial difficulties, which led Stella to train as a secretary in London, very much against the will of her father. She first met her future husband while she was working as a secretary – for his first wife, Alice. This meeting took place in India, during his tour of duty as Viceroy between 1921 and 1925. When the Readings returned to England, Stella worked for Lord Reading as his private secretary, at his home on Curzon Street in London and at the headquarters of the Imperial Chemical Industries (ICI), of which he was President. They fell in love and were married in 1932, when he was seventy and she was thirty-seven. The transition from secretary to marchioness was a formidable challenge, but one that Stella managed with her characteristic resourcefulness. 'When she came to live at that house with butler, footman etc.', commented her private secretary, Peggy Blampied, 'she must have felt nervous and apprehensive, but she kept her dignity and they soon learnt she was the boss and respected and took her to their hearts.' The Readings used to have 'grand dinner parties, lunches at Curzon Street with Maharajas etc.', added Miss Blampied, 'and she adapted herself quickly as though she had done it all her life. She looked wonderful the day she came down the stairs to be presented at Court, white satin and ostrich feathers, very regal.'[5] It was Stella's ability to adapt quickly to new situations and to move comfortably in all kinds of social contexts that made her ideal for the role that was pressed on her by Samuel Hoare in 1938.

On 16 May, Hoare held a small meeting at the Home Office to discuss the proposed formation of the 'WVS', as it quickly became known. As well as Stella, Lady Reading, those present included other women who were key figures in the prominent women's organizations: Lady Ruth Balfour, the vice-chairman of the National Council of Women; Eva Hubback, a leading figure in the Family Endowment Society and the Children's Minimum Council; Miss Caroline Haslett (later Dame Caroline Haslett), who had founded the Women's Engineering Society; and Miss Philippa Strachey, who was active in the National Society for Equal Citizenship. Everybody gave their approval to Lady Reading's plan. A few days later, Hoare sent Lady Reading a letter that formally invited her to form an organization that would:

provide a channel through which women could enrol in the Air Raid Precaution Services; bring home to every household in the country what air attack would mean; and make known to every household what it could do for its own protection and to help the Community.[6]

The plan was to cast a net all over Britain, in which representatives of counties, county boroughs, and urban and rural districts would work in co-operation with the local authority.

'I had one of the best ideas of my life in thinking of Stella, Lady Reading for the Chairmanship of the new organisation', wrote Sir

Samuel Hoare in his memoir of the period.[7] Especially valuable was her experience in the Personal Service League of organizing women in different parts of Britain to work together for a common cause. The League had been set up to help the victims of unemployment in distressed areas and was run from its offices in Grosvenor Road by volunteer ladies who collected second-hand clothes for the unemployed. 'It was a big clothing campaign', recalled Lady Holland-Martin, a member of the League: as well as collecting clothes, 'endless garments were cut out and sent up to the North where they were made up. They were expertly cut out and we used to fold and pack them up.'[8] The League was not connected with the local authorities, but had representatives in every county and in 1933 managed to clothe 5,000 men, women and children each week.[9] Lady Londonderry was the first chairman but she retired in 1932 and asked Lady Reading to take it on – which she did, with tremendous success, until 1938. 'Lady Reading is absolutely first class', praised Lady Londonderry (who was not given to empty compliments).[10]

Within three years of its foundation, more than a million women, mostly housewives working part-time, were members of the WVS. To recruit them, Lady Reading spoke in her role as chairman of the organization at 98 meetings all over Britain between April and December 1938.[11] These meetings were open to the public but with a special invitation to prominent women: the Mayor would take the Chair and then Lady Reading would speak. Generally, a WVS office would open the next day to enrol new volunteers. One recruit later recalled: 'Early in the summer of 1939 I was persuaded to attend a WVS Meeting in London – I went unwillingly, as apparently did most of the other women – but after Lady R. had spoken, we were all queuing to enrol.'[12] Local and national newspapers covered the meetings in late 1938 and 1939, urging women to join. By the end of 1938, enrolments in the WVS had reached 32,329[13] and this number rose in a sharp curve after the publication in January 1939 of *The National Service Handbook*, which gave special prominence to the WVS.

Its first really big challenge was the evacuation of city schoolchildren and mothers with babies. On 1 September 1939, Germany invaded Poland, with the result that Great Britain and France, bound by a treaty of alliance with Poland, declared war on Germany on 3 September. The WVS had been promised 24 hours' notice of the intended exodus and on receipt of a 'most immediate' message from the Ministry of Health, telegrams were sent to the regional administrators. Within fourteen hours, 120,000 members had been alerted, 17,000 of them for escort duties.[14] During these three days, 1.25 million children and mothers were evacuated from the big cities to the country. As the weeks passed and the Germans showed no signs of bombing the cities, many evacuees returned – only to be re-evacuated in June 1940 after Dunkirk. The WVS provided nurseries, social clubs for mothers and much-needed support.[15] The next major demand on the WVS came in May 1940, when Germany invaded the Low Countries and refugees fled to Britain; this was followed in September by the blitzkrieg on London, in November by heavy raids on Coventry and Birmingham, and in December by the bombing of ports. Food and clothing were provided for refugees and bombed-out families and WVS staff manned the nine large reception centres set up by the London County Council, at which the refugees were fed, given baths, medically examined and registered, and then passed on to the borough councils for billeting.

The chief function of the WVS was, of course, civil defence. When the ARP service first began, there was an assumption that it would be composed mostly of men. Women were allowed to enrol as wardens, but some doubt was felt about their physical endurance under heavy raiding: in one London borough, where a practical exercise for wardens was accompanied by a gramophone record of the sounds to be expected during an air attack, the explosions of mock bombs were modified to gentle popping noises when ladies were present.[16] However, this attitude swiftly disappeared once the WVS got underway. Women were called on to work in any of thirty-eight branches of ARP work, including 'Social Organizers', 'Advisors on Food Supplies', 'Optical Assistants', 'Watch Room Attendants', 'Transport Drivers', 'Switchboard Operators' and 'X-ray Mechanics'. Training was a priority and courses were set up for women in ARP, First Aid, anti-gas and fire fighting; in London, courses were arranged not only in English but also in Italian, French, Spanish, Dutch and Yiddish, at times to suit women working in the West End shops and other daily workers. At first, training was in accordance with the programmes arranged for volunteers in the regular civil defence services, but their scope was rapidly enlarged. Many women were nervous about taking the qualifying examination and one husband reported that his wife was 'wrestling in agony with the problems which she anticipates that her A.R.P. Examiners may put before her at the test which she has to pass'.[17]

Members of the WVS worked at incident inquiry points, collecting information from air raid wardens after a bomb or a rocket had been dropped and passing this on to relatives and friends who were desperate for news. They served thousands of meals to shocked and distressed people at rest centres and provided clothes and washing facilities. After air raids WVS mobile canteens brought hot drinks and sandwiches to rescue workers, firemen and those who had been bombed out of their homes. Journeys at night had to be made without headlights and it was difficult to avoid bomb craters and unexploded bombs. When thousands of people started to spend every night in the shelters, WVS volunteers fortified their spirits with tea and cake.

It was fundamental to Lady Reading's vision of the WVS that it should operate as a voluntary organization. 'I should hope to be able to do the greater part of the job on a voluntary basis', she wrote to Sir Samuel Hoare, when plans for the WVS were first underway. 'It will probably be a bit more untidy on these lines', she added, 'but if we succeed in getting the women interested they will feel that the whole thing belongs to them in a real sense more than if it were run for them by paid people or by officials.'[18] Out of the million or more members, there was a steady average of only 700 members who received a monetary grant; of these, barely 200 workers were given more than out-of-pocket expenses. But this voluntary system was absolutely dependent for the basic machinery of its structure on funding from national and local government. The total cost to government was considerable: at headquarters, it had to cover office accommodation and maintenance, equipment, telephone services, postage and related expenses, and a number of salaries; and in each region, there was one full-time paid organizer, travelling and other expenses for centre organizers, and the provision of offices and equipment by local government. Without this financial underpinning, it would not have been possible for the WVS to develop so swiftly into an efficient and massive national service.

Insofar as it did not pay its volunteers, the WVS drew on a long tradition of voluntary service in Britain. But this time it was different – because the volunteers were doing military service. They had put themselves at the disposal of the government authorities and had to follow orders, even if this meant doing a job that was unpleasant. They were organized from the WVS section of the ARP offices of the Home Office at 41 Tothill Street in London, which soon became known as 'Totters'. The administrative machinery had a firm hierarchy and was based on the twelve Civil Defence Regions instituted by the Home Office and then subdivided into counties and county boroughs or their Scottish equivalents. The head office made no attempt to foster democratic participation: volunteer regional administrators were assisted by paid organizers overseeing the work of its local centre organizers and these officials were all appointed by a committee of senior officers under Lady Reading. In this way, the WVS operated quite differently from other women's organizations with a tradition of voluntary service, such as Women's Institutes (the WI), Towns-women's Guilds or Women's Co-operative Guilds.[19] Whereas the WI and the Guilds were organized in such a way as to meet the interests of their members, the WVS had been specifically created as a wartime service to do what had to be done – even jobs that were unpleasant. Efforts were made to soften the military aspect of the WVS, though, to ensure that volunteers felt they were being treated as individuals. There were no rules on how to wear the WVS hat, for example, and a story is told that when the Prime Minister Winston Churchill watched a group of WVS members on parade, he turned to Lady Reading and complained that their hats were all at different angles. She replied: 'Here is a case of individuality in operation, but uniformity of pattern.'[20]

Great emphasis was laid on the importance of the WVS outside London and Lady Reading spent at least one-third of her time touring the country, investigating problems and meeting members. A Cardiff newspaper announced on 23 January 1940 that 'Dowager Lady Reading [was] Staggered by the Courage of the Women of South Wales', while the *Southend Times* reported on 28 February 1940 that 'Lady Reading Thanks Southend W.V.S'. As a way of integrating the different regions into one organic whole, Lady Reading sent a Christmas card to every WVS Centre Organizer and any other person in the country who carried some organizational responsibility. One member who had formerly been a secretary to Sir John Simon, the Lord Chancellor, said that Lady Reading used to spend three months every year giving birth to her Christmas message, but that it was not always effective. 'The letters, to me, and to many other people', she said, 'were incomprehensible. One couldn't get to the thinking of what it was about. I remember on one occasion she wrote, "This year I am sending you a packet of seed" and then she went on and on about the seeds, and any amount of people wrote and said, "But you forgot to enclose the seed." The whole thing was a parable.'[21] Another member recalled that, 'One year she sent us candles and she told us all that the candles could do. Not real candles. This allegorical business never struck a chord with me, and I am sure it didn't with the average WVS member.'[22]

The 'average WVS member' was often a member of the Housewives Service, which was the linchpin of the organization. When the air raid warning sounded, the 'Housewives' were responsible for finding out how many children were in the street and how many old people were alone. It was a genuine street service that assisted the police and air raid wardens and helped in all sorts of ways, sometimes by answering queries from men abroad who had heard about a raid on their home towns. In the event of bombing, they had to provide in their own homes a boiling kettle always ready for tea for the wardens or casualties, blankets, and a bucket of water and a bucket of sand on the doorstep for fire prevention. Early in 1940 the Ministry of Home Security recognized the status of the Housewives Service by authorizing a standard blue card for display in a window; and before Christmas approximately 191,500 Housewives had enrolled, some 49,000 of them in London and 10,000 in Scotland. In 1942 the name of the service was changed to 'Housewives Section of the WVS' and the Housewives were properly trained. About 20 per cent of the entire WVS membership was in the Housewives Section and blue window cards were displayed from more than three-quarters of a million homes.[23] A Housewives' Assistant was normally included in the staff at a WVS Centre and news travelled fast down this channel to street level and back up again. This provided an effective means for members to share with each other the benefits of their experience and to enable the organization to evolve in the most appropriate way. This was invaluable because both the organization and the situation were without precedent and everyone had to learn from their mistakes: for example, the country was saturated with gas masks at the start of the war, but they were never actually needed.

In the English district of the Holme Valley, most WVS volunteers joined the Housewives Service, so their work illustrates the nature of responsibilities taken on by the Housewives. These covered every kind of war work: camouflage netting; running a mobile canteen; emergency cooking for the Home Guard; mending chores; collecting cash for the Wings For Victory fund and for National Savings; collecting bones and tins from dustbins for the salvage drive; help with the billeting of evacuees; and setting up rest centres. They kept records of the residents on every street for the Searcher Service, which was invaluable when V-bombs (or doodle-bugs as they were called) were dropped on the area. There was a Volunteer Car Pool listing seventeen members who were always on call. A clothing exchange was set up, where garments could be exchanged for a different article or credited for their value in 'points'; this was a great help to mothers with growing children, since new clothing was rationed. Special attention was paid to the needs of servicemen home on leave and bicycles were bought for the use of those who were stranded because their train arrived after the last bus had left. 'During the war', recalled one WVS member, 'we had a soldier every Sunday for dinner.' In 1944, the Holme Valley WVS won the Regional Make Do and Mend Competition.[24] Some of the entries for Make Do and Mend Competitions were ingenious: first prize for the garment category in the 1945 national competition was awarded for 'a Tyrolean jacket, made entirely from the tops and legs of grey socks'.[25]

In the Holme Valley WVS, residents of council houses worked alongside the clergyman's wife, and a teacher. It was the same all over Britain, because the Women's Voluntary Service was an organization without rank and titles. This meant, theoretically, that a charwoman and a highborn lady could work on an equal footing. It was rare – but it *did* happen. The wife of the Director General of the Post Office, for example, chose to 'humbly start at the bottom of the ladder' when she joined the WVS.[26] For this was an organization where eligibility for membership did not depend on who you were, or your social status, but on what you could do and on your willingness to work hard. This democratic aspect of WVS was carefully nurtured by Lady Reading, who had a strong distaste for the kind of snobbery and patronage that had informed the workings of the Personal Service League. There was a time, said Lady Reading, 'when society could count on volunteers coming from the leisured class . . . the Lady Bountiful sort of thing. Now that is past.'[27] The absence of rank was reflected in the uniform, a fetching outfit in green, with grey woven through it. There was a WVS badge on the sleeve, as well as a small flash indicating the region from which the wearer came, but there was no other mark to distinguish one woman from another. Lady Reading wore her uniform at all times, as did other high officers; members wore it when on duty. It was designed by Norman Hartnell, a top couturier, as clothing that would be feminine, smart, hardwearing – and, above all, classless.

Lady Reading never isolated herself within the tiny class to which she belonged after her marriage to the Marquess. After Lord Reading's death and just before the Second World War she motored across the United States under the assumed name of 'Mrs Reed', lodging in private houses where tourists were accommodated at a dollar a night, or in camps or hotels. She managed to belong to the elite, but somehow to remain detached: her step-granddaughter recalls that she had no patience for pomposity and enjoyed serving sweetcorn to arrogant guests, who would then have to eat with their fingers.[28] 'When Sir Samuel Hoare saw me in the first place', recalled Lady Reading later, 'he said to me, "I think you ought to have the status of a Deputy Under Secretary of State."' But she refused:

I said, 'I don't want any status, I think I'm much better off without status'. . . I didn't even know what a Deputy Under Secretary of State was. I knew about a Permanent Secretary, and I had no idea at all whether a Principal or Deputy Under Secretary of State was of higher status, but the answer was that when we started at Totters, the men who came to furnish my room were very insistent that I ought to have the sort of stuff that went into a Deputy Under Secretary's room, because they had been told so! I eliminated this from the start because I was quite certain it was wrong to have status or any sort of grade . . .[29]

But to get the WVS started, it had been necessary for Lady Reading to resort to the traditional methods of setting up a voluntary organization – using the patronage of the nobility and the royal family. At the end of the Thirties, it was still not enough to have the backing of the government: she needed ladies with titles, too. Stella well understood how this system worked as a result of her experience as chairman of the Personal Service League. Wherever possible, she had utilized her social prestige – as the wife of the Marquess of Reading – for the benefit of the League. One such occasion was a fund-raising auction in 1933 at Bridgewater House, which was lent for the purpose by Lord Ellesmere; the House itself was a great draw, not least to see the paintings by Poussin. The gifts poured in and Queen Mary gave some Japanese objects in jade and came to a private view, in order to show her interest. This gave Lady Reading the courage to visit Sir Harry Verney, Queen Mary's Secretary, to tell him that she did not think the items donated by Queen Mary quite represented the impor-tance that she felt sure the Queen would intend. As a result, the Queen went to Bond Street that afternoon and bought a splendid clock to add to her other gifts. Encouraged by this, Lady Reading then went to see Lord Stamfordham, the King's Secretary, to tell him what the Queen had given and to inquire what *he* was planning to give. The King responded with a number of fine shawls that had been presented to him as a tribute from Kashmir. These impressive royal donations meant that when the evening of the auction arrived, £2,000 had been taken at the door in entrance fees before the event had even started. Miss E. Wade, who helped with the cataloguing at this event, later recalled that

Mr Seymour Leslie, Appeal Secretary for Queen Charlotte's Hospital, came up to me and said 'you and I have to struggle to get *one* royalty – she's got the lot', and she had – Queen Mary, the Duke and Duchess of York, Prince and Princess Arthur of Connaught, Princess Alice and Lord Athlone, and Princess Marie Louise and Princess Helena Victoria.[30]

Contacts like these – and a flair for managing them – were invaluable in the early development of the WVS. 'She was so close to the powers that be,' observed one of the early regional administrators, 'that she made all these contacts, so of course she could do [all sorts of difficult things]. If you read about her you find it seems all the time to be leading up to this tremendous job [WVS] that she took on.'[31] As a first step in setting up the WVS, Lady Reading approached the Lords Lieutenant and their ladies, as well as her own circle of well-connected friends. Lady Hillingdon, a Labour intellectual who had been at school with the Queen Mother, became a vice-chairman. The social seal of approval was stamped on the organization by the Queen's readiness to become President and her wholehearted support.[32]

Throughout the 1940s, 30–40 per cent of the regional administrators were titled ladies; Lady Reading also managed to get hold of a number of 'debutantes'.[33] It was not always easy to find a role for interested members of the upper classes, however. One of these was Lady Mountbatten, who asked Lady Reading at the beginning of the war what she could do to help but 'didn't know about anything practical', recalled a member of the headquarters team later. Eventually, Lady Reading 'got her down on the ground and she did some very good things after that. Once it was something to do with a typewriter: Lady Reading said, "You must have some carbon-paper", and Lady Mountbatten said, "What is carbon-paper?" She hadn't a clue'.[34]

The noble ladies brought into the top tier of management, however, were carefully chosen for their expertise. One such women was Lady Iris Capell, the daughter of the Earl of Essex, who joined the WVS in its first month, when she was forty-three. Iris Capell had many skills: she had been a member of the Voluntary Aid Detachment during the 1914–18 war and spent many years of her life in the support of hospital administration; she was also a gifted theatrical director and producer. But the expertise that was most valuable to the WVS was that of motor mechanics. A skilful driver, she had set up and run the first 'Drive-Yourself' service in London after the war and had competed in many trials and rallies. Her car service was not successful as a business venture, but she was able to draw on this experience to start the WVS Transport Department, of which she became the head. She was in her element: a reluctant debutante who preferred cars to parties, she had found a niche where she could use her mechanical skills for a worthwhile purpose. From her Transport Department in Tothill Street, Iris Capell managed all the transport services and mobile canteens. She also worked with the Ministry of Home Security to devise and organize the Volunteer Car Pool, which enabled volunteers to keep their cars on the road with extra petrol rations, in order to be available for any kind of emergency service. Under this scheme, 20,000 owner-drivers, men and women from all parts of England, covered 60 million miles, often on secret service missions for the government.[35] According to Lady Norman, who was a vice-chairman from 1938 to 1941, Lady Iris was 'always an individualist and wore uniform only when it was "de rigueur"'.[36] But she was invaluable to the organization of the WVS, because she understood completely that transport was one of the keys to its success. She was appointed a vice-chairman in 1941.

Other members of the 'Totters' team included the chairman's secretary, Miss Blampied; her step-granddaughter Joan Zuckerman; the Hon. Sylvia Fletcher-Mouton, a barrister involved with Anglo-American work; Mrs Catherine Benn, who had been information officer for the Personal Service League and took on similar work for the WVS; and Mrs Montagu Norman (later Lady Norman), the wife of the governor of the Bank of England, who became a WVS vice-chairman with special responsibility for London. Another vice-chairman was Miss Marjorie Maxse, Lady Milner's sister-in-law, who had been a senior Conservative Party organizer since the 1920s. Mrs Lindsey Huxley, Honorary Treasurer for the National Federation of Women's Institutes, soon joined the team as chief regional administrator. For her general secretary, however, Lady Reading wanted a woman with something more than a background in voluntary service or social connections, who would be able to handle government officials in a professional manner. She insisted on having Miss Mary Smieton, a young Oxford graduate at the Ministry of Labour (who went on to a distinguished career in the civil service after the war).

As general secretary between 1938 and 1940, Miss Smieton had the task of harnessing this new source of energy to the old machinery of civil service procedure and local government administration. This was a considerable challenge – not least because, as noted by Hoare's biographer, the Home Office did not welcome the creation of a special corps of women volunteers or the initial accommodation of Lady Reading and her small headquarters staff in the Home Office.[37] Civil servants were unhappy, too, about the cosy relationship between

Hoare and Lady Reading (which continued with future Home Secretaries) and relations were often strained. The government officials, recalled Miss Blampied later, were 'always doing what was right, but [were] plodders and red tape', while Lady Reading 'wanted to rush everything, in case there was no tomorrow to do it'.[38] An official at the Ministry of Food was irritated by Lady Reading's demand for rationed food for nutrition demonstrations and complained that 'Lady Reading refused to be put off!';[39] these demonstrations generated further bad feeling between the WVS and the Board of Education.[40] What especially concerned Miss Smieton, though, was Lady Reading's failure to conform to civil service procedure. Having gone away on a short holiday, she returned to find the chairman in the process of putting the WVS into uniform – but without having obtained prior permission from the Home Office, who 'might be startled to find that they had created a new uniformed corps'.[41] When this was pointed out to Lady Reading by Miss Smieton, she simply went to see Sir Wilfred Eady, the under-secretary in charge, to get his approval – which he gave. 'Of course', commented Miss Smieton drily, Eady was 'an old friend'.[42]

The same directly personal approach was employed by Lady Reading in her dealings with local authorities. Keeping them happy was essential to the work of the WVS, since they were responsible for civil defence locally and it was only through them that the WVS could have any scope or status, let alone office accommodation or the use of a telephone. According to Miss Smieton, 'she used every weapon, all her vigour and drive, all her charm, all the "blackmail" of her personal position and influence and her practical commonsense'.[43] It worked: as early as 1939, many local authorities had been made aware of the WVS and its aims and they were generally supportive. Eady commented in a Home Office memo that, 'though one still hears occasional stories that a local authority here or there has no use for the WVS and regards them as useless busybodies, the fact remains that local authorities in increasing numbers are calling on WVS to do particular jobs on their behalf or look after one or other of the functions which have been heaped upon them'.[44]

Lady Reading had a strong sense of solidarity with her volunteers, which was largely informed by the fact that they were all women, working together. Described by Doreen Harris as 'Too feminine to be a feminist', Stella was of the opinion that 'It isn't women who need equality: it's men!'[45] Like Mrs Baldwin, she believed that women were superior to men in capability and endurance. According to another close friend, who first met Lady Reading at a country house party and was 'slightly mesmerized' by her,

she was a feminist, of course, but in the old-fashioned sense. While convinced that women could do most things as well as men, she always insisted that a wife's priority was her husband. She was not an advocate of women leaving their menfolk night after night to work in factories or canteens. She once said to me she thought women were far more practical than men, but that men had more vision.[46]

However, husbands and family were not *always* seen as a priority. On one occasion, Lady Reading told her members to 'put first things first. Leave the beds undone, leave the house dirty; and don't cook your husband's meal – let him jolly well get on with a piece of bread.'[47]

Food played a key role in WVS work. Richard Titmuss suggests in *Problems of Social Policy*, his history of the wartime years, that in the development of wartime feeding schemes, such as British Restaurants, food convoys and canteens, the contribution made by voluntary workers, notably the WVS, 'was, perhaps, greater in this field of war-time service than in any other'.[48] But the organization did not stop at meals: it also provided education about food values and ways of making the best use of the limited foods now available to housewives. Every month the WVS *Bulletin* included a section on 'Food News', with advice on nutrition and ways of cooking the rationed food to produce healthy meals. It sang the praises of National Bread and offered recipes in which Spam (a tinned pork luncheon meat sent to Britain from the USA) was a regular feature. As a special meal for Christmas in 1944, it recommended 'Smothered Rabbit', which was soaked overnight in salted water and then dipped in reconstituted egg, or 'Barbecued Spam', in which a tin of Spam was not actually barbecued but fried in two tablespoonfuls of frying-fat, then garnished with boiled shallots or onions. 'Very few of us', added the *Bulletin* apologetically, 'can hope to find a fat goose for our Christmas table, but we have been promised extra rations.' These extra rations included an extra half-pound of margarine 'for one week only', as well as an extra half-pound of sweets 'for children between 6 months and 18 years'.[49] For American Thanksgiving in 1943, the *Bulletin* urged housewives to welcome American soldiers into their home and offer them a festive meal of 'Mock Turkey (otherwise Baked Rabbit)' or 'Barbecued Spam' (in this recipe, the Spam is baked rather than fried), with 'MockCream' for dessert. As some kind of recompense for this less-than-appetizing fare – and acknowledging the American distaste for the warm drinks enjoyed in Britain – it recommends giving GIs a 'cup of *hot* coffee or a really *cold* drink (sic)'.[50]

In October 1942, the Birmingham branch of the WVS reported on a new scheme to pass on food news to housewives: 'At least 150 Food Leaders are now enrolled and trained, and requests for the training talks are coming in steadily. The Education Department and the Ministry of Food Advice Centre at Worcester are encouraging WVS co-operation in this scheme and a WVS representative has been appointed to the Birmingham Food Committee.'[51] Lady Reading then suggested to Lord Woolton, who was Minister of Food, that he sponsor a national campaign along these lines, using WVS Housewives. The national scheme was jointly announced in February 1944 by the Ministry of Food and the Board of Education. Within a year, 15,000 food leaders were at work throughout the country, most of them WVS volunteers, distributing advice from the Ministry of Food and information about the need for fuel economy.

However, there was often tension between the WVS and Ministry of Food officials, who regarded the women volunteers as amateurs and thought they took too much credit for the nutrition work that was done. Typically scathing was a Ministry of Food memorandum about a WVS recipe book for wartime: 'The [experimental] kitchen do not consider the book sound at all. Dishes too elaborate and very complicated. Ingredients very often unobtainable. Badly set out. In their own words, "*Very* W.V.S." [sic]'.[52] Another memorandum comments with some satisfaction that, 'It would appear as if the Bristol WVS are on the threshold of a big row among themselves. This might, of course, prove quite helpful in the long run, if they have one and reorganize.'[53] When the WVS asked the Ministry of Food Advice

Division for a 'policy decision' on whether it should extend its pie-making activities to jam tarts,[54] the Ministry sent a brisk response:

So far as publicity for jam tarts is concerned, I think that the Public Relations have felt that it would be much better not to have too much, particularly because it might lead to a demand for jam tarts all over the country which your people would be unable to satisfy.[55]

The irritation of the Ministry was perhaps understandable on those occasions when it was presented by the WVS with recipes like 'Crepes Jeanne-Marie (French)' and 'Zillertaler Krappen (Tyrolese)',[56] which were submitted for the national good by the Hon. Mrs E—-W— of the Cheshire county office.

Few complaints were made by anybody, however, about the hard work of the mass of WVS members 'in the field'. They knitted up millions of socks, sweaters, scarves, balaclavas, mittens, turning 1,000,000 pounds of khaki wool into warm caps. After negotiations with the War Office, the WVS 'adopted the feet of the Army' on an official basis and in one year the WVS centres mended a million pairs of socks, as well as quantities of other garments.[57] The official scheme for sock mending by the WVS was welcomed as a kind of recognition of the work that had been done, although there was some resentment at the elaborate records that now had to be kept to justify the issue of mending wool (which in any case was generally considered to be of such inadequate quality that many housewives continued to buy wool rather than waste work). Another sewing task was the attaching of divisional 'flashes' and other marks of identity or rank to soldiers' uniforms; and a 'Make Do and Mend' party was organized at almost every clothing exchange. The WVS even organized a circulating library service, which was funded by the Pilgrim Trust: shelved boxes were built and thousands of books were chosen to form travelling libraries which could be left at military posts until the units exhausted their contents and needed a new box. Soon there were over 300 Pilgrim Trust boxes in circulation. From 1943 onwards, Sunday papers were sent to all the fighting fronts and altogether some 13.5 million papers were handled.[58]

As a sideline, the WVS organized the collection of aluminium, a metal which contains bauxite and was an essential material for fighter aircraft. This contribution to the war effort, which led to the collection of 1,000 tons of aluminium, was the result of a phone call from Lord Beaverbrook to Lady Reading, in which he suggested that the WVS collect every kind of aluminium pot and pan in the country. To start the campaign, Lady Reading broadcast an appeal over the wireless and within an hour the Skegness WVS Organizer had arranged for the appeal to appear on the screens of local cinemas. For weeks afterwards, the WVS offices were inundated with saucepans, kettles and jelly moulds.[59]

The WVS was always busy with new and original ideas – which reflected Lady Reading's own capacity for taking the initiative and her motto, 'Not Why We Can't But How We Can'. During the 'phoney' war she wrote each week to her friend Eleanor Roosevelt, giving her confidential news and telling her about shortages and what things were urgently needed by ordinary people. This meant that when the real war started, the American Red Cross had already sent over a vast amount of essential items: dried milk, clothing, toilet articles for babies, and bags packed ready to be given to those who had lost all their belongings. Lady Reading appeared to be a woman of endless practical resourcefulness: in 1939, a newspaper informed its readers that 'Lady Reading sticks her postage stamps on with jam when they are not gluey enough'.[60] When she heard in 1946 that a WVS member cooked five meals in her kitchen and delivered them to neighbouring old people in a pram, she thought of developing Meals on Wheels; this was the origin of a service that by the end of the century was providing over 100,000 house-bound pensioners and invalids with over 12 million hot meals a year, by 68,000 trained food volunteers. This model – as well as the name 'Meals on Whels' – has been adopted and is used by a number of countries throughout the world, including Australia, Japan, Denmark, Kenya and the USA.

The story of Dunkirk – how Churchill's fleet of 'Little Ships' brought back to England 224,584 British and Dominion and 112,546 Allied soldiers – usually ends with the disembarkation of the rescued troops. But it was only then that the work of the WVS began. Canteens were opened at the ports and railway stations and tea and sandwiches were provided for the exhausted men, who were accommodated in churches, halls and cinemas, falling asleep where they stood. The women of the WVS rolled them into lines, removed their equipment, took off their boots and washed their feet as they lay, then washed their socks. The mayor of one of the coastal towns involved said later, 'I thought how much the men's feet had bled. But then I looked again and saw that it was not stale brown blood, but fresh red blood that came from the women's hands.'[61] A special postcard service was organized to enable every soldier to write a personal message to his relatives, with the news of his safe return. All servicemen and -women knew that if they applied to a WVS Centre for help, they could rely on it being given within the limits of possibility. An extract from a Huntingdonshire report in July 1940 reveals the extent of WVS assistance to soldiers:

Tea at an hour's notice for any number between forty and four hundred has become a commonplace. Baths, laundry, salads, RAF pullovers and socks to men, altar flowers for chaplains, floral decorations for Officers' Messes, interior decorations for the same, together with the upholstery of chairs and sofas, provision of furniture on a hire purchase system, cakes and sandwiches for special Sunday teas, fresh fruit, arrangements for Concert parties, billets for wives and children . . .[62]

The WVS established dormitories in railway stations for the men on leave who were in transit and had nowhere to rest. They set up Welcome Clubs for Americans troops landing in England and manned air-raid enquiry points. They served in canteens, clubs and leave centres for the troops.

In late 1943, the WVS extended its troop welfare services to the combat zones. Members first went in small numbers to Algiers and Italy, then later to France and Greece; in 1945, they went into Germany and Burma to help prisoners-of-war who had just been set free. A branch of the WVS was started in India in 1940, working in close association with the WVS in Britain. Over 100 centres were established to care for patients in military hospitals, assist families of Indian servicemen and undertake any kind of welfare work required for refugees, abandoned families and servicemen. At its peak it had a membership of over ten thousand. WVS (India) closed down in 1955, when most of its members had returned home and the need for services welfare had ceased. But in the autumn of 1962, under the threat of border welfare, Indian women restarted the West Bengal branch.

It is extraordinary that the women of the WVS worked so hard – and for no pay. Of course, they were working not simply for an organization, but for the safety of their country, which was under the very real threat of defeat by Germany. But it is unlikely that their enthusiasm would have been harnessed to such good effect without the motivation provided by Lady Reading. She was a born leader: according to a woman who worked for her from 1940 until her death, she

lit a spark wherever she went and no matter whom she met. To this day, old hands light up when her name is mentioned . . . she gave you a job and made you feel you were just the one to do it! If you did your best she backed you to the hilt – always being several steps ahead in future planning – and when things began to go smoothly and you relaxed with a sigh, lo, she immediately gave you another job! True, she was a dictator, but only because she had such faith in herself and in you as part of herself.[63]

With a handsome and imposing presence and a deep, almost manly voice, she managed to combine charisma with efficiency. 'The action went at a cracking pace', remembered Doreen Harris, who helped to launch the WVS in 1938 and was Lady Reading's special assistant. 'From her desk', said Mrs Harris, 'flowed a stream of memos with the footnotes PSM – Please See Me. Always there was the personal touch. In every letter she sent, the typed content was "topped and tailed" with greeting and farewell in her own hand. Her energy was legendary.'[64]

In effect, the WVS provided a domestic and nurturing service to the nation that was not so different from the one its individual volunteers gave to their families at home, as wives and mothers. But this was domestic work on a massive scale: its wardrobe of clothes for the dispossessed, for example, was a national wardrobe. The fact that this work was done in the public sphere gave it a new value and prestige. A diary kept for Mass Observation by Nella Last, a lower middle-class woman in her early fifties who worked for the WVS in Barrow, tells a story of increasing self-confidence and the giving up of the 'slavery years of mind and body' that had gone into looking after her family in the 1930s. She developed a wholly new perspective on her domestic skills, even her ability to 'make do'. Through working in a WVS canteen, she realized 'what a knack of dodging and cooking and managing I possess, and my careful economies are things to pass on, not hide as I used to!'[65] Many housewives, like Mrs Last, were surprised to discover through their work for the WVS that they possessed gifts of organization and leadership.

Lady Reading had drawn upon and exploited the traditional aspects of voluntary service – patronage and social prestige – in order to create the WVS. But she then proceeded to transform the voluntary idea into something very different. The WVS was 'not patronage by the few', observed the Conservative MP, W. F. Deedes, 'but personal service by the many.'[66] This quality helps to explain the ability of the WVS to survive the early postwar period, which was a time in British history when notions of 'charity' and voluntary service were widely unpopular. When the National Health Service began in 1948, a leaflet explaining its operation promised that 'Everyone – rich or poor, man, woman or child – can use it or any part of it . . . *it is not a "charity"*.'[67] In this climate of opinion, the Charity Organization Society sensibly changed its name to the Family Welfare Association and many other organizations, such as the British Hospitals Association, simply wound themselves up. If the Personal Service League had survived the war, it would not have lasted very long. The future of the voluntary sector looked bleak. Some government spokesmen pledged to protect it: 'We must watch', warned Herbert Morrison, 'for the State to take over more and more what formerly was done by voluntary action . . . even where there would not be much financial saving, there are strong arguments for keeping the voluntary spirit alive.'[68]

In this context, the WVS – based on the principle of equality and need – was uniquely placed to offer an example of voluntary service that might successfully replace old-fashioned, discretionary organizations. Also, it had demonstrated an ability to work closely with government services. As Lady Reading told Chuter Ede, the Labour Home Secretary, in 1948: 'The days of "charity" and patronage are a thing of the past, but there is in the WVS a body of women in every part of the country and of all classes who are ready and willing to carry on this new . . . service to the community if the right channels for voluntary activity in the modern state can but be joined to the greatly increased flow of provision by the State.'[69] In 1972, Lord Henry Brooke of Cumnor, who had been Conservative Home Secretary in the early 1960s, commented that the organization was 'something quite new to Britain'. It was 'not only', he said, 'that Lady Reading inspired, directed and regulated the spirit of voluntary service among so many people', but also that she

forged this instrument to complete the partnership between Voluntary Service and the work of the statuary bodies and I think that she was very far-seeing in this. I think we all agree that as the so-called Welfare State has developed in the years since the end of the war, the job can only be done effectively if there is real intelligent partnership between volunteer organisations and the statutory bodies.[70]

However, the early postwar years were a struggle for the WVS, as there was fatigue throughout the service. One regional administrator recalled that after the war, she was constantly asked, 'How long?'[71] Opposition to the idea of survival was especially strong in Scotland, from where Lady Ruth Balfour, chairman of the WVS in Scotland, warned Lady Reading in July 1945 that she was 'faced with what is really widespread revolt amongst the W.V.S. members over the possibility of indefinite continuance of W.V.S. work'.[72] On top of this was the problem that Lady Reading had given an undertaking in 1938 to Mrs Huxley, the treasurer for the Women's Institute, that the WVS would not go on after the war. Mrs Huxley had died, but government records reveal that other members of the WI were not happy with the continuation of the WVS.[73] This was not surprising, as the WI had largely sunk their identity in order to help the other organization with its war work.

But Lady Reading had absolutely no intention of allowing the WVS to be a wartime wonder and it quickly proved to the public its value in peacetime. In 1953 violent gales hit Britain, causing homelessness and other emergencies – which the WVS was expertly trained to meet. This was the first national disaster after the war and the WVS showed itself to be indispensable. The organization became the Women's *Royal*

Voluntary Service (WRVS) in 1966 and Lady Reading continued as chairman until her death in 1971 at the age of seventy-seven. Today, members deliver a broad range of services, ranging from Meals on Wheels to prison welfare, and the organization has served as a pattern for similar organizations in many other countries, including Portugal, Australia and the United States. Lady Reading developed her theories on voluntarism in a booklet called *Voluntary Service*, which was distributed to all members of the WRVS. With chapters like 'Philosophy of Voluntary Service', the booklet offers a kind of rubric for voluntary work: it argues that the years of wartime effort had pushed the concept forward, so that it became a direct response to need rather than simply an effort to raise cash. Service like this is conspicuously lacking in glory and easy gratification, observed Lady Reading, since 'old people are cantankerous, the making of endless tea is monotonous; [and] the baking of endless home-made cakes can get tedious'.[74] But this service to the community, she added, was 'very like love, it transcends things'.[75]

Afterword

'TURNED INTO ORNAMENTS'

The history of women is the 'accumulation of unrecorded life', commented Virginia Woolf in *Three Guineas*. 'For all the dinners are cooked', she explained, and 'the plates and cups washed; the children sent to school and gone out into the world. Nothing remains of it all. All has vanished. No biography or history has a word to say about it.'[1] The first half of Woolf's statement has little relevance to the seven women of this book, who may never have cooked a single dinner or washed a single plate. But the second half certainly does, because they too have been overlooked in most accounts of the past. Typically, a *Guardian* editorial in 1996 observed that 'Lucy Baldwin, who first caught Stanley's eye while making a dashing fifty in a ladies' cricket match was a cherished partner but *no natural campaigner*'.[2] But Mrs Baldwin was a natural and a successful campaigner. Her efforts to make pain relief available to all women in childbirth may have been forgotten, but they were driven by a campaigning zeal that transformed public opinion in Britain on this important and controversial issue.

Lady Londonderry, too, has been largely absent from conventional histories of the period and from studies of Ramsay MacDonald. The official biography of *Ramsay MacDonald* (1977) by David Marquand records the intimacy of her relationship with MacDonald but does not attach any real importance to it. 'MacDonald's friendship with Lady Londonderry did great damage to his reputation at the time and, in some quarters at least, it has dogged his memory ever since', writes Marquand, but adds that, 'It is pleasant to record that it brought him at least some happiness, at a time when he got little from anywhere else. And, for that, she deserves the credit.'[3] This is a gallant tribute to Edith, but it does not take her seriously enough. She is mentioned in only eleven of Marquand's 800 pages of text, even though she was MacDonald's closest and most trusted friend when he was Prime Minister. 'In any case', observes Marquand specifically in connection with Lady Londonderry, 'there is no evidence that MacDonald's non-political friendships made any difference to his behaviour'.[4] Marquand is surely mistaken in this implication that the friendship between Lady Londonderry and MacDonald – a famed Tory hostess and the Prime Minister – was 'non-political'. More recently, the socialist historian Austen Morgan has commented in his book, *J. Ramsay MacDonald* (1987), that 'MacDonald's "love" affair with the wife of one of his Conservative ministers was a symptom, rather than a cause, of his political betrayal of the working class'.[5] There has been an oddly persistent refusal to *'chercher la femme'*.

Someone who has taken a different view is Harold Macmillan, who located Edith Londonderry at the very centre of things. As 'Harold the Hummingbird' in the Ark Club and a Conservative politician between the wars, he was no stranger to the world in which Lady Londonderry moved. In his view, she 'became an intimate friend of Ramsay Mac-Donald, and many people believed that she had a great part in his decision to form the National Government of 1931. Whether this be true or exaggerated, she certainly did not need to be given a Parliamentary vote or be allowed to stand for the House of Commons to enhance her persuasive charm.'[6] It was Macmillan's belief that Edith Londonderry 'exercised more political power in the Conservative Party than Lady Astor achieved by her membership in the House of Commons'. In spite of his deep affection for Lady Astor, he said, he was doubtful whether her political power was much enhanced by her parliamentary status. It was rather the case, said Macmillan, that she would be remembered as 'a notable hostess' – as a woman who knew how to make the best possible use of her highly placed connections.[7]

The Duchess of Atholl, elected like Lady Astor as a Conservative Member of Parliament, made strenuous efforts to exercise political power in the House of Commons. More than any of the ladies of influence in this book, she sought to operate within the public world of men on its own terms. In 1929, with the support of Eleanor Rathbone, a fellow woman MP, she forced the attention of Parliament on the horrors of female circumcision. But as the following extract from

Hansard indicates, she had to cope with considerable obstruction from some of her male colleagues:

DUCHESS OF ATHOLL: I submit that the particular point with which I am trying to deal is of such tremendous importance –

MR MAXTON: On a point of Order. While the Deputy-Speaker has given a ruling that this does come within the scope of the Motion, and anything about black men would be within its scope, yet there is in these things a certain perspective, and I put it to –

MISS RATHBONE: Women do not count!

MR MAXTON: Surely that is unfair! [HON. MEMBERS: 'No!'] Well, then, I –

DUCHESS OF ATHOLL: If the House will allow me I will show that this is a very urgent question . . .[8]

Kitty Atholl's campaign probably achieved less for maternal welfare in Kenya than Joan Grigg's more old-fashioned efforts, which relied for their effect on the influence she derived from her husband's status as Governor and her social rank. Kitty appears to have believed that without a parliamentary role, she would have no real influence on national life. It is arguable, though, that she might have been *more* successful at influencing Conservative Party policy on matters of importance – like female circumcision, Spain and appeasement – if she had *not* become an MP but had relied instead on her privileged social status as the wife of a duke.

But in any case, British society changed beyond recognition after the 1939–45 war. The lavish receptions of the social hostess were suddenly over: 'The pattern of the "London Season", of public occasions and private entertaining', wrote John Buchan's son William, 'continued until the first days of September 1939, and then, like a cobweb, was blown clean away.'[9] The Season did in fact start up again soon after the end of the war, but it was never quite the same again. The Labour Party swept to power with its first clear majority in 1945 and this, together with the new economic reality, stripped away many of the privileges enjoyed by upper-class families between the wars. This spelt ruin for the role of the society hostess, which was fundamentally undemocratic. The arts of artistic patronage, too, became a thing of the past. 'The great days of patronage . . . are over', lamented Nancy

Mitford in the 1950s, 'though there are country houses which still shelter some mild literary figure as librarian.'[10]

Meanwhile, the British Empire was being dismantled and the imperial mission pursued by Violet Milner was giving way to the more nebulous framework of the British Commonwealth. The significance of this shift is illustrated by the sharp contrast between the lives of Lord Reading's first wife, Alice, and his second wife Stella, the last lady of influence discussed in this book. Between 1921 and 1925, when Lord Reading was Viceroy of India, Alice Reading lived in Viceregal luxury. 'I was carried in a red and gold sedan chair arrangement', she wrote in a letter home about a visit to Jaipur, where Lord Reading shot his first tiger. 'The rest rode on elephants', added Lady Reading, 'all covered in scarlet and gold. It looked so wonderful – the procession up and up with these huge creatures. My chairmen in every colour of the rainbow.'[11] Like Joan Grigg, Alice Reading used her role as the proconsular wife to promote maternity and baby welfare work for the native population. Despite weak health, she raised funds to set up and improve hospitals and nursing hostels and also instituted the Baby Week Movement in 1924 to draw attention to the needs of mothers and babies. 'Often and often', wrote Lady Reading's secretary, 'people have said to me, "You don't know the good she has done", and they mean not only amongst the European community but amongst Indians of every class.'[12]

In 1947, India obtained independence from Britain. This radically altered the map of the world and relegated to history the roles of Viceroy and Vicereine. For Lord Reading's second and much younger wife, Stella, there was already a different set of opportunities for social action. It is true that she relied on connections based on social status and wealth to create her Women's Voluntary Service in 1938, but she developed it into a massive organization in which women from every kind of social background worked together for the good of the nation. Unlike the voluntary organizations and imperial benevolence of interwar Britain, it was based firmly on the principle of equality and cooperation.

In the era of postwar Britain, people expected to see an end of Want, Disease, Ignorance, Squalor and Idleness, the five Giant Evils identified by Beveridge, which had divided the nation into rich and poor. The creation of the welfare state removed the need for phil-anthropy (theoretically, at least) and Ladies Bountiful were generally seen as redundant. There was no longer a place in British society for the 'unofficial pioneer workers' referred to in *Working-Class Wives*, whose 'wisdom and foresight ... led the way to our Maternity and Child Welfare Service'. These pioneer workers were typically privi-leged women like Lucy Baldwin, who were concerned about the welfare of women in less fortunate circumstances. 'It seems fitting and proper', wrote Janet Campbell, Senior Medical Officer in the Department of Maternal and Child Welfare at the Ministry of Health, that

the voluntary effort of women deeply concerned to bring greater happiness to other women less fortunate than themselves should point [the] gap in our social services, and should contribute many practical suggestions for the remedy of ills which, once recognised, we must all deplore and desire to remove.[13]

But after the war, there was a new way of doing things, in which the state took responsibility for health and welfare provision.

People were less bothered about who your husband was and whether or not you had a title. 'The aristocrats, as they lost their power and turned into ornaments', commented C. P. Snow in 1956, 'shut themselves up.'[14] The Paris exhibition of 1937 had presented British life as a country-house games room with Neville Chamberlain, the Prime Minister, in knickerbockers and fishing hats and surrounded by dogs. But just fifteen years later, at the Festival of Britain in 1951, there were no more country houses and no more country-house life. Rather, there was a massive celebration of science and technology, which were seen to symbolize every hope for the future of the twentieth century.[15] Notwithstanding the ambivalence created by the dropping of atomic bombs on Hiroshima and Nagasaki in 1945, there was immense public faith in the power of science for good. This faith created a world in which social reformers like Joan Grigg and Lucy Baldwin were no longer taken seriously but were regarded as dabbling amateurs. Instead, expert professionals and scientists – C. P. Snow's 'New Men' – became pre-eminent. There were New Women, too (even if Snow showed less interest in them), who were now moving into positions of influence based on merit and qualifications.

In 1938, Virginia Woolf had described the 'daughters of educated men' as being located 'in a moment of transition on the bridge'. They were gazing from a distance at the world of men, she said, 'from the bridge which connects the private house with the world of public life'.[16] Woolf urged her readers to ask themselves whether they *really* wanted to join the 'procession' of men and, if so, on what terms. With a scornful reference to the regalia and costumes of the public world, she asked, 'Who can say whether, as time goes on, we [too] may not dress in military uniform, with gold lace on our breasts, swords at our sides, and something like the old family coal-scuttle on our heads?'[17] This warning had little resonance, though, for the elite women who are the subjects of this book. They were more or less comfortable in the public world on their own terms and were already wearing whatever they liked. Mrs Baldwin wore majestic hats, Lady Londonderry glittered with diamonds ('a diamond necklace, a diamond rivière, and long diamond-drop earrings'),[18] while Lady Grigg cut a slim and dashing figure in her very fetching safari outfits.[19] Nancy Cunard, in a sartorial reference to the discovery of Tutankhamen's tomb in 1923, looked 'very Egyptian, with Nefertiti's long upper lip and slightly pouting mouth, which she paints like a crimson scar across her face'.[20] These women were not trapped on any threshold of domestic life. Enabled by their wealth and social rank, they were citizens of just about everywhere: the private home, the public world and the reaches of the empire.

But after the war, the ladies of the elite lost their special place in British society. It was now their turn to gaze from the sidelines, as Virginia Woolf's daughters of educated men moved swiftly across the bridge between the private house and public life into positions of power and importance. Of course, traditional patterns of female influence have continued to prevail in certain situations and women will always influence men in power. But there has been a significant shift in how things are done. It would no longer be acceptable for Lady Londonderry to hold one of her eve-of-session receptions for a government today. This does not mean, however, that her influence on the social and political landscape of interwar Britain should be overlooked, nor should that of the other ladies in this book. The social hostesses, proconsular wives and patronesses of the period wielded an influence that may have been indirect and not easily visible, but it constituted a very real power. This power had an unmistakable impact on national life.

Notes

Introduction

1. Virginia Woolf: *Three Guineas*, p. 22.
2. Winifred Holtby: *Women and a Changing Civilization*, p. 5.
3. Virginia Woolf: *Three Guineas*, p. 19.
4. The Duchess of Atholl: *Women and Politics*, p. 177.
5. The Countess of Oxford and Asquith: *Off The Record*, p. 126.
6. Virginia Woolf: *Three Guineas*, p. 6.
7. 'Lady Castlereagh's Views', Letter to the Editor, *The Times*, 1 April 1912.
8. Harold Macmillan: *The Past Masters*, p. 209.
9. The Marchioness of Londonderry: *Retrospect*, p. 251.
10. Ellen Wilkinson MP: *Peeps at Politicians*, p. 99.
11. Violet Milner, Editorial in the *National Review*, August 1934.
12. Edith, Marchioness of Londonderry: *Frances Anne. The Life and Times of Frances Anne, Marchioness of Londonderry and her husband Charles, Third Marquess of Londonderry*, p. viii.
13. Alison Macfarlane and Miranda Mugford: *Birth Counts. Statistics of Pregnancy and Childbirth*, p. 271.
14. Bessborough to Manningham-Buller: July 1930, NBTF, F5/1/2.
15. Quoted in Pamela Brookes: *Women at Westminster*, p. 67.
16. *Evening Standard*, 20 November 1928.
17. Report of NBTF fund-raising dinner at the Guildhall on 8 May 1934, NBTF, G7/4(1).
18. *Hansard*, 7 July 1936, col. 1109.
19. 'Colonial Policy – Coloured Races', *Hansard*, 11 December 1929, col. 611.
20. Joan Grigg to Lady Islington: 2 November 1925, Private Collection.
21. Margery Spring Rice: *Working-Class Wives*, pp. 15 and 96.
22. 'Stead's Penny Poets' in *Maternity. Letters from Working-Women*, collected by the Women's Co-operative Guild, p. 47.
23. Ibid. p. 47.
24. *Daily Mail* Centenary CD ROM (Associated Newspapers Holdings Ltd.,

1996); Currency Calculator using data supplied by the Office of National Statistics.

25. Mrs Cork to Margaret Edmonds, 1990s.
26. Joan Grigg to Lady Islington: 5 November 1925, Private Collection.
27. The Marchioness of Londonderry: *Retrospect*, p. 50.
28. E. M. Delafield: *The Diary of a Provincial Lady*, p. 5.
29. Mrs Baldwin: Diary entry, 4 April 1884, Private Collection.
30. Mrs Baldwin: Diary entry, 31 January 1928, Private Collection.

1. 'A GREAT POLITICAL HOSTESS'

Further Reading

Documents and letters

Ramsay MacDonald's letters to Lady Londonderry are held by the Public Record Office of Northern Ireland in Belfast (PRONI, D.3099/3/10). There are over 400 of these letters, from 1924 to 1937. About 90 of her letters to him are held in the MacDonald papers in the Public Record Office at Kew (PRO, PRO 30/69).

Further papers for Edith Londonderry are held in the Londonderry collection in the Durham County Record Office. These include a notebook listing the members of The Ark, with their Ark names.

'Lady Castlereagh's Views', Letter to the Editor, *The Times*, 1 April 1912. In this long letter Lady Londonderry (then Edith Castlereagh) explains her support for women's suffrage. For her articles and speeches on the suffrage issue between 1909 and 1913, see PRONI, D.3099/3/6.

Books by Lady Londonderry and Lord Londonderry

Edith, Marchioness of Londonderry: *Henry Chaplin. A Memoir*, London, Macmillan, 1926. An account of the life of Lady Londonderry's father.
— *Character and Tradition*, London, Macmillan, 1934.
— *Retrospect*, London, Frederick Muller, 1938. This memoir is a source of information on the role of women in the First World War. See pp. 223–8 for a description of MacDonald and their friendship.
— *Mount Stewart*, privately printed, 1956.
— *Frances Anne. The Life and Times of Frances Anne, Marchioness of Londonderry and her husband Charles, Third Marquess of Londonderry*, London, Macmillan, 1958.
Charles, Marquess of Londonderry, *Ourselves and Germany*, London, Robert

Hale, 1938; Penguin Books, 1938. This book advocates *détente* with Germany and was serialized in the *Evening Standard*.
— *Wings of Destiny*, London, Macmillan, 1943. Lord Londonderry's memoir.

Biographies and useful books

Anne de Courcy, *Circe. The Life of Edith, Marchioness of Londonderry*, London, Sinclair-Stevenson, 1992. The only book-length biography of Lady Londonderry.

H. Montgomery Hyde, *The Londonderrys. A Family Portrait*, London, Hamish Hamilton, 1979. The official biography of the Londonderry family from the time of the eighteenth century.

David Marquand, *Ramsay MacDonald*, London, Jonathan Cape, 1977. The official biography of MacDonald.

Philip Williamson, *National Crisis and National Government. British Politics, the Economy and Empire 1926–1932*, Cambridge University Press, 1992.

1. The Marchioness of Londonderry: *Retrospect*, pp. 11–12 and 255.
2. Ibid., p. 255.
3. 'Receptions. Londonderry House,' *The Times*, 7 February 1928.
4. Lucy Baldwin to Louisa Baldwin: 12 February 1924, Private Collection.
5. 'London Fashions. At Londonderry House', *The Times*, 8 February 1928.
6. William Buchan: *John Buchan. A Memoir*, p. 191.
7. Patrick Donner: *Crusade*, p. 105.
8. 'Dowager Lady Londonderry. A Great Political Hostess', *The Times*, 24 April 1959.
9. The Marchioness of Londonderry: *Retrospect*, p. 40.
10. The Marchioness of Londonderry: *Retrospect*, p. 46.
11. R. Blake: *The Unknown Prime Minister*, p. 88.
12. William Buchan: *John Buchan. A Memoir*, p. 191.
13. Viscount Castlereagh: Memorandum on a discussion in [February or March] 1936, written in August 1936, Private Collection.
14. 'Episodes of the Month', *National Review*, September 1930, pp. 575–6.
15. 'If Gossip we must,' *Bystander*, 4 November 1931.
16. The Marchioness of Londonderry: *Retrospect*, p. 253.
17. Virginia Woolf to Ethel Sands: 24 April 1929, in Nigel Nicolson (ed.): *A Reflection of the Other Person. The Letters of Virginia Woolf*, Vol. IV, p. 45.
18. Harold Acton: *More Memoirs of an Aesthete*, p. 35.

19. Daphne Fielding: *Emerald and Nancy*, p. 102.

20. The Marchioness of Londonderry: *Retrospect*, pp. 236–8.

21. William Buchan: *John Buchan. A Memoir*, p. 192.

22. The Marchioness of Londonderry: *Retrospect*, p. 223.

23. Anne de Courcy: *Circe*, p. 190.

24. Margaret Cole (ed.): *Beatrice Webb's Diaries 1924–1932*, entry for 5 September 1930.

25. Quoted in H. Montgomery Hyde: *Baldwin*, p. 237.

26. Quoted in Anne de Courcy: *Circe*, p. 300.

27. Quoted in Anne de Courcy: *Circe*, p. 73. De Courcy gives a full account in *Circe* of Charley's philandering and Edith's attempts to cope with it.

28. Ibid., p. 247.

29. Quoted in H. Montgomery Hyde: *Baldwin*, p. 203.

30. The Marchioness of Londonderry: *Retrospect*, p. 225.

31. Quoted in Anne de Courcy: *Circe*, p. 237.

32. Lucy Baldwin: Diary entry, 16 October 1935, Private Collection.

33. Lady Londonderry to MacDonald: 8 August 1933, PRO, PRO 30/69/755.

34. The Marchioness of Londonderry: *Retrospect*, pp. 223–4.

35. Lady Londonderry to Ramsay MacDonald: [1932], PRO, PRO 30/69/754.

36. Ramsay MacDonald to Lady Londonderry: 9 October 1932, PRONI, D.3009/3/10/215; emphasis added.

37. Quoted in H. Montgomery Hyde: *The Londonderrys*, p. 241.

38. Quoted in William Buchan: *John Buchan. A Memoir*, p. 192.

39. Viscount Castlereagh: Memorandum on a discussion in [February or March] 1936, written in August 1936, Private Collection.

40. Margaret Cole (ed.): *Beatrice Webb's Diaries 1924–1932*, entry for 14 February 1928.

41. Quoted in William Buchan: *John Buchan. A Memoir*, p. 192.

42. B. Seebohm Rowntree: *The Human Needs of Labour*, pp. 9–10.

43. Katherine Dayus: *Where There's Life*, p. 188.

44. Notes made on 26 May 1993 by Mrs D—B—, Derby, for the author.

45. Lady Londonderry to MacDonald: 2 May 1931, PRO, PRO 30/69/753.

46. Ramsay MacDonald: Diary entry for 9 November 1930, quoted in David Marquand: *Ramsay MacDonald*, p. 577.

47. Notes made on 26 May 1993 by Mrs D—B—, Derby, for the author.

48. MacDonald to Lady Londonderry: 10 August 1931, quoted in the Public Record Office of Northern Ireland, *Guide to Sources for Women's History*, pp. 27–8.

49. C. R. Attlee: *The Labour Party in Perspective*, p. 9.

50. H. Montgomery Hyde: *The Londonderrys*, p. 192.

51. Quoted in H. Montgomery Hyde: *Baldwin*, p. 192.

52. Ramsay MacDonald to Lady Londonderry: 27 December 1931, quoted in David Marquand: *Ramsay MacDonald*, p. 690.

53. Quoted in Anne de Courcy: *Circe*, p. 217.

54. MacDonald to Lady Londonderry: October 1931, quoted in the Public Record Office of Northern Ireland: *Guide to Sources for Women's History*, p. 28.

55. Virginia Woolf: *Three Guineas*, p. 18.

56. In Nigel Nicolson (ed.): *A Reflection of the Other Person. The Letters of Virginia Woolf*, Vol. IV, pp. 132 and 133, Virginia Woolf to Sybil Colefax, 3[?] February 1930.

57. Ibid., Virginia Woolf to Ethel Smyth, [19 June 1931].

58. Ibid., Virginia Woolf to Clive Bell, 6 February 1930.

59. Austen Morgan: *J. Ramsay MacDonald*, p. 9.

60. Quoted in H. Montgomery Hyde: *The Londonderrys*, pp. 193–4.

61. The Countess of Oxford and Asquith: *Off The Record*, p. 68.

62. 'Eve of the Session. Reception at Londonderry House', *The Times*, 2 February 1932.

63. Lady Londonderry to MacDonald: 31 [April] 1932, PRO, PRO 30/69/754.

64. Lady Londonderry to MacDonald: 21 June [1932], PRO, PRO 30/69/754.

65. Lady Londonderry to Ramsay MacDonald: 9 July 1932, quoted in David Marquand: *Ramsay MacDonald*, p. 689.

66. Ramsay MacDonald to Lady Londonderry: 27 March 1932, quoted in David Marquand: *Ramsay MacDonald*, pp. 690–91.

67. Ramsay MacDonald to Lady Londonderry: 21 May 1932, quoted in David Marquand: *Ramsay MacDonald*, p. 691.

68. Thomas Jones: *A Diary with Letters, 1931–1950*, p. 100.

69. Quoted in Anne de Courcy: *Circe*, p. 248.

70. Anne de Courcy: *Circe*, p. 229.

71. See 'The Master of the Commons', in Michael and Eleanor Brock (eds.): Part I, *H. H. Asquith. Letters to Venetia Stanley*, p. 3.

72. Asquith to Venetia Stanley, in Michael and Eleanor Brock (eds.): Part I, *H. H. Asquith. Letters to Venetia Stanley*, letter 96.

73. The Countess of Oxford and Asquith: *Off The Record*, p. 122.

74. Beatrice Webb to Friends of Seaham, quoted in Anne de Courcy: *Circe*, p. 218.

75. Ibid., p. 218.

76. Anne de Courcy: *Circe*, p. 228.

77. Harold Laski, 'Ramsay MacDonald: a portrait', *Harper's Magazine*, 21 September 1932.

78. Philip, Viscount Snowden: *An Autobiography. Volume Two 1919–1934*, p. 957.

79. Quoted in Keith Middlemas and John Barnes: *Baldwin. A Biography*, p. 806.

80. Lord Londonderry to Clementine Churchill: 1 January 1942; Clementine Churchill to Lord Londonderry: 5 January 1942, PRO, PREM 4/6, 12.

81. Lady Londonderry to Ramsay MacDonald: 29 August 1932, PRO, PRO 30/69/1442.

82. Thomas Jones: *A Diary with Letters, 1931–1950*, p. 100.

83. The popularity of the National Government is established on the basis of Gallup polls of voting intention in 1939 and 1940 by W. D. Rubinstein in 'Britain's Elites in the Interwar Period, 1918–1939' in Alan Kidd and David Nicholls (eds.): *The Making of the Middle Class*, p. 200.

84. Quoted in H. Montgomery Hyde: *The Londonderrys*, p. 236.

85. Londonderry to MacDonald: 13 November 1936, PRO, PRO 30/69/683.

86. Quoted in H. Montgomery Hyde: *Baldwin. The Unexpected Prime Minister*, p. 542.

87. Harold Nicolson: Diary entry for 20 February 1936 in Nigel Nicolson (ed.): *Harold Nicolson. Diaries and Letters 1930–1939*, p. 245.

88. Viscount Castlereagh: Memorandum on a discussion in [February or March] 1936, written in August 1936, Private Collection.

89. As noted by David Marquand in *Ramsay MacDonald*, p. 783.

90. Quoted in Anne de Courcy: *Circe*, p. 281.

91. The Marchioness of Londonderry: *Retrospect*, p. 224.

92. Londonderry House to Riddick: 18 January 1955, NBTF, G28.

2. 'DAILY, HOURLY . . . ''OVER THE TOP'''

Further Reading

Documents and letters

Lady Baldwin's papers are held privately. They include her correspondence and a series of leather-backed miniature diaries, with her pet name 'Cissie' inscribed on their covers. The series runs from 1894 to 1945 and is complete, apart from 1901; there is an additional and large diary for 1888.

An extensive correspondence to and from Lady Baldwin on issues of maternal welfare is contained in the archive collection of the National Birthday Trust Fund (NBTF). Section H of the archive is exclusively about the campaign for obstetric anaesthesia. This set of papers is held by the Contemporary Medical Archives Centre (CMAC) at the Wellcome Institute for the History of Medicine in London.

The Public Record Office at Kew in London holds several files related to the Thorneycroft Bill: PRO, MH 134/141, 144, 145.

Biographies

No biography of Lady Baldwin has yet been written, but key biographies of her husband Stanley are:

Keith Middlemas and John Barnes: *Baldwin. A Biography*, London, Weidenfeld & Nicolson, 1969.

Philip Williamson: *Stanley Baldwin. Conservative Leadership and National Values*, Cambridge University Press, 1999.

A. Susan Williams: *Women and Childbirth in the Twentieth Century*, Stroud, Sutton Publishing Ltd., 1997. This is a 'biography' of the National Birthday Trust Fund from its foundation in 1928 until its merger with WellBeing in 1993.

Related novels

Vera Brittain: *Honourable Estate*, London, Victor Gollancz, 1936. A major theme of this novel is the physical pain of childbirth.

— *Testament of Experience*, London, Victor Gollancz, 1957.

On pain relief in labour

British College of Obstetricians and Gynaecologists: *Investigation into the Use of Analgesics Suitable for Administration by Midwives*, 1936. This is an account of the results of a survey funded by the NBTF and is held in the archives of the Royal College of Obstetricians and Gynaecologists in London.

'Chloroform Capsules during Labour', *British Medical Journal*, 29 October 1933.

'Obstetric Analgesia', *British Medical Journal*, 22 April 1939.

Ellen P. O'Sullivan, 'Dr Robert James Minnitt 1889–1974: A Pioneer of Inhalational Analgesia', *Journal of the Royal Society of Medicine*, 82, April 1989.

A. Susan Williams, 'Pain relief for childbirth in 1930s Britain', in *The History of Anaesthesia. The Fourth International Symposium on the History of Anaesthesia*, edited by Jochen Schulte am Esch and Michael Goerig, Lübeck, DragerDruck, 1998, pp. 483–92.

1. Keith Middlemas and John Barnes: *Baldwin. A Biography*, p. 28.

2. Betty Cowell and David Wainwright: *Behind the Blue Door. The History of the Royal College of Midwives 1891–1991*, p. 58.

3. Lucy Baldwin: Diary entry, frontispiece, 31 December 1928, Private Collection.

4. Keith Middlemas and John Barnes: *Baldwin. A Biography*, p. 36.

5. 'Draft of Mrs Baldwin's Speech at the Mansion House', 11 December 1929, NBTF, G1/2(2).

6. Lucy Baldwin: Diary entry, 25 January 1894, Private Collection.

7. Lucy Baldwin: Diary entry, 25 January 1896, Private Collection.

8. Gertrude Tuckwell to Lady Rhys Williams: 6 December 1934, NBTF, R8/1/1(5).

9. 'Draft of Mrs Baldwin's Speech at the Mansion House', 11 December 1929, NBTF, G1/2(2).

10. 'Safer Motherhood' [1939], NBTF, G4/1.

11. Virginia Woolf: *Three Guineas*, p. 79.

12. The Book of Genesis 2:21.

13. Report of London County Council Central Public Health Committee, October 1933, NBTF, H1/5.

14. 'Draft of Mrs Baldwin's Speech at the Mansion House', 11 December 1929, NBTF, G1/2(2).

15. Cutting from *The Times*, 1939, in NBTF, P15 (emphasis added).

16. Oatley to NBTF: 19 January 1938, NBTF, H3/2/1.

17. 'Obstetric Analgesia', *British Medical Journal*, 22 April 1939.

18. Lucy Baldwin: Diary entry, 10 July 1896, Private Collection.

19. Lucy Baldwin: Diary entry, 4 March 1899, Private Collection.

20. Lucy Baldwin: Diary entry, 12 March 1899, Private Collection.

21. Lucy Baldwin: Diary entry, 20 March 1904, Private Collection.

22. Lucy Baldwin: Diary entry, 21 March 1904, Private Collection.

23. Lucy Baldwin: Diary entry, 22 March 1904, Private Collection.

24. Transcript of Mrs Baldwin's Wireless Appeal, 24 February 1935, NBTF, G7/5 [emphasis added].

25. Thomas Jones: *A Diary with Letters 1931–1950*, pp. 515–16.

26. Reported in *The Times*, 22 March 1929.

27. Manningham-Buller to J. M. Jackson: 13 March 1929, NBTF, F3/2/1.

28. Lady George Cholmondeley to Lady Londonderry: 14 March 1929, NBTF, F11/1(9).

29. Lady George Cholmondeley to Lady Londonderry: 18 March 1929, NBTF, F11/1(9).

30. Transcript of Mrs Baldwin's Wireless Speech, given 28 April 1929, with pencil annotations showing 'As Spoken', NBTF, F3/2/1 (emphasis added).

31. Transcript of Mrs Baldwin's Wireless Appeal, 24 February 1935, NBTF, G7/5.

32. Viscount Castlereagh: Memorandum [February or March] 1936, written in August 1936, Private Collection.

33. Duff Cooper: *Old Men Forget*, p. 177.

34. *Daily Express*, 13 December 1928.

35. Jacques Gélis: *History of Childbirth*, p. 152.

36. Letters received in response to an appeal in the press, 1930, NBTF, F3/2/2(1).

37. From 'A Mother in Stockton-on-Tees', 17 June 1931, NBTF, F3/2/2(1).

38. See samples of stamps and flags in file NBTF, G6/4.

39. Goodhart to Baldwin: 12 November [1936], NBTF, H3/2/1.

40. 'A Small Giver' to Lucy Baldwin: n.d., NBTF, F3/2/2(1).

41. Mrs C— L— to Lucy Baldwin: 5 March 1935, NBTF, F3/2/3(2).

42. Robert McDougall to Lady Londonderry: 24 November 1936, NBTF, D4/1.

43. Meeting of NBTF Finance Committee, 21 April 1936, NBTF, A2/1. The comparison in value is based on information provided by the Office of National Statistics and allows for inflation.

44. Samples of Brisettes and Zombs are held in NBTF, H1/7.

45. Ross to NBTF: 9 October 1933, NBTF, F/6/6.

46. Completed forms on the effectiveness of the capsules are in NBTF, H1/6(10).

47. Elder to NBTF: 21 June 1933, NBTF, H1/1.

48. Mentioned in NBTF to Matron, 4 November 1932, NBTF, H1/1.

49. Ellen P. O'Sullivan, 'Dr Robert James Minnitt 1889–1974: A Pioneer of Inhalational Analgesia', *Journal of the Royal Society of Medicine* 82, April 1989, p. 221.

50. Greasley Nursing Association to NBTF: 7 July 1938, NBTF, H3/3(2).

51. Shearing to Baldwin: 3 February 1937, NBTF, H3/2/1.

52. McVicker to Baldwin: 15 November 1938, NBTF, H3/2/1.

53. Jones to Williams: 8 March 1937, NBTF, H3/2/1.

54. NBTF: 'Report on Gas/Air Analgesia' [1948], NBTF, H2/5.

55. Diana Palmer: 'Women, Health and Politics, 1919–1939: Professional and Lay Involvement in the Women's Health Campaign', PhD thesis, p. 268.

56. Oatley to 'Lucy Baldwin's Birthday Trust Fund': 19 January 1938, NBTF, H3/2/1.

57. Report of London County Council Central Public Health Committee, October 1933, NBTF, H1/5.

58. Vera Brittain: *Testament of Experience*, p. 52 [emphasis added].

59. *The Times*, 18 March 1931.

60. *The Times*, 19 March 1931.

61. Hardy to the Minister of Health: 4 July 1938, PRO, MH 55/625.

62. H. Crichton-Miller: 'Preserving the Race in Post-War Reconstruction', *British Medical Journal*, 7 March 1942, p. 337.

63. Bennett to Rhys Williams: 22 March 1945, NBTF, H2/2(1).

64. Keith Middlemas and John Barnes: *Baldwin. A Biography*, p. 29.

65. Kenneth Young: *Stanley Baldwin*, p. 10.

66. Lucy Baldwin to Louisa Baldwin: 10 March 1923, Private Collection.

67. Lucy Baldwin to Louisa Baldwin: 27 October 1923, Private Collection.

68. Lucy Baldwin: Diary entry, 31 May 1929, Private Collection.

69. A. W. Baldwin: *My Father, The True Story*, p. 116 [emphasis added].

70. Lucy Baldwin: Diary entry, 10 March 1923, Private Collection.

71. Lucy Baldwin to her daughter Margot: 7 November 1930, Private Collection.

72. Lucy Baldwin to Louisa Baldwin: 9 February 1923, Private Collection.

73. Lucy Baldwin to Louisa Baldwin: 10 March 1923, Private Collection.

74. Lucy Baldwin: Diary entry, 2 December 1928, Private Collection.

75. Lucy Baldwin: Diary entry, 31 January 1928, Private Collection.

76. Lucy Baldwin: Diary entry, 12 July 1929, Private Collection.

77. Lucy Baldwin to Louisa Baldwin: 15 December 1924, Private Collection.

78. Lucy Baldwin to Louisa Baldwin: 19 February 1923, Private Collection.

79. Lucy Baldwin: Diary entry, 11 February 1935, Private Collection.

80. Nigel Nicolson (ed.): *Harold Nicolson, Diaries and Letters 1930–1939*, p. 32.

81. Ibid., pp. 220–21.

82. Ibid., p. 373.

83. Mary Soames: *Clementine Churchill*, p. 51.

84. Quoted in Mary Soames: *Clementine Churchill*, p. 249.

85. Violet Bonham Carter: *Winston Churchill as I Knew Him*, p. 384.

86. Derby to N. Chamberlain: 25 February 1931, quoted in H. Montgomery Hyde: *Baldwin*, p. 318 [emphasis added].

87. L. S. Amery: *My Political Life. Volume Two: War and Peace 1914–1929*, p. 296.

88. 'Medical Notes in Parliament', *British Medical Journal*, 5 August 1939.

89. Camp to NBTF: 10 August 1939, NBTF, H3/1/1.

90. Frank Honigsbaum: *The Division in British Medicine*, pp. 158–9.

91. 'The Midwife as Anaesthetist', *Lancet*, 29 July 1939.

92. Frank Honigsbaum: *The Division in British Medicine*, p. 159.

93. Joint Committee of the Royal College of Obstetricians and Gynaecologists and Population Investigation Committee: *Maternity in Great Britain*, p. 78.

94. Virginia Woolf: *Three Guineas*, note 19, pp. 183–4.

95. Joint Committee of the Royal College of Obstetricians and Gynaecologists and Population Investigation Committee: *Maternity in Great Britain*, pp. 82–3.

96. Joint Committee of the Royal College of Obstetricians and Gynaecologists and Population Investigation Committee: *Maternity in Great Britain*, p. 86.

97. Women's Co-operative Guild: Annual Report for 1946, p. 46.

98. Ibid.: Annual Report for 1947, p. 49.

99. Joint Committee of the Royal College of Obstetricians and Gynaecologists and Population Investigation Committee: *Maternity in Great Britain*, p. 80.

100. Mass Observation: *Britain and her Birth-Rate*, p. 113.

101. Letter to *The Lady*, 21 May 1942.

102. *Hansard*, 15 March 1949.

103. *Sketch*, 14 September 1949.

104. See the letters in the following files: PRO MH 134/141, 144, 145.

105. *Hansard*, 4 March 1949.

106. *Hansard*, 4 March 1949.

107. For example, Watson at the Ministry to Swindale: 7 April 1949; the substance of this letter was replicated many times, PRO, MH 134/145.

108. 'Analgesia births more than doubled, progress under National Health Service', 221/12/49, no. 8, PRO, MH 134/141.

109. *Hansard*, 1 July 1949, 8 July 1949.

110. Hall to Bevan: 11 March 1949, PRO MH 134/144.

111. Lawrence to Bevan: 8 March 1949, PRO, MH 134/145.

3. 'A BRITISH RACE PATRIOT'

Further Reading

Documents and letters

Violet Milner's papers are held by the Bodleian Library, Oxford University. Her diaries running from 1926 to 1958 are held in VM 4–7.

A copy of ' "Credo". Lord Milner's Faith' is held in VM 13.

Some useful books

Lord Edward Cecil: *The Leisure of an Egyptian Official*, London, Hodder and Stoughton, 1921.

Rudyard Kipling: *Stalky & Co.*, 1899; London, Macmillan, 1924.

The Viscountess Milner: *My Picture Gallery 1886–1901*, London, John Murray, 1951. This is a memoir of her life as a girl and young woman and of the people she knew in Victorian days.

Biographies

No biography of Lady Milner has been written, but the following biographies of the men in her life contain some useful information:

Kenneth Rose: *The Later Cecils*, London, Weidenfeld & Nicolson, 1975.

A. G. Gollin: *Proconsul in Politics. A Study of Lord Milner in Opposition and in Power*, London, Anthony Blond, 1964.

John A. Hutcheson: *Leopold Maxse and the* National Review, *1893–1914. Right-Wing Politics and Journalism in the Edwardian Era*, New York and London, Garland Publishing Inc., 1989.

1. 'Viscountess Milner. Brilliant Talker and Hostess', *The Times*, 11 October 1958.
2. '"Credo". Lord Milner's Faith', *The Times*, 27 July 1925.
3. Rudyard Kipling: *Stalky & Co.*, pp. 210–16.
4. The Duchess of Atholl: *Women and Politics*, p. 2.
5. Stanley Baldwin: *On England*, p. 214.
6. 'Countess Baldwin is Dead in England', *The New York Times*, 19 June 1945.
7. *National Review*, March 1932, No. 589, pp. 309ff.
8. Patrick Donner: *Crusade*, pp. 108–9.
9. 'Viscountess Milner', *The Times*, 15 October 1958.
10. Violet Milner: Diary entry, 12 May 1926, VM 4–7.
11. Violet Milner: Diary entry, 3 May 1926, VM 4–7.
12. Violet Milner: Diary entry, 4 May 1926, VM 4–7.
13. Violet Milner: Diary entry, 15 May 1926, VM 4–7.
14. Obituary in *The Times*, 11 October 1958.
15. David Cecil: *The Cecils of Hatfield House*, p. 14.
16. Quoted in Kenneth Rose: *The Later Cecils*, p. 192.
17. Quoted in Kenneth Rose: *The Later Cecils*, p. 193.
18. Quoted in Kenneth Rose: *The Later Cecils*, p. 195.

19. Lord Edward Cecil to Lady Edward Cecil: 6 July 1900, VM 62/C705/272.

20. Lady Edward Cecil to Lord Edward Cecil: 23 November 1914, VM 62/C705/272.

21. Louise Dawkins to Lady Edward Cecil: 19 October 1899, VM 39/C259/1.

22. Lord Milner to Lady Edward Cecil: 5 August 1917, VM 30/C110/61.

23. William Buchan: *John Buchan. A Memoir*, p. 104.

24. Quoted in Kenneth Rose: *The Later Cecils*, p. 218.

25. Lord Edward Cecil: *The Leisure of an Egyptian Official*, pp. 11–15.

26. Robert Graves and Alan Hodge: *The Long Week-End*, pp. 125–6.

27. Lord Edward Cecil: *The Leisure of an Egyptian Official*, pp. iii–v.

28. Viscount Milner: *England in Egypt*, pp. 5 and 376–8.

29. Ibid., pp. 376–8.

30. Lord Milner to Lady Edward Cecil: 9 August 1920, VM 30/C110/124.

31. Lord Milner to Lady Edward Cecil: 7 August 1920, VM 30/C110/123.

32. Lord Milner to Lady Edward Cecil: 23 January 1920, VM 30/C 110/117.

33. John Evelyn Wrench: *Geoffrey Dawson And Our Times*, p. 210.

34. Lord Milner to Lady Milner: 27 October 1921, VM 30/C110/156.

35. Lord Milner to Lady Milner: 30 October 1921, VM 30/C110/156.

36. Violet Milner: Diary entry, 11 January 1926, VM 4–7.

37. Violet Milner: Diary entry, 13 February 1926, VM 4–7.

38. Violet Milner: Diary entry, 21 April 1926, VM 4–7.

39. John Barnes and David Nicholson (eds): *The Leo Amery Diaries, Vol. 1*, entry for 14 May 1925.

40. Ibid., entry for 16 May 1925.

41. J. A. Spender: *Life of Sir Henry Campbell-Bannerman*. Vol. 1, p. 264.

42. A. G. Gollin: *Proconsul in Politics. A Study of Lord Milner in Opposition and in Power*, p. 606.

43. Violet Milner: Diary entry, 19 March 1932, VM 4–7.

44. 'The Junior King's School', *Kentish Observer*, 19 July 1928. The author is grateful to Mrs Margaret Edmonds for sending her a copy of this article.

45. Violet Milner: Diary entry, 8 December 1926, VM 4–7.

46. Violet Milner: Diary entry, 21 April 1926, VM 4–7.

47. *The Nation*, 15 February 1913.

48. Donald Read: *Edwardian England*, p. 61.

49. John A. Hutcheson, *Leopold Maxse and the* National Review, *1893–1914. Right-Wing Politics and Journalism in the Edwardian Era*, p. xiii.

50. Nicholas Hiley, 'You Can't Believe a Word You Read': Newspaper reading in the British Expeditionary Force, 1914–1918', *Studies in Newspaper and Periodical History. 1994 Annual*, p. 91.

51. *National Review*, September 1930, pp. 573–4.

52. Violet Milner: Diary entry, 4 February 1930, VM 4–7.

53. Violet Milner: Diary entry, 21 January 1932, VM 4–7.

54. The Countess of Oxford and Asquith: *Off The Record*, pp. 26–7.

55. Violet Milner: Diary entry, 11 February 1932, VM 4–7.

56. Violet Milner: Diary entry, 11 February 1932, VM 4–7.

57. Violet Milner: Diary entry, 19 February 1932, VM 4–7.

58. Violet Milner: Diary entry, 15 March 1932, VM 4–7.

59. Violet Milner: Diary entry, 26 March 1933, VM 4–7.

60. Patrick Donner: *Crusade*, p. 110.

61. Violet Milner: Diary entry, 5 February 1932, VM 4–7.

62. Violet Milner: Diary entry, 17 February 1933, VM 4–7.

63. *National Review*, July–December 1933.

64. John Barnes and David Nicholson (eds.): *The Leo Amery Diaries, Vol. 1*, pp. 56–7.

65. Patrick Donner: *Crusade*, p. 111.

66. George Ambrose to Lady Milner: 19 January 1931, VM 45/C420/2.

67. 'Episodes of the Month', *National Review*, August 1939, p. 164.

68. *National Review*, March 1933, p. 343.

69. 'Germany Tells the World', *National Review*, October 1938, p. 457.

70. Brigadier General John Hartman Morgan to Lady Milner: 13 March 1936, VM 47/480/3.

71. 'Episodes of the Month', *National Review*, January 1939.

72. 'Episodes of the Month', *National Review*, August 1934.

73. 'Episodes of the Month', *National Review*, August 1939, p. 163.

74. Violet Milner: Diary entry, 3 September 1939, VM 4–7.

75. Murrow made this comment to John Grigg in 1962, when he was Head of the United States Information Agency in the John F. Kennedy administration. John Grigg to the author: 9 September 1999.

76. Iverach McDonald to Lady Milner: 29 November 1949, VM 45/C441/16.

77. The Viscountess Milner: *My Picture Gallery 1886–1901*, p. ix.

78. ' "Credo". Lord Milner's Faith', *The Times*, 27 July 1925.

4. 'TO THE WOMANHOOD OF DARK AFRICA'

Further Reading

Documents and letters
Lady Grigg's papers are held privately. They include letters, personal notes and a number of annual reports for the Lady Grigg Welfare League. There

are a few documents relating to the Lady Grigg Welfare League in the Cabinet Office files at the Public Record Office.

The papers of Sir Edward Grigg relating to his governorship of Kenya are held by Rhodes House Library at Oxford University. His general papers are available on microfilm at the Bodleian Library at Oxford, in Nairobi at the University of Kenya, and at the Universities of Harvard, Duke and Kingston, Ontario.

Books relating to Kenya between the wars

Lord Altrincham (Sir Edward Grigg), *Kenya's Opportunity. Memoirs, Hopes and Ideas.* London: Faber & Faber, 1955. Sir Edward reflects in this book on his time as governor of Kenya and on the future of East Africa.

Karen Blixen, *Out of Africa*, 1937. Karen Blixen, who also wrote under the name of Isak Dinesen, was a friend of Joan Grigg.

John A. Carman, *A Medical History of the Colony and Protectorate of Kenya.* London: Rex Collins, 1976. A personal memoir by a doctor who went to Kenya in 1926 to work as a Medical Officer.

James Fox, *White Mischief.* London: Jonathan Cape, 1982. This background to the murder of Lord Erroll in 1941 gives a flavour of the 'Happy Valley' set, but is misleading about the settler community as a whole.

Norman Leys, *A Last Chance in Kenya.* London: The Hogarth Press, 1931. The publication of this critical account of the conditions of the African population in Kenya caused a stir in Britain.

On diplomatic wives

Katie Hickman, *Daughters of Britannia.* London: HarperCollins, 1999. This book looks at the lives and experiences of nearly fifty (touching on a further fifty) wives of British diplomats abroad, from the mid seventeenth century to the end of the twentieth century. Five of the book's principal women, including Vita Sackville-West, belong to the interwar period.

1. John Grigg to the author: 27 November 1999.
2. *Dictionary of National Biography*, entry for Grigg, William Edward Macleay, p. 440.
3. Lady Grigg to Lady Islington: 5 October 1925, Private Collection.
4. Lady Grigg to Lord and Lady Islington: November 1925, Private Collection.
5. Lady Grigg to Lord and Lady Islington: 8 December 1925, Private Collection.
6. Lady Grigg to Lady Islington: 8 October 1925, Private Collection.

7. Ann Beck: *Medicine, Tradition and Development in Kenya and Tanzania, 1920–1970*, pp. 15–17.

8. John A. Carman: *A Medical History of the Colony and Protectorate of Kenya*, London, Rex Collins, 1976, pp. 16ff.

9. Lady Grigg to Lady Islington: 27 November 1925, Private Collection.

10. L. S. Amery to Prime Minister, 24 September 1923, quoted in Dennis Dean: 'The Contrasting Attitudes of the Conservative and Labour Parties to Problems of Empire 1922–1936', PhD thesis, pp. 281–2.

11. Norman Leys: *A Last Chance in Kenya*, p. 15.

12. 'Farewell Speech in Nairobi', 23 September 1930, Appendix J in Lord Altrincham: *Kenya's Opportunity*, pp. 292–9.

13. John Grigg to the author: 21 November 1999.

14. Lady Grigg to Lord and Lady Islington: November 1925 (emphasis added), Private Collection.

15. Lady Grigg to Lord and Lady Islington: 8 December 1925 (emphasis added), Private Collection.

16. Lord Altrincham: *Kenya's Opportunity*, p. 82.

17. Ibid., pp. 73–6.

18. Ibid., pp. 73–4.

19. James Fox: *White Mischief*, p. 31.

20. See Katie Hickman: *Daughters of Britannia*.

21. Vera Brittain: *Testament of Youth*, p. 423.

22. John Grigg to the author: 27 November 1999.

23. Lady Grigg to Lord and Lady Islington: n.d., Private Collection.

24. Lady Grigg: personal note for 6 October 1925, Private Collection.

25. Lady Grigg to Lady Islington: 8 October 1925, Private Collection.

26. Lady Grigg: personal note for 30 October 1925, Private Collection.

27. Lady Grigg: personal note for 2 November 1925, Private Collection.

28. Lady Grigg: personal note for 7 December 1925, Private Collection.

29. Lady Grigg to Lady Islington: 5 February 1926, Private Collection.

30. Sarah Tooley: *The History of Nursing in the British Empire*, pp. 338–69.

31. Lord Altrincham: *Kenya's Opportunity*, p. 99.

32. Lady Grigg to Lady Islington: 5 October 1925, Private Collection.

33. Lady Grigg to *The Times*: 13 April 1927.

34. Currency Calculator using data supplied by the Office of National Statistics.

35. Lady Grigg to *The Times*: 11 June 1927.

36. A College Member, 'Midwifery in East Africa', *The Nursing Times*, 14 July 1934.

37. G. V. Anderson, 'Problems of Native Maternity Work, with a Review of Two Hundred Cases', *Kenya and East African Medical Journal*, Vol. VI, 1929–30, pp. 63–4.

38. Lord Altrincham: *Kenya's Opportunity*, p. 101.

39. Frans Lasson (ed.), translated by Anne Born: *Isak Dinesen. Letters from Africa 1914–1931*, p. 268.

40. Currency Calculator using data supplied by the Office of National Statistics.

41. Frans Lasson (ed.), translated by Anne Born: *Isak Dinesen. Letters from Africa 1914–1931*, p. 273.

42. John A. Carman: *A Medical History of the Colony and Protectorate of Kenya*, p. 22.

43. Annual Reports of the Lady Grigg Welfare League: the African Section, 1929, Indian Section, 1929, and European Branch, 1932, Private Collection.

44. Annual Report, African Section, 1930–31, NBTF, F6/6.

45. Lady Grigg to Lady Islington: November 1925, Private Collection.

46. Lady Grigg: personal note for 15 May 1926, Private Collection.

47. Lady Grigg: personal note for 10 September 1927, Private Collection.

48. 'Written Answers: East Africa. Dispensaries and Maternity Centres', statement by Dr Shiels, *Hansard*, 16 December 1929, col. 1002.

49. G. V. Anderson, 'Problems of Native Maternity Work, with a Review of Two Hundred Cases', *Kenya and East African Medical Journal*, Vol. VI, 1929–30, pp. 62–73.

50. Lady Grigg Welfare League, African Section, Annual Report 1929, Private Collection.

51. G. V. Anderson, 'Problems of Native Maternity Work, with a Review of Two Hundred Cases', *Kenya and East African Medical Journal*, Vol. VI, 1929–30, pp. 62–73. The Kikuyu people, who were 20 per cent of the population, practised circumcision, while the Luo, about 15 per cent of the population, did not practise either male or female circumcision.

52. Material collected for essay on female circumcision by C. G. Richards, 1923–1930, mss Afr.S633, file 3, Coryndon Papers, Rhodes House Library, Oxford University.

53. 'Written Answers: Kenya. Pre-Marriage Rite', statement by Dr Shiels, *Hansard*, 23 December 1929, col. 1948.

54. Lord Altrincham: *Kenya's Opportunity*, p. 98.

55. Ibid., p. 98.

56. Jomo Kenyatta: *Facing Mount Kenya*, pp. 130–31.

57. Secretary of State for the Colonies to the Duchess of Atholl, 1 January 1931, PRO, CO 533/394, 11.

58. Lady Grigg Welfare League, African Section, Annual Report 1929, Private Collection. African Section, Annual Report 1930–31, NBTF, F6/6.

59. Irvine Loudon: *Death in Childbirth*, p. 218.

60. Lady Grigg Welfare League, Indian Section, Annual Report 1929, Private Collection.

61. Lord Altrincham: *Kenya's Opportunity*, p. 233.

62. Frans Lasson (ed.), translated by Anne Born: *Isak Dinesen. Letters from Africa 1914–1931*, p. 369.

63. 'A Brief History of the Lady Grigg Welfare League in Mombasa, Kenya', (30 June 1932), p. 5, Private Collection.

64. *Coast Guardian*, 24 October 1936.

65. Muriel Sheridan to Lady Grigg: 30 July 1938, Private Collection.

66. *Annual Report of the Kenya Colony and Protectorate Native Affairs Department*, 1933, p. 56.

67. *Annual Report of the Kenya Colony and Protectorate Native Affairs Department*, 1934, pp. 78–9.

68. G. V. Anderson, 'Problems of Native Maternity Work, with a Review of Two Hundred Cases', *Kenya and East African Medical Journal*, Vol. VI, 1929–30, pp. 62–73.

69. Colonial Office: *Annual Report on the East Africa High Commission 1950*, pp. 47.

70. *Coast Guardian*, 24 October 1936.

71. 'A Brief History of the Lady Grigg Welfare League in Mombasa, Kenya', [30 June 1932], pp. 6–7, Private Collection.

72. *Annual Report of the Lady Grigg Welfare League, African Section, 1931*, pp. 3–4.

73. *Annual Report of the Kenya Colony and Protectorate Native Affairs Department*, 1934, pp. 78–9.

74. Lord Altrincham: *Kenya's Opportunity*, frontispiece.

75. 'Written Answers: East Africa. Dispensaries and Maternity Centres', statement by Dr Shiels, *Hansard*, 16 December 1929.

76. City Council of Nairobi, Kenya: *The Forty-Sixth Annual Report of the Medical Officer of Health*, 1975, p. 58.

5. 'THE RED DUCHESS'

Further Reading

Documents

Most of the Atholl papers are held in the family archive at Blair Castle in Perthshire, Scotland. The papers relating to India are held in the records of the India Office (IO) at the British Library, London.

Key books by the Duchess of Atholl

Katharine, Duchess of Atholl: *The Conscription of a People*, London, Philip Allan, 1931. An account of Soviet labour laws of the time and the labour camps, which was abridged the following year as *The Truth About Forced Labour in Russia* (London: Philip Allan).

— *Women and Politics*, London, Philip Allan, 1931. The Duchess wrote this book to give women a background of political knowledge.

— *Searchlight on Spain*, Harmondsworth, Penguin, 1938.

— *The Tragedy of Warsaw and its Documentation*, London, John Murray, 1945.

— *Working Partnership: Being the Lives of John George, 8th Duke of Atholl, and of his wife, Katharine Marjory Ramsay*, London; Arthur Barker, 1958.

Biographies

S. J. Hetherington: *Katharine Atholl 1874–1960. Against The Tide*. Aberdeen University Press, 1989. This is the only biography of the Duchess of Atholl.

Books about the Spanish Civil War

Tom Buchanan: *Britain and the Spanish Civil War*, Cambridge University Press, 1997.

Valentine Cunningham (ed.): *Spanish Front. Writers on the Civil War*, Oxford University Press, 1986. A wide-ranging anthology of excerpts from writings on the war.

1. The Duchess of Atholl: *Working Partnership*, p. 137.
2. *Spectator*, 23 July 1936.

3. Robert Graves and Alan Hodge: *The Long Week-End*, p. 337.

4. Luigi Villari: 'Italian – and Other – Intervention in Spain', *National Review*, May 1938, p. 594.

5. The Duchess of Atholl: *Working Partnership*, p. 207.

6. A. J. P. Taylor: *English History 1914–1945*, p. 394.

7. Nigel Nicolson (ed.): *Harold Nicolson. Diaries and Letters 1930–1939*, 8 August 1936, p. 270.

8. John Cornford: 'Full Moon at Tierza Before the Storming of Huesca', p. 40.

9. Margaret Wynn to the author: 20 August 1999.

10. Jessica Mitford: *Hons and Rebels*, p. 115.

11. Patrick Donner: *Crusade*, p. 124.

12. Ellen Wilkinson: *Peeps at Politicians*, pp. 35–6.

13. The Duchess of Atholl to Miss Rathbone: 6 September 1929, IO, MSS, EUR D903/1.

14. Ellen Wilkinson: *Peeps at Politicians*, pp. 35–6.

15. The Duchess of Atholl: *Women and Politics*, pp. 1–3.

16. Patrick Donner: *Crusade*, p. 124.

17. John Barnes and David Nicholson (eds.): *The Empire at Bay. The Leo Amery Diaries 1929–1945*, pp. 385–6.

18. The Unknown Diplomat': *Britain in Spain*, p. 12.

19. Quoted in Pamela Brookes: *Women at Westminster*, p. 34.

20. Minute by Sir G. Mounsey, 3 August 1937, PRO FO 371/21343, W14544 17/41 [emphasis added].

21. Edith Summerskill: *A Woman's World*, p. 60.

22. 'Oral Answers: East Africa. Pre-Marriage Initiation Rite', *Hansard*, 11 December 1929, cols. 603–4.

23. 'Written Answers: Kenya (Kikuyu Girl Operation)', *Hansard*, 13 December 1929, col. 844.

24. The Duchess of Atholl: *Working Partnership*, p. 135.

25. Ibid., p. 136.

26. Kitty Atholl to Ted Butler: 30 December 1926, quoted in S. J. Hetherington, *Against the Tide*, p. 122.

27. S. J. Hetherington: *Katharine Atholl 1874–1960. Against the Tide*, pp. 119–24.

28. The Duchess of Atholl: *Women and Politics*, p. 103.

29. The Duchess of Atholl, *Working Partnership*, p. 214.

30. George Orwell: *Homage to Catalonia*, p. 3.

31. See E. H. Carr: *The Comintern and the Spanish Civil War*, edited by Tamara Deutscher, p. 10.

32. Charles Sarolea: *Daylight on Spain. The Answer to the Duchess of Atholl*, p. 67.

33. The Duchess of Atholl: *Women and Politics*, pp. 42–3.

34. Tom Buchanan: *The Spanish Civil War and the British Labour Movement*, pp. 123–4.

35. From G. L. Steer, 'Guernica', quoted in Valentine Cunningham (ed.): *Spanish Front. Writers on the Civil War*, pp. 130–38

36. The Duchess of Atholl: *Searchlight on Spain*, pp. ix–xii.

37. Quoted in Neville Thompson: *The Anti-Appeasers*, p. 121.

38. *Times Literary Supplement*, 18 June 1938.

39. Charles Sarolea: *Daylight on Spain. The Answer to the Duchess of Atholl*, pp. 16–17.

40. Quoted in Anne Chisholm: *Nancy Cunard*, p. 238.

41. Anne Chisholm: *Nancy Cunard*, p. 238.

42. Harold Macmillan: *The Past Masters*, p. 216.

43. Quoted in S. J. Hetherington: *Against the Tide*, pp. 191–2.

44. Quoted in Tom Buchanan: *Britain and the Spanish Civil War*, p. 87.

45. Jessica Mitford: *Hons and Rebels*, p. 123.

46. George Orwell: 'Looking Back on the Spanish Civil War', in Valentine Cunningham (ed.): *Spanish Front. Writers on the Civil War*, p. 376.

47. The Duchess of Atholl: *Working Partnership*, p. 232.

48. Nancy Mitford to Raymond Mortimer: 30 June 1960, in Charlotte Mosley (ed.): *Love From Nancy. The Letters of Nancy Mitford*, p. 453.

49. Mary Stocks: *Eleanor Rathbone*, p. 177.

6. 'THE GIOCONDA OF THE AGE'

Further Reading

Documents and letters

The bulk of Nancy Cunard's papers are held by The Humanities Research Center, University of Texas at Austin, USA.

Correspondence between Nancy Cunard and the Surrealist painter John Banting from 1932 to 1960 is held by the Tate Gallery Archive in London. The Banting collection contains a number of photographs of Nancy Cunard.

Key publications by Nancy Cunard

Outlaws, London, Elkin Matthews, 1921.

Sublunary, London, Hodder & Stoughton, 1923.

Parallax, London, Hogarth Press, 1925.

Poems (Two) 1925, London, Aquila Press, 1930.

(ed.): *Black Man and White Ladyship*. Privately printed in Toulouse 1931. Printed in full in *Nancy Cunard: Brave Poet, Indomitable Rebel* (see below).

(ed.): *Negro Anthology*, London, Wishart & Co., 1934.

(ed.): *Authors Take Sides on the Spanish War*, London, Left Review, 1937.

(with George Padmore): *The White Man's Duty*, London, W. H. Allen, 1943.

(ed.): *Poems for France. Written by British Poets on France Since the War*, London, La France Libre, 1944.

G. M.: Memories of George Moore, London, Rupert Hart-Davis, 1956.

These Were The Hours, Southern Illinois University Press, 1969. This book is a history of the Hours Press.

Books on Paris between the wars

Gertrude Stein: *Paris France*, 1940; rpt. London, Clerkenwell Green, 1983.

Noel Riley Fitch: *Sylvia Beach and the Lost Generation*, Harmondsworth, Penguin, 1983.

Ernest Hemingway: *A Moveable Feast*, New York, Charles Scribner's Sons, 1964.

Biographical studies

Charles Burkhart: *Herman and Nancy and Ivy. Three Lives in Art*, London, Victor Gollancz, 1977.

Anne Chisholm: *Nancy Cunard*, London, Sidgwick & Jackson, 1979. An outstanding biography: well researched, readable and thorough.

Daphne Fielding: *Emerald and Nancy. Lady Cunard and Her Daughter*, London, Eyre & Spottiswoode, 1968. Daphne Fielding (the Marchioness of Bath) was a friend of Lady Cunard.

Hugh Ford (ed.): *Nancy Cunard: Brave Poet, Indomitable Rebel*, London, Chilton Book Company, 1968. Ford and some other friends of Nancy produced this book because they were afraid that Fielding's *Emerald and Nancy* would not give an accurate impression of Nancy's life.

1. Harold Acton: *Memoirs of an Aesthete*, p. 149.
2. Gertrude Stein: *Paris France*, pp. 36–7.

3. Robert Graves and Alan Hodge: *The Long Week-End*, p. 125.
4. Note by John Banting [1960s], Tate Gallery, 779.5.35.
5. Cecil Beaton: *The Book of Beauty*, p. 63.
6. Reported by John Banting in Notes [1960s], Tate Gallery, 779.5.35.
7. Anne Chisholm writes in her biography, *Nancy Cunard*, that when Nancy was twenty-four, in 1920, she had a hysterectomy in Paris, which was followed by severe complications. The hysterectomy was possibly treatment for the results of a problematic abortion or miscarriage. After this, Nancy was unable to have children (pp. 67–8).
8. Nancy's gynaecological illness is discussed by her biographer Anne Chisholm in *Nancy Cunard*, chapter 7.
9. Harold Acton: *Memoirs of an Aesthete*, p. 149.
10. George Moore to Maud Cunard: 26 January 1905, in Rupert Hart-Davis (ed.): *George Moore. Letters to Lady Cunard 1895–1933*, p. 38.
11. George Moore to Maud Cunard: March 1917, in Rupert Hart-Davis (ed.): *George Moore. Letters to Lady Cunard 1895–1933*, pp. 94–5.
12. Nancy Cunard: *Black Man and White Ladyship*, p. 105.
13. Ruth Brandon: *Surreal Lives*, p. 3.
14. Harold Acton: *Memoirs of an Aesthete*, p. 226.
15. All three quoted in Philip Ziegler: *Osbert Sitwell*, p. 69.
16. George Moore to Maud Cunard: 5 March 1921, in Rupert Hart-Davis (ed.): *George Moore. Letters to Lady Cunard 1895–1933*, p. 111.
17. Harold Acton: *Memoirs of an Aesthete*, p. 149.
18. Robert Graves and Alan Hodge: *The Long Week-End*, p. 197.
19. Note by John Banting, crossed out, [1960s], Tate Gallery, 779.5.35.
20. Michael Arlen: *Piracy*, p. 7.
21. Nancy Cunard: 'To the Eiffel Tower Restaurant' in *Sublunary*.
22. Note by John Banting, crossed out, [1960s], Tate Gallery, 779.5.35.
23. Daphne Fielding: *Emerald and Nancy. Lady Cunard and Her Daughter*, p. 74.
24. Harold Acton: *Memoirs of an Aesthete*, pp. 223–4.
25. Michael Arlen: *Piracy*, p. 7.
26. Robert Graves and Alan Hodge: *The Long Week-End*, p. 192.
27. Quoted in Robert Graves and Alan Hodge: *The Long Week-End*, p. 352.
28. Hugo Vickers: *Cecil Beaton. The Authorized Biography*, p. 89.
29. Harold Acton: *Memoirs of an Aesthete*, pp. 223–4.
30. Quoted in J. H. Willis, Jr.: *Leonard and Virginia Woolf as Publishers: The Hogarth Press, 1917–41*, pp. 116–17.
31. Diana Cooper: *The Rainbow Comes and Goes*, pp. 103–4.
32. Ibid., p. 82.

33. William Buchan: *John Buchan. A Memoir*, pp. 190–91.

34. Nancy Cunard: *These Were the Hours*, p. 123.

35. Quoted in Ruth Brandon: *Surreal Lives*, p. 47.

36. Harold Acton: *Memoirs of an Aesthete*, p. 224.

37. Ernest Hemingway: *A Moveable Feast*, p. 36.

38. Noel Riley Fitch: *Sylvia Beach and the Lost Generation*, p. 101.

39. Nancy Cunard: *These Were the Hours*, pp. 110–11 and 118.

40. Ernest Hemingway: *A Moveable Feast*, p. 110.

41. Michael Reynolds: *Hemingway: The Paris Years*, pp. 99–100.

42. Nancy Cunard: *These Were the Hours*, p. 129.

43. *The Times Literary Supplement*, 1 January 1931, p. 8.

44. Reported by Anne Chisholm: *Nancy Cunard*, p. 81.

45. Quoted in Nancy Cunard: *These Were the Hours*, p. 8.

46. J. H. Willis, Jr.: *Leonard and Virginia Woolf as Publishers: The Hogarth Press, 1917–41*, p. 41.

47. Robert Graves and Alan Hodge: *The Long Week-End*, p. 426.

48. Charles Burkhart: *Herman and Nancy and Ivy: Three Lives in Art*, p. 15.

49. Charles Burkhart: *Herman and Nancy and Ivy*, p. 110.

50. Nancy Cunard: *These Were the Hours*, pp. 172–3 (emphasis added).

51. Charles Burkhart: *Herman and Nancy and Ivy*, p. 118.

52. Quoted in Nancy Cunard: *These Were the Hours*, pp. 82–3.

53. Reported by Stefan Collini, 'Oh, a genius, darling', in the *Guardian*, 5 September 1998, p. 10.

54. Cecil Beaton: *The Book of Beauty*, p. 36.

55. Nancy Cunard: *These Were the Hours*, p. 26.

56. Circular printed by Nancy Cunard [April 1931], Tate Gallery, 779.7.22.

57. Thomas Jones: *Whitehall Diary*, Vol. II 1926–30, edited by Keith Middlemas, p. 126.

58. Una, Lady Troubridge: *The Life and Death of Radclyffe Hall*, p. 19.

59. Nancy Cunard: *Black Man and White Ladyship*, p. 103.

60. Quoted in Daphne Fielding: *Emerald and Nancy*, p. 107.

61. Daphne Fielding: *Emerald and Nancy*, p. 108.

62. *The Times*, 15 July 1933.

63. Nancy Cunard (ed.): *Negro Anthology*, p. 181.

64. Ibid., p. iii.

65. Nancy Cunard: *Black Man and White Ladyship*, p. 108.

66. Nancy Cunard: *These Were the Hours*, pp. 128–9.

67. See James R. Hooker: *Black Revolutionary. George Padmore's Path from Communism to Pan-Africanism*, pp. 27 and 30.

68. Nancy Cunard (ed.): *Negro Anthology*, pp. iii and 75.

69. Nancy Cunard to Charles Burkhart, 1955, quoted in Charles Burkhart: *Herman and Nancy and Ivy*, p. 116.

70. Nancy Cunard: *These Were the Hours*, p. 29.

71. Quoted in Anne Chisholm: *Nancy Cunard*, p. 244.

72. Nancy Cunard: 'The Question', in Valentine Cunningham (ed.): *Spanish Front*

73. Anne Chisholm: *Nancy Cunard*, p. 241.

74. Harold Acton: *More Memoirs of an Aesthete*, pp. 33–4 and 143–4.

75. Daphne Fielding: *The Rainbow Picnic*, p. 125.

76. Nancy Mitford to Violet Hammersley: 24 July 1960, in Charlotte Mosley (ed.): *The Letters of Nancy Mitford*, p. 454.

77. Charles Burkhart: *Herman and Nancy and Ivy*, p. 58.

78. D[ouglas] C[ooper] to John Banting: [10 March 1966], Tate Gallery, 779.1.126.

79. Nancy Cunard (ed.): *Poems for France. Written by British Poets on France Since the War*, p. 87.

7. 'NOT WHY WE CAN'T BUT HOW WE CAN'

Further Reading

Documents and letters

The WRVS archive is held by the organization at its Head Office in Oxfordshire. It contains a mass of papers relating to Lady Reading and her role in the organization.

Correspondence between WVS/WRVS and the government is held by the Public Record Office. Documents of particular relevance are to be found in the files of the Home Office (HO) and the Ministry of Agriculture and Fisheries (MAF).

Books about the WVS/WRVS

Charles Graves: *Women in Green (The Story of the WVS)*, London, Heinemann, 1948. A detailed account of the first eight years of the organization.

Katharine Bentley Beauman: *Green Sleeves. The Story of WVS/WRVS*, London, Seeley Service, 1977.

Virginia Graham: *The Story of WVS*, London, HMSO, 1959. This account is illustrated with numerous photographs.

WVS. Report on 25 Years' Work, London, HMSO, 1963.

Writings by Stella Reading

Stella, Lady Reading. *Voluntary Service*, privately printed, n.d. [1950s]. This booklet sets out Lady Reading's philosophy of voluntary service.

It's the Job that Counts, Vols. I and II. A Selection from the Speeches and Writings of the Dowager Marchioness of Reading, Baroness Swanborough 1954–1971, privately printed, 1972.

About Stella Reading

Stella Reading. *Some Recollections by her friends*, privately printed [1979].

1. *National Review*: March 1933, No. 601, p. 343.
2. Hoare to Lady Reading: 4 May 1938, PRO, HO 356/2/54374.
3. Stella Reading to Margaret Hickey in 'We must pay for our own room on earth', *Ladies Home Journal*, USA, August 1951.
4. Katharine Bentley Beauman: *Green Sleeves. The Story of WVS/WRVS*, p. 6.
5. Statement by Mrs Sullivan (Peggy Blampied) in *Stella Reading. Some Recollections by her friends*, p. 7.
6. Hoare to Reading: 20 May 1938, WRVS, A1/38.
7. Viscount Templewood (Sir Samuel Hoare): *Nine Troubled Years*, p. 238.
8. Lady Holland-Martin to WRVS: 24 March 1976, WRVS, A1/38.
9. 'Catalogue of the Personal Service League Auction', 14 December 1933, PRO, PRO 30/69, 1443 (pt. 2), 55310.
10. Lady Londonderry to Ramsay MacDonald: 1 September 1932, PRO, PRO 30/69, 1442.
11. Katharine Bentley Beauman: *Green Sleeves. The Story of WVS/WRVS*, p. 16.
12. Mrs Richard to WRVS: n.d., WRVS, A1/38.
13. Charles Graves: *Women in Green*, p. 19.
14. Katharine Bentley Beauman: *Green Sleeves. The Story of WVS/WRVS*, p. 19.
15. 'Note on the activities of the WVS during the last fortnight', 15 September 1939, WRVS, A1/38.
16. Charles Graves: *Women in Green*, p. 10.
17. Director General of the Post Office to Lady Reading: 4 July 1938, WRVS, A1/38.
18. Lady Reading to Hoare: 29 April 1938, PRO, HO 356/2/54374.
19. James Hinton, 'Voluntarism and the Welfare/Warfare State. Women's Voluntary Services in the 1940s', in *Twentieth-Century British History* 9, (1998) pp. 282–3.

20. Charles Graves: *Women in Green*, p. 31.

21. Mrs Carroll-Marks to WRVS: 5 March 1975, WRVS, A1/38.

22. Miss Halpin to WRVS: 5 March 1975, WRVS, A1/38.

23. Charles Graves: *Green Sleeves*, p. 41.

24. Patricia Andrews (compiler): *WRVS The Story of The Women's Royal Voluntary Service in the Holme Valley 1938–1988*, pp. 1–8.

25. *The Bulletin*, No. 66, April 1945.

26. Director General of the Post Office to Lady Reading: 4 July 1938, WRVS, A1/38.

27. Stella Reading to Margaret Hickey in 'We must pay for our own room on earth', *Ladies Home Journal*, USA, August 1951.

28. Lady Zuckerman to the author: 16 February 1999.

29. Lady Reading to Mrs Harris: 15 August 1962, WRVS, A1/38.

30. Miss E. Wade to WRVS: n.d., WRVS, A1/38.

31. Mrs Darling to WRVS: 15 January 1975, WRVS, A1/38.

32. Katherine Seymour, Lady in Waiting, to Lady Reading: 22 September 1939, WRVS, A1/38.

33. Statement by Mrs Sullivan (Peggy Blampied), in *Stella Reading. Some Recollections by her friends*, p. 7.

34. Mrs Carroll-Marks and Miss Halpin to WRVS: 5 March 1975, WRVS, A1/38.

35. Iris Capell: *Myself When Young and Other Writings*, p. 57.

36. 'A Transcript of the Words Spoken at the Thanksgiving for the Life of Iris Capell at The Church of St Lawrence-Jewry in the City of London', 28 November 1977, p. 5, Private Collection.

37. J. A. Cross: *Sir Samuel Hoare: A Political Biography*, p. 278.

38. Statement by Mrs Sullivan (Peggy Blampied), in *Stella Reading. Some Recollections by her friends*, p. 8.

39. Minutes, Ministry of Food: 13 October 1944, PRO, MAF 102/12.

40. Minutes, Ministry of Food: 15 October 1944, PRO, MAF 102/12.

41. Statement by Dame Mary Smieton, in *Stella Reading. Some Recollections by her friends*, p. 14.

42. Ibid., p. 14.

43. Ibid., p. 14.

44. Eady to Wood 30 August 1939, PRO, HO 356/3.

45. 'Lady Reading: Unforgettable Founder of the WVS', p. 67.

46. Statement by Mrs Antony Thesiger, in *Stella Reading. Some Recollections by her friends*, p. 20.

47. 'Nation Before Husband', *Surrey County Herald*, 2 June 1944.

48. Richard Titmuss: *Problems of Social Policy*, p. 267.

49. *Bulletin*, No. 62, December 1944.

50. *Bulletin*, No. 49, November 1943.

51. Quoted in Katharine Bentley Beauman: *Green Sleeves. The Story of WVS/ WRVS*, p. 46.

52. Minute, Ministry of Food, 6 January 1943, PRO, MAF 102/11.

53. Lister to Walker: 27 July 1943, PRO, MAF 102/12.

54. Memo, Ministry of Food, 12 May 1942.

55. L. Cooper, Ministry of Food, to A. Rowe, WVS: 30 May 1944, PRO, MAF 102/11.

56. Hon. Mrs E—-W—, WVS, to Ministry of Food: 30 November 1943, PRO, MAF 102/11.

57. Charles Graves: *Women in Green*, p. 151.

58. Virginia Graham: *The Story of WVS*, p. 15.

59. Ibid., pp. 11–12.

60. 'Lady Reading Uses Jam for Sticking Stamps', *Daily Mail*, 8 February 1939.

61. Charles Graves: *Women in Green*, p. 65.

62. Ibid., p. 69.

63. Mrs Tingey to WRVS: n.d., WRVS, A1/38.

64. Reported in Doreen Harris, as told to Peter Browne: 'Lady Reading: Unforgettable Founder of the WVS', *Reader's Digest*, October 1972, p. 65.

65. R. Broad and S. Fleming (eds.): *Nella Last's War. A Mother's Diary 1939–45*, p. 168.

66. W. F. Deedes: 'Welfare: one woman's way', *Daily Telegraph*, 22 June 1971.

67. Cover of leaflet, 'The New National Health Service', 1948, Private Collection (emphasis added).

68. Morrison to Cripps: 15 January 1949, PRO, T 227/79.

69. Lady Reading to Chuter Ede: WRVS, A1/38/6.

70. Lord Brooke of Cumnor to WRVS: 18 May 1972, WRVS, A1/38.

71. Miss E. Wade to WRVS: n.d., WRVS, A1/38.

72. Ruth Balfour to Stella Reading: 23 July 1945, WRVS, A1/38.

73. See correspondence in PRO, HO 356/2.

74. *It's the Job that Counts, Vol. II. A Selection from the Speeches and Writings of the Dowager Marchioness of Reading, Baroness Swanborough 1954–1971*, pp. 40–41.

75. Stella Reading: 'Introduction', *Report on 25 Years' Work*, p. iv.

Afterword

1. Virginia Woolf: *Three Guineas*, p. 89.

2. David McKie: 'Trouble and strife in the premiership', *Guardian*, 4 September 1996 (emphasis added).

3. David Marquand: *Ramsay MacDonald*, p. 692.

4. Ibid., p. 406.

5. Austen Morgan: *J. Ramsay MacDonald*, p. 226.

6. Harold Macmillan: *The Past Masters*, pp. 210–16.

7. Ibid., pp. 210–16.

8. 'Oral Answers: East Africa. Pre-Marriage Initiation Rite', *Hansard*, 11 December 1929, cols. 603–4.

9. William Buchan: *John Buchan. A Memoir*, p. 190.

10. Nancy Mitford, 'U and Non-U', in Alan S. C. Ross *et al.*: *Noblesse Oblige*, p. 53.

11. Iris Butler: *The Viceroy's Wife. Letters of Alice, Countess of Reading, from India, 1921–1925*, p. 69.

12. Ibid., p. 62 and *passim*.

13. Dame Janet Campbell, 'Introduction' in Margery Spring Rice: *Working-Class Wives*, p. xviii.

14. C. P. Snow: *Homecomings*, p. 227.

15. Publicity leaflet about the Festival of Britain, 1951, PRO, T 227/77.

16. Virginia Woolf: *Three Guineas*, p. 22.

17. Ibid., pp. 71–2.

18. 'Receptions. Londonderry House', *The Times*, 7 February 1928.

19. This observation is based on photographs of Lady Grigg on safari (Private Collection).

20. Cecil Beaton: *The Book of Beauty*, p. 63.

Archive Sources

Where archive collections have played a particular role, these are identified below. Family papers relating to Lucy Baldwin, Iris Capell, Joan Grigg and Stella Reading are held privately.

The Archives of the Dukes of Atholl, Blair Castle, Blair Atholl, Pitlochry, Perthshire, Scotland PH18 5TL
  Papers of Katherine, Duchess of Atholl

Bishopsgate Institute, 230 Bishopsgate, London EC2M 4QH
  Women's Co-operative Guild papers, including annual reports

Bodleian Library, Oxford University, Broad Street, Oxford OX1 3BG
  Violet Milner papers

British Library, London – India Office Records, 96 Euston Road, London NW1 2DB
  Papers relating to the Duchess of Atholl and India

Contemporary Medical Archives Centre (CMAC), Wellcome Library, 183 Euston Road, London NW1 2BE
  National Birthday Trust Fund (NBTF) archive

London Metropolitan Archives, 40 Northampton Road, London EC1 OHB
London County Council (LCC) records

London School of Hygiene and Tropical Medicine, University of London, Keppel Street, London WC1
   Miscellaneous papers on East Africa

Public Record Office (PRO), Kew, Surrey TW9 4DU
   Records of UK central government
   Private papers of Ramsay MacDonald

Public Record Office of Northern Ireland (PRONI), 66 Balmoral Avenue, Belfast BT9 6NY
   Edith, Lady Londonderry papers

Royal College of Obstetricians and Gynaecologists, 27 Sussex Place, Regent's Park, London NW1 4RG
   Papers of the British College of Obstetricians and Gynaecologists

Tate Gallery Archive, Tate Gallery, Millbank, London SW1P 4RG
   John Banting collection

Women's Royal Voluntary Service, Head Office, Milton Hill, Abingdon, Oxfordshire OX13 6AF
   Papers relating to WVS, WRVS and Lady Reading

Bibliography

Acton, Harold: *Memoirs of an Aesthete*, London, Methuen & Co., 1948.

— *More Memoirs of an Aesthete*, London, Methuen & Co., 1970.

Altrincham, Lord (Sir Edward Grigg): *Kenya's Opportunity. Memoirs, Hopes and Ideas*, London, Faber & Faber, 1955.

Amery, L. S.: *The Empire in the New Era*, London, Edward Arnold & Co., 1928.

— *My Political Life. Volume Two War and Peace 1914–1929*, London, Hutchinson, 1953.

Andrews, Patricia (compiler): *WRVS The Story of The Women's Royal Voluntary Service in the Holme Valley 1938–1988*, Huddersfield, privately printed, 1988.

Arlen, Michael: *Piracy*, London, William Collins, Son & Co., 1922.

Asquith, Margot: *Off The Record*, London, Frederick Muller, 1943.

Duchess of Atholl, MP, Katharine: *The Conscription of a People*, London, Philip Allan, 1931.

— *Women and Politics*, London, Philip Allan, 1931.

— *Searchlight on Spain*, Harmondsworth, Penguin, 1938.

— *The Tragedy of Warsaw and its Documentation*, London, John Murray, 1945.

— *Working Partnership, Being the Lives of John George, 8th Duke of Atholl and of his wife Katharine Marjory Ramsay*, London, Arthur Barker, 1958.

Attlee, C. L.: *The Labour Party in Perspective*, London, Victor Gollancz, 1937.

Baldwin, A. W.: *My Father – The True Story*, London, George Allen & Unwin, 1955.

Baldwin, Stanley: *On England*, London, P. Allan & Co., 1926.

Barnes, John and Nicholson, David (eds.): *The Leo Amery Diaries, Vols. 1 and 2*, London, Hutchinson, 1980.

Beaton, Cecil: *The Book of Beauty*, London, Duckworth, 1930.
— *The Years Between, Diaries 1939–44*, London, Weidenfeld & Nicolson, 1965.
Beauman, Katharine Bentley: *Green Sleeves. The Story of WVS/WRVS*, London, Seeley Service, 1977.
Beck, Ann: *Medicine, Tradition and Development in Kenya and Tanzania, 1920–1970*, Waltham, Mass.: Crossroads Press, 1981.
Blake, R.: *The Unknown Prime Minister. The Life and Times of Andrew Bonar Law*, London, Eyre & Spottiswoode, 1955.
Blixen, Karen (Isak Dinesen): *Out of Africa*, 1937, Harmondsworth, Penguin, 1954.
Bonham Carter, Violet: *Winston Churchill as I Knew Him*, 1965; London, Weidenfeld & Nicolson, 1995.
Brandon, Ruth: *Surreal Lives. The Surrealists 1917–1945*, London, Macmillan, 1999.
Brittain, Vera: *Testament of Experience*, London, Victor Gollancz, 1957.
—*Honourable Estate*: London, Victor Gollancz, 1936.
Broad, R. and Fleming, S. (eds.): *Nella Last's War. A Mother's Diary 1939–45*, 1981; London, Sphere Books, 1983.
Brock, Michael and Eleanor (eds.): Part I, *H.H. Asquith. Letters to Venetia Stanley*, Oxford University Press, 1982.
Brookes, Pamela: *Women at Westminster*, London, Peter Davies, 1967.
Buchan, William: *John Buchan, A Memoir*, London, Buchan & Enright, 1982.
Buchanan, Tom: *The Spanish Civil War and the British Labour Movement*, Cambridge University Press, 1991.
—*Britain and the Spanish Civil War*, Cambridge University Press, 1997.
Burkhart, Charles: *Herman and Nancy and Ivy. Three Lives in Art*, London, Victor Gollancz, 1977.
Bush, Julia: *Edwardian Ladies and Imperial Power*, London, Leicester University Press, 2000.
Butler, Iris: *The Viceroy's Wife. Letters of Alice, Countess of Reading from India, 1921–25*, London, Hodder & Stoughton, 1969.
Cannadine, David: *Aspects of Aristocracy*, New Haven, Conn., Yale University Press, 1994.
Capell, Iris: *Myself When Young and Other Writings*, Ontario, Canada, privately printed, n.d.
Carman, John A.: *A Medical History of the Colony and Protectorate of Kenya. A personal memoir*, London, Rex Collins, 1976.
Carr, E. H.: *The Comintern and the Spanish Civil War*, edited by Tamara Deutscher, London, Macmillan, 1984.

Cecil, David: *The Cecils of Hatfield House*, London, Book Club Associates, 1973.

Cecil, The Late Lord Edward: *The Leisure of an Egyptian Official*, 1921; London, Hodder & Stoughton, 1931.

Chisholm, Anne: *Nancy Cunard*, London, Sidgwick & Jackson, 1979.

Cole, Margaret (ed.): *Beatrice Webb's Diaries 1924–1932*, London, Longman, Green and Co., 1956.

Colonial Office: *Annual Report on the East Africa High Commission 1950*, London, HMSO, 1951.

Cooper, Diana: *The Rainbow Comes and Goes*, London, Rupert Hart-Davis, 1958.

Cooper, Duff: *Old Men Forget. The Autobiography of Duff Cooper*, London, Rupert Hart-Davis, 1953.

Cornford, John: 'Full Moon at Tierza before the Storming of Huesca', 1936, in *Understanding the Weapon, Understanding the Wound, Selected Writing of John Cornford*, edited by Jonathan Galassi, Manchester, Carcanet New Press, 1976

de Courcy, Anne: *Circe. The Life of Edith, Marchioness of Londonderry*, London, Sinclair-Stevenson, 1992.

Cowell, Betty and Wainwright, David: *Behind the Blue Door. The History of the Royal College of Midwives 1891–1991*, London, Baillière Tindall, 1981.

Cross, J. A.: *Sir Samuel Hoare: A Political Biography*, London, Jonathan Cape, 1977.

Cunard, Nancy: *Outlaws*, London, Elkin Matthews, 1921.

— *Sublunary*, London, Hodder & Stoughton, 1923.

— *Parallax*, London, Hogarth Press, 1925.

— *Poems (Two) 1925*, London, Aquila Press, 1930.

— *Black Man and White Ladyship*, Toulouse, privately printed, 1931.

— (ed.) *Negro Anthology*, London, Wishart & Co., 1934.

— (ed.) *Authors Take Sides on the Spanish War*, London, Left Review, 1937.

— with Padmore, George: *The White Man's Duty*, London, W. H. Allen, 1943.

— (ed.) *Poems for France. Written by British Poets on France Since the War*, London, La France Libre, 1944.

— G. M.: *Memories of George Moore*, London, Rupert Hart-Davis, 1956.

— *These Were The Hours. Memories of My Hours Press, Réanville and Paris 1928–31*, Southern Illinois University Press, 1969.

Cunningham, Valentine (ed.): *Spanish Front. Writers on the Civil War.* Oxford University Press, 1986.

Dayus, Katherine: *Where There's Life*, 1985; London; Virago, 1989.

Dean, Dennis: 'The Contrasting Attitudes of the Conservative and Labour Parties to Problems of Empire 1922–1936', PhD thesis for the University of London, 1974.

Delafield, E. M.: *The Diary of a Provincial Lady*, London, Macmillan, 1930.

Dick-Read, Grantley: *Natural Childbirth*, London, Heinemann, 1933.

— *Childbirth without Fear*, London, Heinemann, 1942.

Dinesen, Isak (Karen Blixen): *Letters from Africa 1914–1931*, edited by Frans Lasson, translated by Anne Born, London, Weidenfeld & Nicolson, 1981.

Disraeli, Benjamin: *Sybil; or the Two Nations*, 1845; London, Oxford University Press, 1975.

Donner, Patrick: *Crusade*, London, Sherwood Press, 1984.

Dos Passos, John: *Adventures of a Young Man*, New York, Harcourt, Brace & Co., 1939.

Douglas, Ann: *Terrible Honesty. Mongrel Manhattan in the 1920s*, 1995; London, Papermac, 1997.

Fielding, Daphne: *Emerald and Nancy. Lady Cunard and Her Daughter*, London, Eyre & Spottiswoode, 1968.

— *The Rainbow Picnic: A Portrait of Iris Tree*, London, Eyre Methuen, 1974.

Fitch, Noel Riley: *Sylvia Beach and the Lost Generation*, Harmondsworth, Penguin, 1983.

Ford, Hugh (ed.): *Nancy Cunard: Brave Poet, Indomitable Rebel*. London, Chilton Book Company, 1968.

Foreman, Amanda: *Georgiana, Duchess of Devonshire*, London, Harper-Collins, 1998.

Fox, James: *White Mischief*, London, Jonathan Cape, 1982.

Gelis, Jacques: *History of Childbirth*, Cambridge, Polity Press, 1991.

Gerard, Jessica: *Country House Life. Family and Servants 1815–1914*, Oxford, Blackwell, 1994.

Gilbert, Martin: *Winston S. Churchill*, Vol.V, 1922–39, London, Heinemann, 1976.

Gollin, A. G.: *Proconsul in Politics. A Study of Lord Milner in Opposition and in Power*, London, Anthony Blond, 1964.

Graham, Virginia: *The Story of WVS*, London, HMSO, 1959.

Graves, Charles: *Women in Green (The Story of the WVS)*, London, Heinemann, 1948.

Graves, Robert and Hodge, Alan: *The Long Week-End. A Social History of Britain 1918–1939*, London, Faber & Faber, 1940.

Harris, Jose: *Private Lives, Public Spirit: Britain 1870–1914*, Penguin, Harmondsworth, 1993.

Hart-Davis, Rupert (ed.): *George Moore: Letters to Lady Cunard 1895–1933*, London, Rupert Hart-Davis, 1957.

Headlam, Cecil (ed.): *The Milner Papers: South Africa*, Vols. I and II, London, Cassell, 1930 and 1933.

Hemingway, Ernest: *For Whom the Bell Tolls*, New York, Charles Scribner's Sons, 1940.

—*A Moveable Feast*, New York, Charles Scribner's Sons, 1964.

Hetherington, Sheila: *Katharine Atholl 1874–1960. Against the Tide*, Aberdeen University Press, 1989.

Hickman, Katie: *Daughters of Britannia*, London, HarperCollins, 1999.

Hiley, Nicholas: ' "You Can't Believe a Word You Read": Newspaper reading in the British Expeditionary Force, 1914–1918', *Studies in Newspaper and Periodical History. 1994 Annual*, Westport, Conn.: Greenwich Press, 1996.

Hinton, James: 'Voluntarism and the Welfare/Warfare State. Women's Voluntary Services in the 1940s', *Twentieth Century British History 9*, 1998.

Holtby, Winifred: *Women and a Changing Civilization*, London, John Lane, 1934.

Honigsbaum, Frank: *The Division in British Medicine. A History of the General Separation of General Practice from Hospital Care 1911–1968*, London, Kogan Page, 1979.

Hooker, James R.: *Black Revolutionary. George Padmore's Path from Communism to Pan-Africanism*, London, Pall Mall Press, 1967.

Hutcheson, John A.: *Leopold Maxse and the* National Review, *1893–1914. Right-Wing Politics and Journalism in the Edwardian Era*, New York and London, Garland Publishing Inc., 1989.

Hyde, H. Montgomery, *Baldwin. The Unexpected Prime Minister*, London, Rupert Hart-Davis, 1973.

— *The Londonderrys. A Family Portrait*, London, Hamish Hamilton, 1979.

Jones, Thomas: *A Diary with Letters 1931–1950*, London, Oxford University Press, 1954.

— *Whitehall Diary*, Vol. II 1926–30, edited by Keith Middlemas, London, Oxford University Press, 1969.

Kenyatta, Jomo: *Facing Mount Kenya*, 1938; London, Secker & Warburg, 1953.

Kidd, Alan and Nicholls, David (eds.): *The Making of the Middle Class*, Stroud, Sutton Publishing Limited, 1998.

Kipling, Rudyard: *Stalky & Co.*, 1899; London, Macmillan, 1924.

Lee, Laurie: *The Sun My Monument*, London, Hogarth Press, 1944.

Leys, Norman: *A Last Chance in Kenya*, London, Hogarth Press, 1931.

Londonderry, Charles, Marquess of: *Ourselves and Germany*, London, Robert Hale 1938; Penguin Books, 1938.
— *Wings of Destiny*, London, Macmillan, 1943.
Londonderry, Edith, Marchioness of: *Henry Chaplin. A Memoir*, London, Macmillan, 1926.
— *Character and Tradition*, London, Macmillan, 1934.
— *Retrospect*, London, Frederick Muller, 1938.
— *Mount Stewart*, privately printed, 1956.
— *Frances Anne. The Life and Times of Frances Anne, Marchioness of Londonderry and her husband Charles, Third Marquess of Londonderry*, London, Macmillan, 1958.
Loudon, Irvine: *Death in Childbirth*, Oxford, Clarendon Press, 1992.
MacFarlane, Alison and Mugford, Miranda: *Birth Counts. Statistics of Pregnancy and Childbirth*, London, HMSO, 1984.
Macmillan, Harold: *The Past Masters. Politics & Politicians 1906–1939*, London, Macmillan, 1975.
Marquand, David: *Ramsay MacDonald*, London, Jonathan Cape, 1977.
Mass Observation: *Britain and her Birth-Rate*, London, John Murray, 1945.
Middlemas, Keith and Barnes, John: *Baldwin. A Biography*, London, Weidenfeld & Nicolson, 1969.
Milner, Viscount: *England in Egypt*, Eleventh edition with additions summarizing the course of events to the year 1904, London, Edward Arnold, 1904.
Milner, The Viscountess: *My Picture Gallery 1886–1901*, London, John Murray, 1951.
Mitchell, David: *The Spanish Civil War*, London, Granada, 1982.
Mitford, Jessica: *Hons and Rebels*, 1960; London, Quartet Books, 1978.
Mitford, Nancy: 'U and Non-U', in Alan S. C. Ross *et al.*, *Noblesse Oblige. An Enquiry into the Identifiable Characteristics of the English Aristocracy*, 1956; Harmondsworth, Penguin Books in association with Hamish Hamilton, 1959.
Morgan, Austen: *J. Ramsay MacDonald*, Manchester University Press, 1987.
Morgan, Janet: *Edwina Mountbatten. A life of her own*, London, HarperCollins, 1991.
Mosley, Charlotte (ed.): *Love from Nancy. The Letters of Nancy Mitford*, London, Hodder & Stoughton, 1993.
Nicolson, Nigel (ed.): *Harold Nicolson. Diaries and Letters 1930–1939*, London, Collins, 1966.
—*A Reflection of the Other Person. The Letters of Virginia Woolf, Vol. IV: 1929–1931*, London, Hogarth Press, 1978.
Orwell, George: *Homage to Catalonia*, London, Secker & Warburg, 1938.

Oxford and Asquith, Countess of: *Off The Record*, London, Frederick Muller, 1943.

Palmer, Diana: 'Women, Health and Politics, 1919–1939: Professional and Lay Involvement in the Women's Health Campaign', PhD thesis, University of Warwick, 1986.

Pottle, Mark (ed.): *Champion Redoubtable: The Diaries and Letters of Violet Bonham Carter 1914–1945*, London, Weidenfeld & Nicolson, 1998.

Public Record Office of Northern Ireland (PRONI): *Guide to Sources of Women's History*, Belfast, n.d.

Pugh, Martin: *Women and the Women's Movement in Britain, 1914–1959*, London, Macmillan, 1992.

Rathbone, Eleanor: *The Disinherited Family*, 1924; Bristol, Falling Wall Press, 1986.

Read, Donald: *Edwardian England*, London, Harrap, 1972.

Reading, Baroness Swanborough, Stella: *Voluntary Service*, privately printed, n.d.

—'Introduction', *WVS, Report on 25 Years' Work*, London, HMSO, 1963.

—*It's the Job That Counts, Vols. I and II. A Selection from the Speeches and the Writings of the Dowager Marchioness of Reading, Baroness Swanborough 1954–1971*, privately printed, 1972.

Stella Reading. Some Recollections by her friends, privately printed, n.d.

Reynolds, Michael: *Hemingway: The Paris Years*, London, Basil Blackwell, 1989.

Rose, Kenneth: *The Later Cecils*, London, Weidenfeld & Nicolson, 1975.

Rowntree, B. Seebohm: *The Human Needs of Labour*, London, Longman, Green and Co., 1937.

The Royal College of Obstetricians and Gynaecologists and Population Investigation Committee, Joint Committee of: *Maternity in Great Britain*, Oxford University Press, 1946.

Sarolea, Charles: *Daylight on Spain. The Answer to the Duchess of Atholl*, London, Hutchinson & Co., 1938.

Snow, C. P.: *The New Men*, Harmondsworth, Penguin, 1954.

— *Homecomings*, 1956; Harmondsworth: Penguin, 1971.

Snowden, Philip: *An Autobiography. Volume Two 1919–1934*, London, Ivor Nicolson and Watson, 1934.

Soames, Mary: *Clementine Churchill*, London, Cassell, 1979.

Spender, J. A.: *Life of Sir Henry Campbell-Bannerman*. Vol. 1, London, 1930.

Spring Rice, Margery: *Working-Class Wives*, 1939; London, Virago, 1989.

Stein, Gertrude: *Paris France*. 1940; London, Clerkenwell Green, 1983.

Stocks, Mary: *Eleanor Rathbone*. London, Victor Gollancz, 1949.

Summerskill, Edith: *A Woman's World*, London, Heinemann, 1967.

Taylor, A. J. P.: *English History 1914–1945*, Oxford University Press, 1965.

Templewood, Viscount (Sir Samuel Hoare): *Nine Troubled Years*, London, Collins, 1954.

Terry, Roy: *Women in Khaki*, London, Columbus Books, 1988.

Thompson, Neville: *The Anti-Appeasers. Conservative Opposition to Appeasement in the 1930s*, Oxford, Clarendon Press, 1971.

Titmuss, Richard M.: *Poverty and Population. A Factual Study of Contemporary Social Waste*, London, Macmillan, 1938.

— *Problems of Social Policy*, London, HMSO and Longman, Green and Co., 1950.

Tooley, Sarah: *The History of Nursing in the British Empire*, London, S. H. Bousfield, 1906.

Troubridge, Lady Una: *The Life and Death of Radclyffe Hall*, London, Hammond Hammond, 1961.

'The Unknown Diplomat': *Britain in Spain. A Study of the National Government's Spanish Policy*, London, Hamish Hamilton, 1939.

Vansittart, Lord: *The Mist Procession*, London, Hutchinson, 1958.

Vickers, Hugo: *Cecil Beaton. The Authorized Biography*, London, Weidenfeld & Nicolson, 1980.

Wilkinson, Ellen: *Peeps at Politicians*, London, Philip Allan, 1930.

Williams, A. Susan: *Women and Childbirth in the Twentieth Century*, Stroud, Sutton Publishing Limited, 1997.

—'Pain Relief for Childbirth in 1930s Britain', *The History of Anaesthesia. The Fourth International Symposium on the History of Anaesthesia*, edited by Jochen Schulte am Esch and Michael Goerig, Lübeck, DragerDruck, 1998.

Williamson, Philip: *National Crisis and National Government. British Politics, the Economy and Empire, 1926–1932*, Cambridge University Press, 1992.

— *Stanley Baldwin. Conservative Leadership and National Values*, Cambridge University Press, 1999.

Willis Jr., J. H.: *Leonard and Virginia Woolf as Publishers: The Hogarth Press, 1917–41*, Charlottesville, Va. and London, University Press of Virginia, 1992.

Woolf, Virginia: *Three Guineas*, 1938; London, Hogarth Press, 1986.

Women's Co-operative Guild (collected by): *Maternity Letters from Working Women*, London, G. Bell and Sons, 1915.

Wrench, John Evelyn: *Geoffrey Dawson and Our Times*, London, Hutchinson, 1955.

WVS, Report on 25 Years' Work, London, HMSO, 1963.
Young, Kenneth: *Stanley Baldwin*, London, Weidenfeld & Nicolson, 1976.
Ziegler, Philip: *Osbert Sitwell*, London, Chatto & Windus, 1998.

Newspapers, periodicals and journals

British Gazette
British Medical Journal (BMJ)
British Worker
Bystander
Coast Guardian (Kenya)
Daily Express
Daily Mail
Daily Telegraph
English Review
Evening Standard
Everyman
Fortnightly Review
Guardian
Hansard
Harper's Magazine
Journal of the Royal Society of Medicine
Kentish Observer
Kenya and East African Medical Journal
Ladies Home Journal (USA)
Lancet
The Nation
National Review
The New York Times
Nursing Times
Pall Mall Gazette
Reader's Digest
Round Table
Signs
Sketch
Spectator
Surrey County Herald
Tatler
The Times
The Times Literary Supplement
Twentieth Century British History
WVS Civil Defence – Bulletin

Index